International Mediation in the South African Transition

This book challenges the conventional understanding of South Africa's transition to democracy as a home-grown process through a comparative analysis of Commonwealth and United Nations mediation attempts.

Approaching power transition through the lens of South Africa, Zwelethu Jolobe raises questions about how methods and types of mediation are understood, and their appropriateness for certain stages of negotiation processes. *International Mediation in the South African Transition* calls into question the generalisations about the determinants of success by international third parties in resolving internal conflicts. It moves from the position that the success of a mediation effort depends on the examination of the time horizon of a conflict and on the contribution the mediation effort plays in improving the relationship between the belligerents. The book argues that the international community, particularly the Commonwealth and the United Nations, played a profound and beneficial role in the political transition to end apartheid.

International Mediation in the South African Transition will be of interest to students and scholars of African politics, conflict resolution, international relations and global governance.

Zwelethu Jolobe is a senior lecturer in political studies at the University of Cape Town, South Africa.

Routledge Contemporary South Africa

#FeesMustFall and Youth Mobilisation in South Africa
Reform or Revolution?
Musawenkosi W. Ndlovu

Rights-based Litigation, Urban Governance and Social Justice in South Africa
The Right to Joburg
Marius Pieterse

Mining and Community in South Africa
From Small Town to Iron Town
Edited by Lochner Marais, Philippe Burger and Deidré van Rooyen

Reversing Urban Inequality in Johannesburg
Edited by Melissa Tandiwe Myambo

Uprooting University Apartheid in South Africa
From Liberalism to Decolonization
Teresa Barnes

International Mediation in the South African Transition
Brokering Power in Intractable Conflicts
Zwelethu Jolobe

International Mediation in the South African Transition

Brokering Power in Intractable Conflicts

Zwelethu Jolobe

Routledge
Taylor & Francis Group
LONDON AND NEW YORK

First published 2019
by Routledge
2 Park Square, Milton Park, Abingdon, Oxon OX14 4RN

and by Routledge
52 Vanderbilt Avenue, New York, NY 10017

Routledge is an imprint of the Taylor & Francis Group, an informa business

British Library Cataloguing-in-Publication Data
A catalogue record for this book is available from the British Library

Library of Congress Cataloging-in-Publication Data
Names: Jolobe, Zwelethu, author.
Title: International mediation in the South African transition: brokering power in intractable conflicts/Zwelethu Jolobe.
Description: New York, NY: Routledge, 2019. | Series: Routledge contemporary South Africa; 6
Identifiers: LCCN 2018059766 (print) | LCCN 2018060797 (ebook) | ISBN 9781351020589 (Ebook) | ISBN 9781351020572 (Adobe Reader) | ISBN 9781351020565 (Epub) | ISBN 9781351020558 (Mobipocket) | ISBN 9781138496804 (hardback)
Subjects: LCSH: South Africa—Politics and government—1948–1994. | South Africa—Politics and government—1994– | Peace-building—South Africa—International cooperation. | Mediation, International.
Classification: LCC DT1945 (ebook) | LCC DT1945.J65 2019 (print) | DDC 968.06—dc23
LC record available at https://lccn.loc.gov/2018059766

ISBN: 978-1-138-49680-4 (hbk)
ISBN: 978-1-351-02058-9 (ebk)

Typeset in Times New Roman
by Apex CoVantage, LLC

MIX
Paper from responsible sources
FSC
www.fsc.org
FSC® C013056

Printed and bound in Great Britain by
TJ International Ltd, Padstow, Cornwall

In memory of my father, Dr Siviwe Jolobe (1944–2018)

Contents

1 Introduction

Conventional wisdom has it that South Africa's negotiated transition to democracy was a home-grown process with no significant international mediation. The general argument is that the two main protagonists, the South African government and the African National Congress (ANC) simply rejected any form of mediation, as a significant and sufficient amount of trust had developed between them, mainly through various confidence-building measures in the 1980s. Authors such as inter alia Sparks (1994), Waldmeir (1997), Harvey (2001) and Esterhuyse (2012) detail such encounters in depth. International participation in the transition in the form of the Commonwealth Eminent Persons Group in 1986, and the United Nations Observer Mission, that intervened after negotiations broke down in 1992, are either viewed as failed attempts, or do not conform to mediation (Saunders, 2014: 4). The conclusion reached is that sufficient trust existed between the parties because of the confidence-building measures among the adversaries before the formal negotiations, and this was enough to make international mediation unnecessary. Further, both parties thought that the likely outcome would be better for them without such mediation (Saunders, 2014: 1).

This book problematises these conceptions about the negotiation process in South Africa on two counts. First, no such trust existed between the government and the ANC throughout the entire negotiation process. While these 1980s encounters did improve understanding between the intermediaries representing government officials, and certain representatives of the ANC, this cannot be equated to trust between the government and the ANC. Building trust was not their function. Their importance was that they were a forum that facilitated the exchange of communication between the government and the ANC in their search for negotiated solutions. These secret forums, the book will argue, are a type or method of mediation. Further, the basic points of discussion in these forums, i.e. linking the release of political prisoners and unbanning of prohibited political parties with the initiation of a political process, emerged within the context of the Commonwealth mission. The Commonwealth's Eminent Persons Group resolving formula, the "Negotiating Concept," was prophetic; it embodied the basic ingredients that formed the basis of negotiations between the ANC and the government, leading to the Groote Schuur Minute on 2 May 1990, and Pretoria Minute on 6 August 1990. In this unfolding political process there was no love lost between the government and the ANC. The book will closely examine this contribution by the Commonwealth and locate the analysis within the negotiation process. The reasons why historians of the South African transition have not examined the significance of the Commonwealth mission, and the way it synchronised crucial preconditions, has to do with the way in which international mediation is understood, the second item of contention.

Second, the South African literature misconceives the complexity of international mediation and fails to problematise it. Thus, when questioning the role of international mediation in the transition, the examination is not done within the context or in relation to the scholarly literature on mediation. Mediation is either defined by a method or individual e.g. a Richard Holbrooke, George Mitchell, Kofi Annan, Thabo Mbeki or a Western Contact Group as in the case of Namibia, where disputants are directly mediated, and its success is equally misconstrued, i.e. it produced an agreement, the parties rejected it, people stopped fighting, etc. Thus, the Commonwealth mission is dismissed because the South African Defence Force sent them packing via air strikes in neighbouring countries, and the United Nations Observer Mission did not directly mediate the Multi-Party Negotiation Process. No attempt is made to evaluate success or failure within the context of scholarly debates on mediation outcomes. Through an examination of these scholarly debates on international mediation, the book will show that international mediation can cover a wide range of third-party activities: from simply providing good offices for the parties to negotiate, to assisting them in creating a resolving formula to their conflict, in which the mediator uses resources to leverage an agreement. Mediation is a political process and the mediator can assume different roles in that process, and there is no obligation on the part of the conflicting parties to accept the mediation ideas or proposals. Therefore, the task is to understand what type or method the Commonwealth's mediation was, and how it performed in that phase of the conflict. Similarly, the United Nations Observer Mission was created by a Security Council Resolution. There was a political process that occurred before that involving discussions between the international community, the conflicting parties and the deployment of a Special Representative. This was equally a distinct type or method of mediation.

Further, there is no consensus in the literature on the criteria for success. Some scholars explain success as a situation in which both parties to the conflict formally or informally accept a mediator. Others measure successful mediation as producing an agreement. Others point out that mediation is successful when it leads to the termination of hostilities and the advent of democratic governance. Distinguishing success from failure is further complicated when a mediation effort produces a ceasefire without achieving a lasting resolution for the conflict, i.e. the issues remain, and the violence flares up. Others point to a more long-term perspective on mediation success that goes beyond the ending of violence and examine the contribution of international mediation to the conflict-resolution process. The point is that if the two significant international interventions in the South African transition (the Commonwealth and United Nations missions) are examined within a scholarly canvas, i.e. within the context of scholarly debates, concepts and analytical properties of mediation, very different conclusions about their significance will be reached.

Aims of the book

The aim of the book is to do just that and to make two contributions: (1) to the rich scholarship on the South African political negotiations; and (2) to the rich scholarship on international mediation. The book will examine the two international attempts at mediation in the South African transition. At a first glance, one might expect glaring differences between the approaches of the Commonwealth Eminent Persons Group (EPG) and the United Nations Observer Mission to South Africa (UNOMSA) in assisting the South African negotiated transition. Both occur in different phases of the negotiation process, and the EPG is regarded as a failure and UNOMSA a success. Yet a closer comparison of their approaches along several dimensions illustrates important similarities in the ways and means of third-party actions. While the generally accepted verdict on each differs, the book will argue that the international community, particularly the Commonwealth and the United Nations, played a profound and beneficial role in the political transition to end apartheid.

This book compares these distinct roles and approaches in mediation by the Commonwealth and United Nations. The main question the book addresses is under what conditions international mediation brings about peaceful change. Following William Zartman's approach, international mediation in the South African transition is examined as an exercise in which international organisations had interests and operated in a context of power and cost-benefit calculation. The book argues that the Commonwealth and United Nations had an interest in the conflict and in obtaining an outcome and played distinct roles. The comparative analysis not only contributes to the existing literature on international mediation but also calls into question the generalisations about the determinants of success by international third parties in South Africa's negotiated transition.

Through the comparative analysis, the book will raise general questions about the methods or types of mediation and their appropriateness for certain phases of a conflict-resolution phase and call into question the generalisations about the determinants of success by international third parties in South Africa's negotiated transition. It moves from the position that the success of a mediation effort depends on the examination of the time horizon of a conflict and on the contribution the mediation effort plays in improving the relationship between the belligerents. Through the comparative analysis, the book focuses on success measured in two ways and corresponding to the different stages of the conflict-resolution process. The first success is getting disputing parties to the table. In this stage, the goal of mediation is to get each party to agree that they have a shared understanding of the conflict or problem, a shared understanding that a negotiated solution is possible, to produce a commitment towards a negotiated solution, and to overcome preconditions as a barrier towards the opening of settlement negotiations. The second is success in having the parties reach an agreement because of mediation. Once parties agree that a mutually acceptable resolution to their conflict is possible, the next goal of mediation is to find ways of arriving at an agreement.

Mediators are therefore called upon to do different things for the conflicting parties depending on the history and dynamics of the conflict. For example, if a negotiation process is underway and then subsequently experiences crisis and breakdown, the task of the mediator is to restore communications between the adversaries and explore conditions each was imposing on the resumption of talks (Mitchell, 2003: 80). Under these circumstances, mediation is assessed on its ability to break the deadlock and resume talks, not on its ability to get the parties to reach agreement. By contrast, if belligerents are yet to even explore the possibility of talking, then the task of the mediator is to "sound out both sides to see if there might be any readiness to engage in talks i.e. if the elusive will exists on both sides, and if it did what conditions for meeting might be imposed" (Mitchell, 2003: 83). A third scenario is the task of the mediator once representatives of the parties in conflict are already at the table. Here the methods and skills required would be those akin to a chairperson of the actual face-to-face talks, using power, leverage and the like.

Chapter outline

The book is divided into five chapters. Chapter 2 examines the main research debates regarding international mediation strategies, their efficacy and their consequences for the peace-making process. The chapter will show that while the literature on international mediation has made progress towards understanding the conditions under which mediation processes help resolve conflict, there is a lack of consensus regarding the question of strategy in international mediation, and how to conceptualise success. The challenge is to develop a better understanding of the conditions under which different mediation strategies are more effective, and how they shape the outcome of a conflict management process (Wallensteen and Svensson, 2014). More importantly, it is to also think differently about success, i.e. success should be measured by what contribution the mediation makes to transforming the relationship between the belligerents, and how it does this. This chapter will also explain the research design of the book.

Chapter 3 provides analysis of the South African conflict. This is important; any attempt to understand the negotiation process, and any resolving formula put forward by mediators, must understand what is being negotiated, what are the fundamental issues, and how the resolving formula talks to the issues. It also reveals the complexity of mediation. The chapter will show that the root of the South African conflict was white minority rule. The basic demand of the African National Congress and its allied organisations that resisted racial domination during this period was for the universal franchise and the right to be included as equals in all aspects of society. At the centre of this conflict was the system of apartheid. Successive National Party governments devised various methods to co-opt Africans on unequal terms to maintain white minority rule. These methods were repeatedly rejected and rendered unworkable. The Commonwealth mediation occurs at the point where parties were beginning to explore negotiation possibilities. Its contribution therefore is not only with regards to whether they were able to get parties talking, but what the consequences of its resolving formula were.

Chapters 4 and 5 analyse the case studies. Both chapters will trace and provide a detailed analysis of the stage of the negotiation process in which the mediation occurs. It is important to critically examine the time horizon of the conflict and negotiation process to truly appreciate the contribution the mediation effort plays in altering the relationship between the belligerents. For example, while the EPG may be considered a failure from one respect, if we locate its contribution in terms of the time horizon of the conflict, its resolving formula was prophetic; the resultant secret facilitative mediation by Michael Young had all its elements as the basic points of discussion between government intermediaries and ANC envoys. However, if we merely confine our discussion up to the point where the EPG abort its mission, then it is clearly a failure. In Chapter 4, the discussion will also include the evolution of the South African question in the Commonwealth. The government's response to the EPG was shaped by these politics. Similarly, to understand the success of the United Nations mission in Chapter 5, and its contribution in getting parties to back to the table and then agreement, it is important to trace the negotiation process in South Africa after Mandela was released, and how parties committed to negotiations, and discuss the fundamental issues of contention. The United Nation mediation and formula comes at a specific point in this process. At the heart of the matter was the issue of political violence and its relationship to the negotiation process.

Chapter 6 will contrast these approaches across several dimensions to develop a better understanding of the range of third-party actions that may be appropriate and effective in the different stages of the negotiation process. Moving from Curran et al.'s (2004) comparison of George Mitchell and Richard Holbrooke's mediation in Northern Ireland and Bosnia-Herzegovina respectively, the chapter will offer a set of categories into which the actions of the EPG and the United Nations can be characterised (Curran et al., 2004: 516). These categories are embedded in framework that analyses the basic choices for those involved in third-party roles. Third parties face three decisions (Curran et al., 2004: 516). First, they must "determine their basic objectives," e.g. to get parties to the table, to restore communication between parties once talks have broken, to foster an agreement, to delay the conflict, to model a more constructive process or to break a deadlock. A mediator's objective will be determined by the stage of the conflict-resolution process. Second, mediators must "choose their fundamental role," e.g. neutrality or bias. Mediators must decide how they want to alter the perception and behaviour of the belligerents. Some mediators don't simply listen and suggest; they steer the belligerents towards an agreement and some form of muscle might be necessary (but not always) in the context of an impasse. Third they must consider their "best means of influence on the situation," e.g. forceful, persuasive, facilitative, etc. With these choices, mediators must form a "winning coalition" (i.e. coalition strategy) which contains three overlapping strands: "an issues strategy, with respect to the substantive aspects of the agreements sought, a process strategy with respect to the choices of process for the mediation, and a timing strategy with respect to the timing of their efforts" (Curran et al., 2004: 516).

Bibliography

Curran, D., J. Sebenius and M. Watkins. 2004. "Two Paths to Peace: Contrasting George Mitchell in Northern Ireland With Richard Holbrooke in Bosnia – Herzegovina," *Negotiation Journal* 20(4): 513–537.

Esterhuyse, W. 2012. *Endgame: Secret Talks and the End of Apartheid*. Cape Town: Tafelberg.

Harvey, R. 2001. *The Fall of Apartheid: The Inside Story From Smuts to Mbeki*. Hampshire: Palgrave.

Mitchell, C. 2003. "Mediation and the Ending of Conflicts," in J. Darby and R. MacGinty, eds. *Contemporary Peacemaking: Conflict, Violence and Peace Processes*. New York: Palgrave Macmillan.

Saunders, C. 2014. "The Dog that didn't Bark: The Absence of Significant International Mediation in the South African Transition to Democracy," *Mediation Arguments*, No. 5. Pretoria: Centre for Mediation in Africa.

Sparks, A. 1994. *Tomorrow Is Another Country: The Inside Story of South Africa's Negotiated Revolution*. Sandton: Struik Book Distributors.

Waldmeir, P. 1997. *Anatomy of a Miracle: The End of Apartheid*. New York: Norton.

Wallensteen, P. and I. Svensson. 2014. "Talking Peace: International Mediation in Armed Conflicts," *Journal of Peace Research* 51(2): 315–327.

2 International mediation

Mediation is one of the most common methods of dealing with and resolving social and political conflicts. Irrespective of the society, conflict, or type of organisation, and their location in time, and irrespective of the development of the society, mediation has always been a method of managing conflict and practice of settling disputes through third parties. Mediation is therefore as common as conflict and is more likely to occur in an environment where disputes are long-drawn-out and complex, where the disputants' own conflict management efforts have reached a deadlock, where neither side is prepared to bear further costs or escalation of the dispute, and when disputants are prepared to break their deadlock or stalemate by cooperating with each other and engaging in some communication (Bercovitch, 2011: 1). Mediation as a means of managing disputes has therefore been used extensively across a diverse set of conflicts, from labour disputes to divorce settlements to resolving disagreements between nation-states. Irrespective of the conflict or items of contention, the definitive feature of mediation is the introduction of a third party or external actor into a dispute with the aim of assisting the belligerents to resolve the conflict. Since the field of mediation is so extensive, this book is limited to the concept of international mediation (i.e. mediation by an international actor) in the context of armed conflict, between representatives of the main conflicting actors, and dealing with conflicting issues or incompatibilities including violent behaviour. The book is not concerned with labour management or workplace disputes of any form, divorces, track one-and-a-half disputes or mediation in relation to the humanitarian consequences of war (Wallensteen and Svensson, 2014: 316).

As an instrument of peace-making in armed conflict, international mediation has stimulated an expanding area of research. While the growing literature has made progress towards understanding the conditions under which mediation processes help bring armed conflicts to peaceful ends, it faces problems about the question of strategy in mediation, and how to consequently conceptualise success. The challenge is to develop a better understanding of the conditions under which different mediation strategies are more effective, and how they shape the outcome of a conflict management process. This chapter examines the main research debates regarding international mediation strategies, their efficacy and their consequences for the peace-making process.

Defining mediation

Since the process of mediation is so varied, the concept of mediation has been defined in different ways. One can loosely organise these definitions in the literature between those that examine the formal role of the mediator, those that highlight the process in which the mediator alters the dynamics between the conflicting parties, and those that describe the different ways in which the mediator assists the parties in settling their conflict. Wall, Stark and Standifer define mediation as the "assistance or some sort of interaction by a third party who does not have the authority to impose an outcome" (Wall et al., 2001: 375). For these authors, mediation is understood as a voluntary process on the part of the belligerents and the mediator: "For mediation to occur, two processes must mesh. First the interacting/disputing parties must request or permit a third party to mediate; second, the third party must agree to mediate" (Wall et al., 2001: 371). The parties in the conflict must believe that they will benefit by accepting mediation. The benefits of accepting mediation may include an end to the conflict, a favourable political settlement or narrower self-serving goals unrelated to the diplomatic initiative. Some belligerents accept mediation to improve or preserve relations with the mediator, while for others it is a strategic or tactical goal to buy the kind of time that is needed for war aims (Richmond, 1998). From this perspective, mediation presents a better alternative than the conflict aims. Bercovitch et al. (1991: 8) put forward a similar definition:

> mediation is a process of conflict management where the disputants seek the assistance of, or accept an offer of help from, an individual, group, state or organisation to settle their conflict or resolve their differences without resorting to physical violence or invoking the authority of the law.

Like Wall et al.'s definition, there is an essential external third party who does not have the authority to impose an outcome but assists belligerents in reaching an agreement. Thus, the act of seeking assistance and its acceptance is central to mediation, and mediators play an active role in the conflict management process.

Other definitions of mediation emphasise mediation as a process where the mediator's role is to change the dynamic between belligerents. The mediator can thus assume multiple roles, functions and activities, and can be carried out by a variety of people (Lederach, 2003: 33). Touval and Zartman (1985: 7) define mediation as "a form of third-party intervention in conflict for abating or resolving that conflict through negotiation." They also understand it as a form of negotiation in which a third party assists conflicting parties to find a solution that they cannot find by themselves (Zartman and Touval, 2007: 438). Like other forms of peace-making, it is an intervention "that must be acceptable to the adversaries in the conflict, who cooperate diplomatically with the intervenor." At the same time, mediation is also distinct from the functions the mediator performs, i.e. "mediators often suggest compromises and may negotiate and bargain with adversaries

[to] induce them to change their stance" (Touval and Zartman, 1985: 7). There are thus different ways in which mediation can occur and each comes with differing structures and techniques. Mediators, for example, not only help adversaries communicate or assist in changing perceptions; mediators often suggest compromises and may negotiate and bargain with adversaries to induce them to change their stance (Touval and Zartman, 1985: 7). Mediation therefore can cover a wide range of third-party activities; from simply providing good offices for the parties to negotiate, to assist them in formulating a resolving formula to their conflict, in which the mediator uses resources to leverage an agreement. Mediation is therefore a political process and the mediator can assume different roles in that process, and there is no obligation on the part of the conflicting parties to accept the mediation ideas or proposals.

Definitions of mediation that describe how third parties conduct this role examine the different ways the presence of the mediator alters the perception and behaviour of the belligerents. These definitions examine the political positioning of the mediator vis-à-vis the belligerents. One definition incorporates the use of force, i.e. mediation with muscle: "mediation is a voluntary process in which the parties retain control over the outcome (pure mediation), although it may include positive and negative inducements (mediation with muscle)" (Miall et al., 1999: 21–22). The point here is that a mediator does not simply listen and suggest; third parties must steer the belligerents towards an agreement and some form of muscle might be necessary in the context of an impasse. While Beardsley (2011: 18) emphasises non-violent tactics, the implications of their definitions are the same; some form of force is incorporated into the definition, i.e. mediation is when conflicting parties are moved to some sort of agreement by a third party. By contrast, Kochan and Jick (2011: 211) incorporate neutrality in their definition; mediation is seen as a "process in which a neutral party attempts to get the direct participants to reach a voluntary agreement." A neutral mediator not only does not favour one side or the other but is perceived as having no interest in either the conflict nor an agreement that would emerge from the mediation. The essential ingredient of neutrality is the issue of trust, i.e. a neutral mediator that is trusted by both sides is at the centre of the mediation process. Neutrality however is relative; if the goal of mediation is to resolve a dispute, then some form of muscle is necessary.

What is clear from the discussion is that mediation is an activity directed towards the peaceful resolution of a conflict. It involves the intervention of an outsider, i.e. a third party that can either be an individual, a group of actors or an organisation in a conflict. The mediator enters the conflict to affect change, resolve, modify or influence the conflict in some way (Greig and Diehl, 2012: 7). In so doing, the mediator uses persuasion rather than coercion and aims to reach a political solution that is acceptable to the belligerent parties. Therefore mediation "aims at conflict resolution and primarily achieves this through negotiations, by resorting to reason and logic and, ultimately, by appealing to the common wishes to end violence and prevent its recurrence" (Wallensteen and Svensson, 2014: 316).

Putting these elements together, Bercovitch (2011: 5–6) summarises the essential characteristics of mediation at all levels:

1 Mediation is generally an extension and continuation of peaceful conflict management. It can take place during violence, but clearly it has much better chances of success if it takes place when violence has ceased.
2 Mediation usually involves the intervention of an outsider, who can be an individual, a group, an organization or even a state, into a conflict between two or more states or other actors.
3 Mediation may be undertaken by a single actor at a time, or multiple actors. There are advantages and disadvantages associated with each form.
4 The essence of mediation is that it is a generally facilitative, non-coercive and non-binding form of social behaviour. Mediation is there to help parties, not to force them into submission.
5 Mediators enter a conflict, whether internal or international, to affect it, change it, resolve it, modify it or influence it in some way. It is important to recall that mediators want to terminate or resolve a conflict. They do not get involved in other people's conflicts just for sake of it. They have objectives, goals and interests.
6 Mediators bring with them, consciously or otherwise, ideas, knowledge, resources and interests of their own or of the group or organization they represent. Mediators often have their own assumptions and agendas about the conflict in question. In other words, mediators do not enter a conflict with a "blank slate"; they may well have their own agenda and interests. It would be good to try to ascertain what these are.
7 Mediation is a voluntary and confidential form of conflict management. Parties in the conflict involved retain control over the outcome (if not always over the process) of their conflict, as well as the freedom to accept or reject mediation or anything that flows from it.
8 Mediation usually takes place on an ad hoc basis only. Mediators are appointed or invited to deal with a conflict. Once their efforts are concluded, successfully or not, they go back to their own policy or organization.
9 Parties enter a mediation process because the process usually works and is an effective way of dealing with many conflicts.

Mediation has important consequences for the structure of a conflict; it transforms it from a dyad into a triangle. Touval and Zartman (1985: 10) write that the outcome of the contest is as a consequence determined by a formation of a coalition of two against one:

> it becomes the parties' interest to reconvert the triadic relationship back into a dyad by forming a subtle coalition with the mediator, bringing the latter in on one side without destroying its appearance of neutrality, and thereby effecting a solution that is both favourable and preferable to continued conflict.

For the mediation process to succeed, neither side must prevail making a mutual stalemate necessary; it is in the interest of the mediator that the parties continue to look to the mediator for a way out of the stalemate. The triangular structure is necessary for mediation: to produce an agreement, the mediator must use this triangular structure to move the parties to agreement. This means maintaining a stalemate, preserving the triangular relationship and not allowing one party to end the conflict by victory (Touval and Zartman, 1985: 11). For Touval and Zartman (1985: 11), stalemate is necessary for mediation, just as mediation is necessary to overcome a stalemate:

> to achieve that stalemate, the mediator must often reinforce the weaker party. This reinforcement can take the form of tangible support during the conflict, or it can be verbal, but it must not be unconditional. It needs to be tied to movement toward agreement.

Strategies and outcomes of mediation

Since mediators need to use their resources to maintain a stalemate and preserve the triangular relationship, moving parties to agreement, a basic problem is identifying the optimal strategy. This is key to the outcome and, as will be discussed, how we think about success. There is no consensus in the literature about what the most effective strategy or method of mediation is. One way to think about methods and strategy is to conceive of mediator activities along a continuum of roles derived from the parties' needs and in order of the mediator's degree of involvement. Touval and Zartman (1985) distinguish between three methods: communication, facilitation and manipulation. The mediator as communicator approaches the conflict as a breakdown in the ability of the parties to communicate with each other. They act as telephone wires, establishing contacts and carrying messages. Their role is procedural, "with no substantive contribution by the mediator, and completely passive, only involving carrying out the parties' orders for delivery of messages" (Zartman, 1996: 211). Such mediation would be appropriate in a conflict where parties are locked in a situation which they cannot extricate themselves simply because they cannot contact each other directly (Touval and Zartman, 1985: 11). In such a conflict, parties may be willing to provide concessions as a means of resolving the conflict, but these depend on the parties' ability to communicate their willingness to compromise without losing face. Mediators here are the target of concessions, as parties cannot communicate, and the receiver of concessions, as parties cannot give in to each other. As a result, their importance is that they package concessions together to present to the parties. The mediator here is therefore a passive conduit and repository: "tact, palatable wording, and sympathetic presentation are as important as, but must not impinge on, accuracy and straightforward presentation" (Touval and Zartman, 1985: 12). A good example of mediator as communicator is the role played by Michael Young, a former executive of mining giant Consolidated Goldfields (discussed in Chapter 4), who set up a secret channel between the ANC and the South African government. Young approached the conflict as a breakdown in the ability of the ANC and South African government to communicate with each other. He acted as a telephone wire, i.e. creating an environment in which the ANC and South African government could establish contact and carry messages. Young's role was thus completely procedural, with no substantive contribution, and completely passive, and only involved carrying out the parties' orders for the facilitation of dialogue and delivery of messages. These series of facilitated meetings had two goals: to improve understanding between the government (through intermediaries) and the ANC by humanising the adversary groups through face-to-face meetings, and to prepare the ground for settlement negotiations by exploring, in an unofficial and informal setting and without commitment, underlying issues and possible solutions (Diamond and McDonald, 1996: 2). These meetings took place in exotic and novel settings: grand estates in the English countryside. These settings were important; they were able to overcome communication-inhibiting conflict norms and promoted learning and new ideas (Kelman and Cohen, 1986: 337). As a result, the meetings all included substantial social interaction, with participants' typically dining and drinking alcohol together. This level of informality and equal status between groups fostered interpersonal bonds and trust and had a significant impact on their perceptions of each other, the conflict, their role in it and anxieties about its resolution.

The mediator as formulator plays a more substantive role. Such mediators are usually innovative thinkers who work out ways to get around the parties' constraining commitments. They not only suggest but persuade; persuasion is a form of power that requires greater involvement from the mediator. Formulation helps parties see a way out of their conflict and is therefore performed by a mediator who "has the confidence of the parties and the imagination to see solutions that they cannot see" (Zartman, 1996: 280). The method is more appropriate in an environment where the breakdown in communication not only impedes but keeps the parties from conceiving a solution to meet the needs of both sides (Touval and Zartman, 1985: 12). This requires tactfulness, sympathy, accuracy, straightforward prodding and the ability to make suggestions to redefine the issues in the conflict and find a formula for its resolution. In this context, parties need help in finding a solution or in constructing a solution from the pieces of the conflict. Mandated by the African Union, Kofi Annan's mediation in the aftermath of Kenya's post electoral crisis in late 2007 and early 2008 is a good example of mediation as formulation. Running a highly pragmatic process and pushing the parties towards a power-sharing agreement from the very beginning, Annan's mediation was instrumental in ending the post-election violence, changing the behaviour of the principals and creating mechanisms to address the root causes of Kenya's governance crisis (Keck, 2011). While the conflicting parties were vehemently opposed to a power-sharing arrangement upon entering negotiations, Annan and his mediation team skilfully employed technical experts to build support for a coalition government (Keck, 2011: 24). Dividing up the issues into categories was also highly pragmatic, as it "enabled the parties to achieve two quick agreements on issues they both agreed upon – ending the violence and addressing the humanitarian crisis." Given the bitter relationship between the parties from the start, "this proved to be an important confidence building moment before turning to agenda three – resolving the political crisis" (Keck, 2011: 24).

It is useful to think of mediator as communicator and formulator as lying on a continuum, from passive facilitation to active formulation. Both are facilitative roles where the mediator works on the parties' perceptions, where the mediator has no interest, except in seeking a solution, and exercises no power except the intangible exercise of power to change people's minds (Touval and Zartman, 1985: 12).

The mediator as manipulator is the maximum involvement of a mediator, making them a party in the solution if not the dispute. In this role, the mediator uses their power to bring the parties to an agreement, i.e. pushing and pulling them away from the conflict and into resolution. This however is not any resolution; the mediator uses the position and other available resources to manipulate parties into an agreement that appears to the most stable or favourable to the mediator. The mediator promotes their formula for a solution and takes measures to make the solution attractive, "enhancing its value by adding benefits to its outcome and distributing them to overcome imbalances that may have prevented one party or another from subscribing to it" (Zartman, 1996: 281). The third party must therefore help improve the attractiveness of a solution and increase the unattractiveness of continued conflict, an involvement that may mean supporting one side or condemning another. This requires leverage that can be brought to bear on the parties to move them to agreement. Leverage is the most elusive element of mediation: "even where the need for a facilitator is glaringly apparent and the would-be mediator's interest in peace very clear, the mediator may have no ability to move the parties in the indicated direction" (Touval and Zartman, 1985: 12). Richard Holbrooke's mediation in Bosnia-Herzegovina is a good example of mediation as manipulation. Holbrooke was less concerned about long-term sustainability and more concerned in getting the deal done (Watkins and Rosegrant, 1999: 2). In adopting an approach of "whatever it takes to force a deal," Holbrooke lowered the value of no-agreement alternatives and influenced dynamics to impose ever high costs on the various parties who refused to play (Curran et al., 2004: 518–519). Further, with the might of the United States and NATO to back up his mediation, he could shape and manipulate the situation through bombing and promised aid and sanctions (Curran et al., 2004: 519).

Most contributions in the literature provide categories that overlap with Touval and Zartman's contribution. Curran et al. (2004) in their comparative analysis of George Mitchell and Richard Holbrooke's mediation strategies in Northern Ireland and Bosnia-Herzegovina respectively, distinguish between forcing and fostering methods. Forcing strategies are characterised by the building of momentum by gaining early wins through agreements on principle. The pace of mediation is accelerated with "a series of partial agreements and forcible actions to prevent backsliding on promises" (Curran et al., 2004: 525). In Bosnia-Herzegovina, Holbrooke used several imposed deadlines (including the threat of bombing) to forge agreement and made well-timed persuasive arguments to force parties to back down (Curran et al., 2004: 525). Holbrooke's forcing strategies would thus be akin to what Touval and Zartman would call manipulation, i.e. the mediator uses the leverage resources of power, influence and persuasion that are brought to bear on the parties to move them to agreement. By contrast, fostering strategies are patient strategies that use time to foster a constructive relationship among the parties in order to increase the parties' sense of respect, obligation, liking and credibility towards the mediator. In Northern Ireland, Mitchell's patient strategy fostered a constructive relationship among the parties, and in so doing, increased their sense of respect, obligation and credibility towards him. Mitchell used this credibility on the final deadline, "which he carefully negotiated with the parties and governments at the talks" (Curran et al., 2004: 525). Mitchell's fostering strategies would be akin to a hybrid version of Touval and Zartman's mediator as communicator and formulator, where the mediator's role lies on a continuum between passive facilitation-communication to active formulation in the final third. Another good example of fostering would be Thabo Mbeki's mediation in the Zimbabwe crisis. Mbeki's mediation in Zimbabwe hinged on facilitative approaches. Defined as a combination of measures comprising behind-the-scenes engagements, secret negotiations and subtle coaxing, Mbeki's controversial mediation in Zimbabwe included: a series of bilateral meetings between Mbeki, Mugabe and senior government officials; Mbeki's defence of Zimbabwe against criticism in international organisations; South Africa's endorsement of questionable election results; persistent negotiations loosely termed "constructive engagement"; and the provision of economic packages in order to facilitate change within Zimbabwe by Zimbabweans (Hove and Ndawana, 2016: 70).

Fisher (2007) also makes an important contribution in this debate. He identifies four methods of mediation: conciliation, consultation, pure mediation and power mediation. Conciliation is a method where "a trusted third party provides an informal communication link between the antagonists for the purposes of identifying the issues, lowering tension and encouraging direct interaction, usually negotiation" (Fisher, 2007: 314). Very similar to mediator as communicator, the mediator, identical to Michael Young in the South African process, is not directly involved in settlement solutions or leverage concessions; the mediator simply provides good offices by arranging meeting places and times to facilitate discussions, and giving belligerents a free hand in discussions (Greig and Diehl, 2012: 7). This is therefore the lowest level of third-party engagement; the mediator or third party simply develops informal communication linkages as a means of reducing tension, and to provide foundations for further negotiations. Consultation is when the mediator "works to facilitate creative problem solving through communication and analysis using human relations skills and social-scientific understanding of conflict etiology and dynamics" (Fisher, 2007: 314). Akin to fostering, the mediator brings their personal skills to problem-solving, but the involvement remains limited; the mediator avoids exerting control over the discussions, changing bargaining positions, or offering carrots and sticks. Rather, the mediator encourages the belligerents to think of common interests that exist in ending the conflict

(Greig and Diehl, 2012: 8). The role of the mediator is therefore more extensive, with a more direct hand in discussions. Mbeki's mediation in Zimbabwe would be consistent with this. In pure mediation, the mediator "attempts to facilitate a negotiated settlement on substantive issues using reasoning, persuasion, the control of information and the suggestion of alternatives" (Fisher, 2007: 314). Akin to Annan in Kenya, the mediator designs innovative solutions to end the conflict to assist the parties in recognising areas of common interest, developing terms of an agreement and encouraging parties to agree on those terms. The mediator thus exerts greater control over negotiations (Greig and Diehl, 2012: 8). The mediator here becomes a solution innovator to the conflict; they might

> limit the range of topics to be conducted in the negotiations in order to increase the chances for their success, excluding some issues from the talks entirely and focusing on others that seem more favourable for agreement or are better tied to the issues under contention.
>
> (Greig and Diehl, 2012: 8–9)

Power mediation goes beyond pure mediation. In this method, the mediator uses leverage and coercion in the form of "promised rewards or threatened punishments and may involve the third party as a monitor and guarantor of the agreement" (Fisher, 2007: 314). Akin to Holbrooke, the mediator is an active participant in the conflict-resolution process; using their leverage, they control the issues under discussion and develop a resolving formula for the final settlement. The mediator uses carrots and sticks to push and pull the belligerents towards a settlement. The mediator therefore not only controls the issues under discussion, and in so doing, develop the terms of settlement; they actively use their resources to leverage an agreement (Greig and Diehl, 2012: 9).

The literature is also no in agreement regarding the most effective strategy. Bercovitch et al. (1991) argue that directive strategies, i.e. forceful strategies tend to be more successful even though facilitative approaches are more common (Curran and Sebenius, 2003). Later, Bercovitch and Diehl (1997) concluded that fostering approaches, i.e. facilitative approaches, were more productive for intractable conflicts. Drawing on peace-making efforts in Africa, Nathan (1999) points to fostering rather than forceful strategies, arguing that the pressure that comes with power or pure mediation has greater potential to be counterproductive. By contrast, Sisk (2009) makes the case for powerful peace-making using incentives and sanctions to leverage parties to peace. In a similar vein Touval (1975: 68) argued that "the more powerful international actors are, the more effective they are as intermediaries." Gelpi (1999) also concluded that great power mediation increases the chances for mediation success.

Other studies point out that mediation can occur in different stages or phases of a conflict. Therefore, the forms or methods of mediation may differ, and outcomes may be determined by whether a method is appropriate for a certain phase of a conflict. For example, getting people to start talking requires a different strategy to packaging a formula for settlement. The forms of mediation may also be determined by the type of conflict. Bercovitch and Gartner (2006) for example make a distinction between high- and low-intensity conflicts, arguing that forceful strategies are more effective in high-intensity conflicts but less effective in low-intensity conflicts where procedural strategies are more appropriate. Greig and Diehl (2012) point out that conflict phases and resolution stages intersect and influence the process and strategies of mediation. Mediation is thus not unique to a certain phase of the conflict but occurs within many different contexts.

The literature generally describes the process of conflict resolution in terms of three phases or stages: getting to the table, getting to agreement and implementing the agreement (Walter, 2002). Zartman and Berman (1982) use different terminology to label essentially the same phases: the diagnostic phase (bringing about negotiations), the formula phase (defining solutions), and the detail phase (working out agreements). These phases or stages intersect and influence the processes and stages of mediation. Thus, a conflict-resolution process may contain a variety of methods of mediation as that process moves through the stages. Given that there are contradictory conclusions regarding the efficacy of mediation strategies, the important task is to develop a better understanding of the conditions under which different mediation strategies are effective in the different phases of a conflict or negotiation process. This also further raises the issue of sequencing, for "the use of a particular mediation strategy rarely occurs in isolation" (Wallensteen and Svensson, 2014: 320). Therefore, depending on the issues before a third party and depending on the different phases of the conflict-resolution process, coercive strategies may include the simultaneous use of softer strategies with the difference being of degree and sequence.

A related question regarding mediation strategies concerns the relationship between mediation strategies and outcomes, i.e. the criteria defining success. When is an attempt at mediation considered successful? Which strategies are more conducive for the successful outcome of a mediation process? Once again there is no consensus in the literature. Frei (1976: 69) explains success as "a situation in which both parties to the conflict formally or informally accept a mediator and a mediation attempt within five days of the first attempt." Bercovitch et al. (1991: 8) measure successful mediation as producing an agreement: "by successful outcomes we mean producing a ceasefire, a partial settlement or a full settlement." Nathan (1999: 3) goes further and defines success as "when it leads to the termination of hostilities and the advent of democratic governance." Other scholars have equated mediation success with effectiveness taking the mediator's objectives as a starting point (Touval and Zartman, 1985).

Distinguishing success from failure is further complicated when a mediation effort produces a ceasefire without achieving a lasting resolution of the conflict. Greig and Diehl (2012: 106) further point out that for some cases of mediation there is no clear delineation between success and failure, arguing that determining the success of a mediation effort depends on the examination of the time horizon of a conflict and on the contribution the mediation effort plays in improving the relationship between the belligerents. This book moves from this position and focuses on success measured in two ways and corresponding to the different stages of the conflict-resolution process. The first success is getting disputing parties to the table. In this stage, the goal of mediation is to get each party to agree that they have a shared understanding of the conflict or problem, a shared understanding that a negotiated solution is possible, to produce a commitment towards a negotiated solution, and to overcome preconditions as a barrier towards the opening of settlement negotiations. The process of getting to the table is the pre-negotiation phase. Pre-negotiation begins with changes in at least one of the parties' perception of the conflict where negotiation is considered as an option and an alternative to the unilateral track. Parties subsequently convey the messages of their intentions to each other. The pre-negotiation stage ends when parties agree to begin negotiating a formula for the resolution of their conflict, or when one party abandons this option altogether. In the process, parties establish whether negotiations are worthwhile and if so, agree on the agenda and the necessary procedure for negotiating a formula for the resolution of their conflict. Pre-negotiations can either be informal and confidential, or they can be formal and well-advertised. However, whether they are formal or informal, public or confidential, pre-negotiations are often more important and far more difficult than is usually supposed.

The second is success in having the parties reach an agreement because of mediation. Once parties agree that a mutually acceptable resolution to their conflict is possible, the next goal of mediation is to find ways of arriving at an agreement. In explaining the political activity in this formula phase, Zartman and Berman (1982: 89) explain two ways in which parties reach agreement. One is to "put the agreement piecemeal, building it primarily through mutual compromise or exchanged concessions on specific items." The other is more deductive, i.e. "to establish first the general principles, or formula, governing the issues susceptible of solution and then work out the implementing details." In the first instance, detailed points of agreement "are arrived at discretely, without specific attention to the broader implications or the relations among these points of agreement." In the second case, the detailed points of agreement "are suggested by the overall framework." These stages however overlap and are related since the same factors and processes that encourage belligerents in seeking mediation also influence their willingness to reach an agreement (Greig and Diehl, 2012: 106).

Mediators are therefore called upon to do different things for the conflicting parties depending on the history and dynamics of the conflict. For example, if a negotiation process is underway and then subsequently experiences crisis and breakdown, the task of the mediator is to restore communications between the adversaries and explore conditions each was imposing on the resumption of talks (Mitchell, 2003: 80). Under these circumstances, mediation is assessed on its ability to break the deadlock and resume talks, not on its ability to get the parties to reach agreement. By contrast, if belligerents are yet to even explore the possibility of talking, then the task of the mediator is to "sound out both sides to see if there might be any readiness to engage in talks i.e. if the elusive will exists on both sides, and if it did what conditions for meeting might be imposed" (Mitchell, 2003: 83). A third scenario is the task of the mediator once representatives of the parties in conflict are already at the table. Here the methods and skills required would be those akin to a chairperson of the actual face-to-face talks, using power, leverage and the like.

Therefore, the task of mediation is varied and is dependent on the phase of the conflict-resolution process. In the pre-negotiation phase, the goal of mediation is to explore possibilities and determine readiness for negotiated solutions, to encourage consensus on core issues and concessions and to initiate the process of talks. During the negotiation process, the goal is to facilitate, provide new options and perspectives, provide new resources, provide insurance against the breakdown of talks and offer to guarantee durable solutions, and to legitimise the negotiated settlement.

The research design of the book

To develop a more thorough understanding of the conditions under which different mediation strategies are most effective, I employ the method of structured focused comparison to study two different episodes of mediation by international organisations in the South African political transition. The structured focused comparison is a method of gaining maximum theoretical utility from a case study. The method is structured in the sense that

> the researcher writes general questions that reflect the research objective and that these questions are asked of each case under study to guide and standardize data collection, thereby making systematic comparison and cumulation of the findings of the cases possible.
>
> (George and Bennett, 2005: 58)

The method is focused in that it "deals only with certain aspects of the historical cases examined." These requirements for structure and focus "apply equally to individual cases since they may later be joined by additional cases" (George and Bennett, 2005: 58). This method is useful for the aims to the book since the number of attempts at mediation is small but the number of possible relevant theoretical variables is large. The comparison of cases is assisted "when the researcher can hold some factors constant among the cases" (Stedman, 1991: 28). Stedman (1991: 28) further writes that under these methodological conditions, the researcher can bolster the yield of the comparison by using process tracing, i.e. "the use of evidence that tells a story that meets the rigorous standards of historical scholarship." Therefore, the reader can judge "whether the historical explanation fits with the explanation suggested by the contrast and comparison of important explanatory variables."

For the objectives of this book, I want to compare an unsuccessful mediation attempt with a successful mediation attempt by two international organisations in the South African political transition. Although there were many mediated attempts to end the South African conflict, the attempts by the Commonwealth and United Nations stand out; they are attractive cases for those interested in getting insights into how failure and success have been understood – the successful

United Nations attempt followed a series of failures and mishaps to an end to the conflict. Therefore, in comparing these two mediation attempts, one can hold some variables constant over subcases and highlight important differences among attempts. Further, since it is a single case, process variables such as learning, changes in actor preferences, and coalition formation among the different parties can be studied. In choosing the South African case study, what the method loses in noncomparability to other countries it gains in "sharpness of focus, subcase comparability, and the opportunity to see the whole process over a variety of mediating efforts" (Stedman, 1991: 29).

To get maximum value from the comparison, I will develop a set of general questions to ask of each case. The following questions will be asked:

1 What is the context of the conflict at the point of mediation? What core issues are at stake or are disputed? What is the structure of the conflict?
2 Who are the main actors? What are their goals? What are their perceptions about their adversaries and the course of the conflict?
3 Who is the mediator? What are the mediator's perceptions about the conflict and the parties within it? What is the mediator's reputation among the parties? Does the mediator have a conception of a possible settlement?
4 What are the mediator's basic objectives? What is their fundamental role? What is their best means of influence on the situation?
5 What is their strategy to form a winning coalition on behalf of the chosen objective?

In the next two chapters, I turn to the respective cases of mediation in the South African transition. The chapters are structured as follows. First, I will trace and provide a detailed analysis of the stage of the negotiation process in which the mediation occurs. It is important to critically examine the time horizon of the conflict and negotiation process to truly appreciate the contribution the mediation effort plays in altering the relationship between the belligerents. For example, while the EPG may be considered a failure from one respect, if we locate its contribution in terms of the time horizon the conflict, its resolving formula was prophetic. Second, I will provide an analysis and examination of the mediators, their reasons for getting involved and their strategy. Third, I will provide an analysis of the political dynamics within the belligerents. Fourth, I will provide a narrative of the mediation process in terms of the questions raised above and examine how the relationship between the belligerents was altered. And fifth, I will examine the broader strategic context in which the mediation took place. The following chapter provides a background to the South African conflict.

Bibliography

Beardsley, K. 2011. *The Mediation Dilemma*. Ithaca: Cornell University Press.

Bercovitch, J. 2011. *Theory and Practice of International Mediation: Selected Essays*. London: Routledge.

Bercovitch, J., T. Anagnoson and D. Wille. 1991. "Some Conceptual Issues and Empirical Trends in the Study of Successful Mediation in International Relations," *Journal of Peace Research* 28(1): 7–17.

Bercovitch, J. and P. Diehl. 1997. "Conflict Management of Enduring Rivalries: Frequency, Timing and Short-Term Impact of Mediation," *International Interactions* 22(4): 299–320.

Bercovitch, J. and S. Gartner. 2006. "Is There Method in the Madness of Mediation? Some Lessons for Mediators From Quantitative Studies of Mediation," *International Interactions* 32(4): 329–354.

Curran, D. and J. Sebenius. 2003. "The Mediator as Coalition-Builder: George Mitchell in Northern Ireland," *International Negotiation* 8(1): 111–147.

Curran, D., J. Sebenius and M. Watkins. 2004. "Two Paths to Peace: Contrasting George Mitchell in Northern Ireland With Richard Holbrooke in Bosnia – Herzegovina," *Negotiation Journal* 20(4): 513–537.

Diamond, L. and J. MacDonald. 1996. *Multi-Track Diplomacy: A Systems Approach to Peace*. Washington, DC: United States Institute for Peace.

Fisher, R. 2007. "Assessing the Contingency Model of Third-Party Intervention in Successful Cases of Prenegotiation," *Journal of Peace Research* 44(3): 311–329.

Frei, D. 1976. "Conditions Affecting the Effectiveness of International Mediation," *Peace Science Society (International) Papers* 26(1): 67–84.

Gelpi, C. 1999. "Alliances as Instruments of Intra-allied Control," in H. Haftendorn, R. Keohane and C. Wallander, eds. *Imperfect Unions: Security Institutions Over Time and Space*. Oxford: Oxford University Press.

George, A. and A. Bennett. 2005. *Case Studies and Theory Development in the Social Sciences*. Cambridge, MA: MIT Press.

Greig, J. and P. Diehl. 2012. *International Mediation*. Cambridge: Polity.

Hove, M. and E. Ndawana. 2016. "Regional Mediation Strategy: The Case of Zimbabwe," *African Security Review* 25(1): 63–84.

Keck, T. 2011. "Mediating Ethnic Conflict: Kofi Annan in Kenya," Selected Works of Trevor Keck, at: https://works.bepress.com/trevor_keck/2

Kelman, H. and S. Cohen. 1986. "Resolution of International Conflict: An Interactional Approach," in S. Worchel and W. Austin, eds. *Psychology of Intergroup Relations*. Chicago: Nelson-Hall.

Kochan, T. and T. Jick. 2011. "The Public-Sector Mediation Process: A Theory and Empirical Examination," *Journal of Conflict Resolution* 22(2): 209–240.

Lederach, J.P. 2003. "Cultivating Peace: A Practitioner's View of Deadly Conflict and Negotiation," in J. Darby and R. MacGinty, eds. *Contemporary Peacemaking: Conflict, Violence and Peace Processes*. New York: Palgrave Macmillan.

Miall, H., O. Ramsbotham and T. Woodhouse. 1999. *Contemporary Conflict Resolution*. Cambridge: Polity.

Mitchell, C. 2003. "Mediation and the Ending of Conflicts," in J. Darby and R. MacGinty, eds. *Contemporary Peacemaking: Conflict, Violence and Peace Processes*. New York: Palgrave Macmillan.

Nathan, L. 1999. "When Push Comes to Shove: The Failure of International Mediation in African Civil Wars," *Track Two* 8(2): 1–23.

Richmond, O. 1998. "Devious Objectives and Disputants' View of International Mediation: A Theoretical Framework," *Journal of Peace Research* 35(6): 707–722.

Sisk, T. 2009. *International Mediation in Civil Wars: Bargaining With Bullets*. London: Routledge.

Stedman, S. 1991. *Peacemaking in Civil War*. Boulder: Lynne Rienner.

Touval, S. 1975. "Biased Intermediaries: Theoretical and Historical Considerations," *Jerusalem Journal of International Relations* 1(1): 51–69.

Touval, S. and I.W. Zartman. 1985. "Introduction: Mediation in Theory," in S. Touval and I.W. Zartman, eds. *International Mediation in Theory and Practice*. London: Westview Press.

Wall, J., J. Stark and R. Standifer. 2001. "Mediation: A Current Review and Theory Development," *Journal of Conflict Resolution* 45(3): 370–391.

Wallensteen, P. and I. Svensson. 2014. "Talking Peace: International Mediation in Armed Conflicts," *Journal of Peace Research* 51(2): 315–327.

Walter, B. 2002. *Committing to Peace: The Successful Settlement of Civil Wars*. Princeton: Princeton University Press.

Watkins, M. and S. Rosegrant. 1999. *Getting to Dayton: Negotiating an End to the War in Bosnia*. Harvard Business School Case 1-800-134. Boston: Harvard Business School Publishing.

Zartman, I.W. 1996. "Bargaining and Conflict Reduction," in E. Kolodziej and R. Kanet, eds. *Coping With Conflict After the Cold War*. Baltimore: John Hopkins University Press.

Zartman, I.W. and M. Berman. 1982. *The Practical Negotiator*. New Haven: Yale University Press.

Zartman, I.W. and S. Touval. 2007. "International Mediation," in C. Crocker, F. Hampso and P. Aall, eds. *Leashing the Dogs of War: Conflict Management in a Divided World*. Washington, DC: United States Institute of Peace.

3 Historical background

The structure of the South African conflict

This chapter will explain the central issues in the South African conflict. The root of the South African conflict in the 20th century was white minority rule. The basic demand of the African National Congress and its allied organisations that resisted racial domination during this period was for the universal franchise and the right to be included as equals in all aspects of society. At the centre of this conflict was the system of apartheid. Successive National Party governments devised various methods to co-opt Africans on unequal terms to maintain white minority rule. These methods were repeatedly rejected and rendered unworkable.

Segregation to apartheid: 1910–1948

The origins of apartheid are in the segregationist policies of the four colonies and republics which combined to form the Union of South Africa in 1910. The Act of Union restricted the franchise to white men and excluded Africans from the political system. After the Act of Union, the building blocks of apartheid evolved through various ad hoc legislative measures in reaction to, and designed to curb, the increased flow of Africans into the towns and cities. In 1922, the Stallard Commission laid down the principle that Africans should only be in urban areas to "minister the needs of the white man and should depart when he ceases to minister" (Lipton, 1985: 18). African men over 16 years had to carry a reference book, known as a pass, which recorded their permission to work and live in a white area. These influx controls managed the flow of African labour into urban areas and allocated labour between sectors and regions.

In the spirit of the Stallard Commission, the 1923 Native Urban Areas Act initiated a policy of urban residential segregation to apply the principles of the 1913 Land Act to urban areas (Davenport, 1970: 77). The Act, however, left it to the discretion of local authorities to implement this policy. As a result, there was considerable variation in its application. This prevented wholesale segregation as some municipalities lacked the means and incentives to provide for the building of new townships to which Africans would have been relocated (Maylam, 1990: 66). Furthermore, official policy discouraged African families and "favoured the mining industry's system of migrant workers housed in all-male compounds, while their families remained in the reserves thus keeping down African numbers and retaining their links with the tribal areas" (Lipton, 1985: 18). These laws hindered Africans wishing to leave white farms or reserves or to enter, or move between, the towns and cities.

The development of large-scale manufacturing during the second quarter of the century, made possible by the installation of a massive domestic steel-and-electricity industrial infrastructure from the 1930s, upset this segregationist dynamic. Many Africans were attracted to the new urban job markets. During this period, the number of urban Africans as a percentage of the total African population doubled from 14 percent to 28 percent (Maylam, 1990: 64). According to the 1946 census, "Africans for the first-time outnumbered whites in all South Africa's major cities" (Posel, 1991: 23–24). Furthermore, manufacturing permitted a relatively permanent and residentially stable African labour force, involving not only the workers themselves but also their families: in metropolitan areas, the percentage of urban Africans living with their families rose from only 30 percent in 1936, to 45 percent in 1951, and to 65 percent in 1960 (Eidelberg, 1997: 93–94).

These developments introduced new ideas in South Africa's liberal intelligentsia and in urban business circles. These were reflected in the publications of important official commissions at the time, such as the van Eck, Smit and Fagan Reports. They argued that

> industrialisation, and the poverty of the crowded reserves, meant that increasing and permanent African urbanisation was inevitable, and that industrialisation required that African workers should be stabilised with their families in the towns and provided with improved education, pay and prospects of promotion that would turn them into the committed, motivated workforce required by modern industry, as well as providing an expanding market for consumer goods.
>
> (Lipton, 1985: 21)

The job colour bar, pass laws and migrant labour were criticised as "unjust and inefficient, deterring ambition and competition." Jan Smuts, the Prime Minister at the time, argued that African urbanisation was inevitable: "you might as well try to sweep the ocean back with a broom" (Smuts, 1942). Jan Hofmeyr, Smuts's deputy, went further and called for the "ultimate removal of the colour bar from our constitution" (Hofmeyr cited in Lipton, 1985: 21).

As a result, the job colour bar was eased, and this was followed by an extension of training facilities for Africans to expand the supply of skilled workers. Through the Wage Board, government policy led to the raising of African wages to such an extent that the black-white wage ratio narrowed. In 1942, the Department of Native Affairs recommended the abolition of pass laws and their implementation was subsequently relaxed resulting in a significant drop in the number of prosecutions.

The ruling United Party went into the infamous 1948 election firmly committed to these ideas and recommendations, which accepted the principle that African workers were a permanent part of urban South African society and migrant labour was economically undesirable. The Fagan Report had concluded that "urbanisation was an economic phenomenon . . . [which] can be guided and regulated" but not prevented and urged that "the policy should be one for facilitating and encouraging stabilisation" (Fagan Report, 1948: 46–50). The Fagan Report also advocated that the mining industry be allowed to provide housing for stabilised labour on the new Orange Free State goldmines.

Early apartheid: 1948–1960

The National Party (NP) that was elected into power under Prime Minister Daniel F. Malan in 1948 reversed the limited reforms of the United Party, and proclaimed their belief in segregation, racial inequality and apartheid. The foundation of their electoral platform was a rejection of the Fagan recommendations and an affirmation of the proposals of the Sauer Commission, an NP commission tasked with formulating NP policy on the racial question. In setting out the terms of the investigation, Malan stated that the commission had to "investigate the implementation of apartheid in the political and industrial terrains and had to consider the question of residential segregation; it had to be practical, positive and constructive, rather than negative and divisionary in character" (cited in Norval, 1996: 117).

The report listed three main aims of apartheid policy:

> first, the maintenance of the white population and a complete eradication of any racial mixing; second, the maintenance of the indigenous non-white racial groups as separate [communities] by working against any influences aiming to undermine those separate identities and by facilitating opportunities to develop each according to its own . . . character; third, the maintenance of the traditional principle of trusteeship, which entailed the fostering of national pride and self-respect for each group, and the encouragement of mutual respect between different racial groups.
>
> (cited in Norval, 1996: 117–118)

To achieve these aims, each racial group had to "have its own territory in which it would be able to develop its inalienable right to self-maintenance and self-determination." Regarding Africans, the report stated that African ethnic groups should each be drawn together territorially so that each could develop as separate tribal units, "offering a spiritual, national and economic home to the natives." This would "encourage 'talented and progressive Natives' to move there to use their initiatives in the service of their own people." When dealing with Africans on farms and in the cities, the commission advocated the continued use of African labour on farms and that urban-based Africans were only temporary visitors to the towns and should never be able to claim equal political rights with whites. Cities "had a 'white character' to be maintained." Consequently, separate African locations had to be developed and steps had to be taken to limit their numbers in cities and reinstate their links with tribal reserves:

> The urbanisation of Natives [conflicts with] the policy of apartheid and the Native can thus never form part of the urban population. The influx into the

> cities has to be subjected to all possible limitations and the Native has to be informed of the disadvantages of urbanisation and the advantages of an own national home.

The report also made a crucial distinction between theoretical and practical apartheid:

> We put as final ideal and aim total separation between Whites and Natives which has to be implemented as far as is practical on a gradual basis, with consideration of the needs of the country and with the necessary prevention of detribalisation of agriculture, industries and general interests.
>
> (cited in Norval, 1996: 117–119)

The government did not want to halt industrialisation and modernisation; it wanted to control it to make it compatible with a hierarchical racial structure and the preservation of white identity. They believed that this required the reinforcement of racial divisions against the social forces released by modernisation. As a result, they drew sharper distinctions between whites and non-whites and resorted to legislation to enforce this. The legislative basis for this was laid by the 1950 Population Registration Act, which classified the whole population by race.

The basis for the creation of separate political systems for Africans was laid by the 1951 Bantu Authorities and 1959 Promotion of Bantu Self-Government Acts, legal interventions whose intention was to convert Africans into foreigners in South Africa. Each of the so-called eight tribes or nations could only exercise political rights in designated and ethnically defined homelands. In 1957, the government stopped all trading by Africans outside the reserves and townships. The 1950 Group Areas Act had already restricted the residential and trading rights of all Africans.

Other existing economic and social controls were tightened. In the public service, hundreds of Africans were dismissed and replaced by whites at higher wages, and job preferences were particularly given to Afrikaners. The Minister of Native Affairs, Hendrik Frensch Verwoerd, spelt out the intention of ensuring job preferences for whites:

> There is no place for [the Bantu] in the European Community above the level of certain forms of labour . . . it is of no avail for him to receive a training which drew him away from his own community and misled him by showing him the green pastures of the Europeans but still did not allow him to graze there. . . . [This led to] the much-discussed frustration of educated natives who can find no employment which is acceptable to them . . . it must be replaced by planned Bantu education . . . [with] its roots entirely in the Native areas and in the Native environment and community.
>
> (cited in Norval, 1996: 24)

Following this, the 1953 Bantu Education Act centralised control of African education and separate "ethnic" universities were set up for each "nation." Migrant labour became the means for reconciling urban capital's need for African labour with the government's determination to limit African numbers and prevent their permanent urbanisation. Regarding Africans already living in urban areas, Verwoerd clearly spelt out the new policy: "The Bantu have no claim to permanency in the European areas, they are in these areas as workers, and therefore own no real estate and can claim any political rights outside of the Bantu reserves" (cited in Norval, 1996: 26). The rights of urban Africans were withdrawn, and thousands of families were forcibly removed from freehold houses to short-term leasehold houses in newly built townships further away from the main cities and towns. Finally, the 1953 Reservation of Separate Amenities Act legalised the provision of unequal facilities for different races. This was followed by the 1957 Native Amendment Act, which extended compulsory segregation into churches, places of entertainment, clubs, buses and sport.

During the early years of NP rule, the pillars of apartheid were enacted. After Verwoerd became prime minister in 1958, apartheid evolved into separate development which served as the structural solution to turn South Africa into a white republic in which Africans would not feature as citizens. Ten homelands would be created to rid South Africa of African citizens. Every African would be assigned a homeland according to their ethnic identity.

Early resistance to segregation and apartheid, 1912–1960

The origins of resistance to white minority rule are in the politics of African nationalism in South Africa. On the 28th of January 1912, South Africa's most prominent African citizens assembled in Bloemfontein and resolved to form the South African Native National Congress (SANNC). For this group, Union was a bitter disappointment: "[despite African] expressions of imperial loyalty . . . the British government made it clear that its paramount concern was with the question of white unity in South Africa" (Lodge, 1983: 1). The Act of Union removed the right of enfranchised Africans to be elected to parliamentary seats and provided for the removal of the franchise from African voters. The first post-Union administration embarked on a path of consolidating this dynamic: the 1911 Natives Land Bill prohibited rural landownership by Africans or occupation outside the reserves, effectively dispossessing many landowners and outlawing tenant farming relationships. The 1913 Land Act destroyed a whole class of peasant producers, and forced them into crowded reserves, driving them into new and arduous social relationships. The group that assembled at Bloemfontein had a concern and fear of a petty bourgeoisie at a time of crisis: "the fear of being thrust back into the ranks of the urban and rural poor" (Lodge, 1983: 2).

The SANNC represented the concerns and anxieties of an African middle class. It retained close ties with the African aristocracy and the rural chieftaincy, who were conservative constituencies concerned with protecting a moral and social order under attack. The SANNC was intended to function as an organised pressure group and planned to agitate for changes through peaceful propaganda, the election of sympathisers to legislative bodies, protests and enquiries, and passive resistance (Carter and Karis, 1971: 118). The SANNC was renamed the African National Congress (ANC) in 1923.

The Communist Party of South Africa (CPSA) was founded in 1921 by small left-wing groups in Cape Town and on the Rand. When the Labour Party split over whether to support the First World War, members who contended that the war was an anti-working-class imperialist struggle broke away to form the International Socialist League (Lodge, 1983: 7). Informed by experiences of eastern European migrants, and the Russian Revolution, the International Socialist League fused together with various Zionist, socialist and Marxist organisations to form the CPSA. Although not a mass-based organisation, it had a well-organised and centralised structure, organised along the lines of a Marxist-Leninist political organisation.

The relationship between the ANC and CPSA dates to 1924. At its 1924 congress, the CPSA's Young Communist wing argued successfully that the CPSA should formally recognise the strategic importance of organising African workers (Ellis and Sechaba, 1992: 15). This brought them into closer contact with other trade unions and political organisations with African members. The most important was the ANC, and the most important leader within the ANC in this regard was Josiah Gumede. The CPSA was later named the South African Communist Party (SACP) after it was banned by the passing of the Suppression of Communism Act in 1950.

The important turning point for resistance happens during the Second World War. This major global event was associated with far-reaching economic and social changes in South Africa; changes that created the conditions for a mass-based African political movement. The growing urbanisation of the African population was the key feature of these changes. Accompanying this increased flow of Africans from the countryside to the towns was another demographic change. Before the war, most African urban migrants were adult males. During the war years, entire families for the first time constituted significant portions of the African urban population. The great majority of these families confronted harsh conditions in the cities: insufficient wages to meet family subsistence needs, and the lack of housing, resulting in families "squatting" in dwellings made of sacking, wood, corrugated iron and cardboard. This new, impoverished and urbanising African population became militant, posing a greater challenge to political authority:

> large-scale squatter movements involving thousands of homeless people took shape during the mid-1940s; Africans in large numbers engaged in a series of bus boycotts to protest increasing fares; and a wave of strikes erupted during the war despite wartime regulations prohibiting them.
>
> (Johns and Davis, 1991: 18)

When the NP won the 1948 election and began implementing apartheid policies, the ANC became more confrontational, responding with a major programme of resistance, the most prominent being the Defiance Campaign of 1952. The Defiance Campaign began the ANC's transformation from a small to a mass-based organisation. Led by a young and charismatic lawyer, Nelson Mandela, and beginning on 26 June 1952, the campaign was one of civil disobedience to confront apartheid laws.

In 1955, the ANC formed additional alliances with the South African Indian Congress, the Congress of Democrats and the South African Coloured People's Organisation into an anti-apartheid coalition, the multiracial Congress Alliance. That same year, the Congress Alliance adopted the Freedom Charter which embodied the ideals of non-racism, a common South African nationhood and equal citizenship. In response to this position, an important group of Africanists led by Robert Sobukwe and Ashby Peter Mda broke away from the ANC to form the Pan-Africanist Congress (PAC) in 1959. At a PAC-organised nation-wide demonstration against pass laws, in the township of Sharpeville, the police took a particularly heavy-handed approach killing 69 protesters and wounding 180. The Sharpeville shootings were a turning point in the South African conflict, "when protest finally hardened into resistance, and when African politicians were forced to begin thinking in terms of a revolutionary strategy" (Lodge, 1983: 225).

Following the events in Sharpeville, the subsequent prohibition of the ANC and PAC, and the state's overall repressive action, both the ANC and PAC produced military offshoots. The ANC formed Umkhonto we Sizwe (MK), meaning "spear of the nation," on 16 December 1961 with Nelson Mandela as its commander, and the PAC formed Poqo, meaning "pure" or "alone" with Potlako Leballo as its commander. MK advocated the "implementation of a carefully controlled campaign of violence which in its initial stages would attempt to avoid bloodshed." Poqo's programme "developed from the same vision of a spontaneous popular uprising which had informed the PAC's conception of their pass campaign" (Lodge, 1983: 231). Poqo was later renamed the Azanian People's Liberation Army (APLA).

Prior to being unbanned in 1960, the ANC had established an external mission headed by its vice president, Oliver Tambo, a Johannesburg lawyer who shared a legal practice with Mandela. After 1960, Tambo set out to organise the ANC internationally and solicit support. By 1962, many of the top leaders of the ANC were arrested at Lilliesleaf farm in Rivonia. The accused, including Nelson Mandela and the entire MK high command, were tried, found guilty of treason in 1964 and imprisoned for life on Robben Island.

The ensuing conflict between the South African government and the ANC lasted from 1961 to the early 1990s. The conflict did not involve MK and the South African Defence Force (SADF) facing each other on a battlefield; rather, it was an internal conflict where the objective for both sides, Stephen Ellis writes, was "the population itself." The conflict, Ellis further points out, was not so much to destroy the enemy as to win political support:

> To be more precise, for more than three decades there was a prolonged confrontation between the apartheid state and a substantial part of the South African population. The ANC, the SACP and some other organisations sought to turn this confrontation into a war that would be fought among the people, by bringing in trained soldiers from outside. They had strictly limited success in

> this endeavour, but some communities in South Africa were in any event disposed to engage in violent protest on their own initiative, notably in 1976 and after 1984. Furthermore, from 1975, the SADF was simultaneously fighting an old-fashioned conventional war in Angola using all the expensive military equipment required.
>
> (Ellis, 2012: 278–279)

The issue of white minority rule was at the centre of the conflict. The basic demand of the ANC was the universal franchise. The government, for its part, devised various methods to include Africans on unequal terms to maintain white minority rule. During this conflict, the ANC was transformed. Before the Defiance Campaign, the ANC had a membership of around 10,000 members. By the time of its banning in 1960, the number had climbed to 100,000. Towards the end of its tenure in exile, the ANC had evolved into a "centralised party with a code of conduct, enforced by severe sanctions, a distinct ideology and a well-defined programme. The ANC had turned itself into a liberation movement" (Ellis, 2012: 279). Nelson Mandela and the SACP played an important role in this process. Mandela emerged as the most decisive ANC leader from the period of the Defiance Campaign up until the Rivonia Trial.

The relationship between the ANC and SACP, and between the SACP and MK, offered the ANC the financial, military and political support of a superpower, the Soviet Union. This in turn brought with it an impressive global infrastructure of solidarity by way of an international alliance of communist and socialist parties. SACP veteran Ben Turok writes that the extent of the SACP's influence over the ANC was "a system without precedence in the history of national liberation movements [in Africa] and arguably no [communist] party has managed to insinuate its presence and influence on such a scale" (Turok, 2003. 118).

Pragmatic apartheid: from Vorster to Botha, 1966–1978

After the death of Verwoerd and the ascension of Balthazar Johannes Vorster to the premiership, apartheid changed "from a missionary sense of purpose to a pragmatic functionalism" (Giliomee and Schlemmer, 1989: 290–291). Whereas Verwoerd projected apartheid as a goal, under Vorster apartheid became perceived as a means to a vaguely defined end. Realising that apartheid was incompatible with winning broad support, Vorster declared apartheid was not the goal, but the means to achieve Afrikaner identity in a white sovereign state (Melunsky, 2002: 72); if this did not work, other means would have to be explored:

> No, chaps, you have got it all wrong. The cardinal principle of the NP is the retention, maintenance and immortalisation of Afrikaner identity within a white sovereign state. Apartheid and separate development is merely a method of bringing this about and making it permanent. If there are other better methods of achieving this end, then we must find those methods and get on with it.
>
> (Vorster cited in Welsh, 1994: 165)

Vorster's style was ad hoc, with no clearly outlined strategic goals, and no certainty about direction (Melunsky, 2002: 73). Giliomee writes that the main goal of government was "*om die fort te hou* – to keep the Afrikaner power base intact" (Giliomee, 1972: 36). While slightly modifying Verwoerdian apartheid by moving away from pervasive social segregation, Vorster sought to retain separate development and not compromise principles. He encouraged contact with English-speakers and the outside world.

The turning point came in the early 1970s, when the government came under pressure. This pressure had three important sources. First, in the beginning of the 1970s, the economy began to experience contradictions. The emergence of manufacturing as the leading sector of the South African economy had implications. The rapid growth of manufacturing undermined the apartheid goal of preventing the development of a large and permanent urban population of Africans. The demand for employment in the urban-based manufacturing sector, and the push of poverty in the rural and depressing homelands "combined to vitiate the elaborate government effort at influx control into the white areas" (Price, 1991: 29). The African population living in urban areas thus tripled in the first two decades of apartheid.

This inability to slow the pace of African urbanisation constituted a failure of one of apartheid's core goals and was expensive. While the social demography of South Africa was changing towards a growing and large permanent urban African population, with the forces of economic development shifting toward a technically skilled and permanent urban-based African workforce, apartheid bureaucracy was working to prevent Africans from acquiring the very skills and technical know-how needed by the most dynamic sector of the economy (Price, 1991: 31–32). This inevitably contributed to low levels of productivity, increased training costs for employers and skills shortages, all of which impinged on prospects for future economic growth and development for the manufacturing sector. The system of influx control also led to the instability of the available workforce. South Africa's new and leading industrialists began to face difficult choices between significant aspects of apartheid and future economic growth and development.

The NP's core Afrikaner constituency also began to change. In 1948, the economic interests of the Afrikaner community had a bias towards agriculture. Most parliamentarians at the time were directly elected from rural constituencies, with many members of parliament themselves being farmers. Giliomee writes that in the late 1940s, Afrikaners controlled 11 percent of the private sector economy outside agriculture (Giliomee, 1979: 171). However, the economic base of the Afrikaner community changed. From agriculture, it shifted into all sectors of the non-agricultural economy including the state bureaucracy. By the mid-1960s, over "one quarter of the private sector outside agriculture was controlled by Afrikaners, and the proportion of Afrikaners in agricultural occupation dropped below 16 percent from over 30 percent in the1940s" (Price, 1991: 38). As white controlled agriculture underwent modernisation during the 1950s and 1960s, i.e. extensive mechanisation and the reduction in reliance on large numbers of African tenant farmers, it began to change its positions on the importance of labour control and repression. Organised agriculture began to relax its insistence that the state exercise more elaborate political control over the African labour market. This reduced the forces pushing for an extension of apartheid and increased those advocating for the reform of apartheid considering economic constraints.

The second source of change was external. A military coup in Portugal on 25 April 1974 precipitated a series of events that changed the political landscape of southern Africa. Before the coup, Angola, Mozambique, Rhodesia (now Zimbabwe) and Namibia were each ruled by a white minority government, had a longstanding working relationship with the South African government and constituted a buffer zone between South Africa and the forces of African nationalism across the Zambezi River (Price, 1991). When the Armed Forces Movement overthrew the Portuguese dictatorship, South Africa's buffer zone collapsed. The new Marxist government in Portugal dismantled its African colonial empire. By the end of 1975, Mozambique and Angola had been granted independence and were controlled by Marxist-Leninist political parties that had a history of opposition to apartheid, had close fraternal ties with the ANC and received substantial assistance from the Soviet Union (Price, 1991: 40).

The third source of change was the revival of black popular protest. This happened in two waves. The first wave began in 1973 when a wave of strikes by black workers swept across South Africa. Although legally constrained from forming trade unions and organising strikes, tens of thousands of black workers put down their tools in a disciplined and successful effort to improve their wages (Price, 1991: 46). The second wave began on 16 June 1976 in Soweto when school children protested the introduction of Afrikaans as the medium of instruction in secondary school courses. They were met by a detachment of police who opened fire, killing several children.

These series of events sparked an unprecedent revolt against the apartheid system, both in its scope and endurance. The revolt, and its suppression, galvanised the attention of international public opinion; it revived the moral issue of the international acceptability of apartheid and subjected South Africa to a different type of world pressure. These pressures transformed entrenched attitudes; "they shaped Afrikanerdom's future leaders, forced a re-think in government policy, and created a generational split" (Melunsky, 2002: 73). Leading Afrikaners began to question apartheid's mission and its ethical basis. The question was no longer whether apartheid was the framework but rather what its alternatives were. Two factors underpinned this debate: the future security of Afrikaners, and that the new order must have moral underpinnings.

Reforming apartheid: the rise of Pieter Willem Botha

It is in this context that Defence Minister Pieter Willem (PW) Botha succeeded Vorster as the prime minister and sought to provide a response to the challenges facing the South African government. Botha was convinced that old-style apartheid had to be discarded. But this realisation did not stem from moral considerations or visions of justice; it stemmed from the stark military, economic and demographic realities of the 1970s. Botha believed that "the unrestrained pursuit of white interests was [not] sustainable and recognised a political formula for urban Africans had to be found" (Schrire, 1991: 47). He realised that Afrikaner political and social isolation was unworkable; allies were needed to secure a more broadly based white dominance. He concluded that classical apartheid was not practical. He told a provincial congress of the NP in the late 1970s that "apartheid was a recipe for permanent conflict [and that] change is the only alternative to revolution." He advised Afrikaners that "the moment you start oppressing people . . . they fight back. We must acknowledge people's rights" (Pottinger, 1988: 72).

The initial move towards reform came in 1977 through a report of the NP parliamentary committee on the constitution, and the appointment of two government commissions: the Riekert and Wiehan Commissions. The Wiehan Commission was charged with investigating industrial relations and trade union rights. It was instructed to make recommendations regarding the adjustment of the existing system for it to respond to changing circumstances. However, it was the Riekert Commission and the report of the NP parliamentary committee under Botha, while serving as defence minister, which had important implications.

The Riekert Commission and the NP constitutional committee

The Riekert Commission was instructed to investigate the systems and procedures that controlled the movement of Africans from the rural homelands to industrial cities. The commission was told to make recommendations "with a view to eliminate bottlenecks and other problems experienced by both employees and employers in the utilisation of labour" (Price, 1991: 81). The impetus for reform was not for moral reasons; it was an attempt to resolve the inefficiencies associated with apartheid's economic contradictions.

The Riekert Commission had two related objectives: to create an environment in respect to labour mobility and African urbanisation that would increase economic efficiency, and through this, reduce political opposition (Riekert Commission Report, 1979). To achieve these objectives, the commission called for major alterations in the system of influx control, and for new legislation that would "explicitly make provision for the social and economic development of urban Black communities that live in the White area" (Riekert Commission Report, 1979: 245). The commission distinguished between the established inhabitants of urban black residential areas and urban residents who were considered commuters, migrants and squatters. This latter and larger category of black urban inhabitants was not entitled to rights of permanent residence. The former category of established residents was defined as those who had acquired residential rights under Section 10 of the Group Areas Act (Riekert Commission Report, 1979: 248–252). The Riekert recommendation, later accepted and implemented by the government, treated the two categories of black urban dwellers very differently. New means were recommended to keep the commuters and migrants out of the urban residential areas, and for the established residents, the commission proposed that residential rights be secured, that other rights and privileges be extended, and that living conditions be improved. Riekert's proposals were designed to create an environment conducive for the emergence of an African middle class in the townships. This social stratum was in turn expected to support the government's efforts to limit the size of the African population in urban areas, for the "outsiders" and revolutionaries would be a threat to the African middle class's newly found stature and lifestyle (Price, 1991: 106).

The report of the parliamentary committee of the NP, issued at the same time as the Riekert commission, also signalled an inclination for political reform. The report introduced a set of constitutional recommendations involving the extension of parliamentary representation to the Indian and coloured population groups. Although excluding the African majority and placing limits on the nature of Indian and coloured representation, these recommendations constituted a significant reversal of the NP's policy of barring Indian and coloured participation in central government (Price, 1980). The strengthening of the reformist drive was marked by the ascension of Botha to the premiership. Botha made domestic reform the centrepiece of his political strategy and defined the purpose of his administration as adaptation and change.

Constitutional reform

In June 1980, in the spirit of reform, the South African parliament passed the Republic of South Africa Constitution Amendment Act. The Act abolished the Senate and replaced it with a multiracial President's Council tasked with agreeing on a new constitution. The council proposed a tricameral legislature with respective chambers for white, coloured and Indian members. This proposal was accepted by the South African parliament when the Republic of South African Constitution Act was passed in late August 1983, and then ratified by a referendum in November 1983.

As for the African majority, the plan was to design separate institutions for them to exercise their rights. Three sets of legislation were drafted in this regard. The Orderly Movement and Settlement of Black Persons Bill and the Black Community Development Bill modified the influx control system by conferring urban status to Africans with stable employment in white areas (Lodge et al., 1991: 35). A system of approved accommodation was introduced to prevent the increase of informal settlements in urban areas, and the Black Local Authorities Act of 1982 gave extra powers to black municipal councils to run township affairs.

With a victory in the referendum of November 1983 behind him, Botha faced two important challenges. First, he had to get the support of urban African leaders to accept the exclusion of Africans from the Tricameral Parliament. Second, he had to persuade them to participate in a negotiating forum on African political rights (Giliomee, 2012: 177). To deal with these twin issues, Botha appointed a special cabinet committee (SKK) five days after the referendum. The SKK was chaired by Botha's close ally, Jan Christiaan (Chris) Heunis, the minister of constitutional development and planning. Botha made his intention clear from the start: "he was opposed to a fourth chamber for blacks, but would support regional development, land consolidation in the homelands and a creation of a constellation of states" (Giliomee, 2012: 177). For the government, the Black Local Authorities Act, and accompanying legislation, was designed to compensate urban Africans from their exclusion from parliament. The system, however, would have an inherent flaw; African local authorities did not have a proper revenue base. Few township residents owned property, revenue from rates were limited and many township beer halls (a major potential source of revenue) had been destroyed in the Soweto uprising in 1976 and the subsequent unrest.

The government was not able to meet the expectations generated by its own discourse and actions. The most important constraint was financial; the cost of improving the physical and social conditions of urban African life were extremely high, and the government had expected to finance the upgrade of African townships out of revenues generated by economic growth. However, for a variety of reasons (falling gold prices, the structural impediments of the South African economy and international economic isolation after the Soweto uprising), the 1980s was a period of economic stagnation for the South African economy. The most important consequence was a decline in the level of African living standards. The recession of the 1980s brought increased levels of unemployment, high rates of inflation and stagnating wages to the urban black population (Seekings, 1988: 60–61).

Increases in rents became a significant threat to the living conditions of township residents. During the 1970s, the finances of the township administrations neared crisis proportions; "costs, driven by inflation, escalated; [the government] seeking to end state subsidisation of township administration, pursued a policy of township self-financing; and township-based revenues, generated largely by liquor taxes and rents, lagged expenditures" (Riekert Commission Report, 1979: 68). By the end of the decade, township administrations were bankrupt. Consequently, pressure mounted to raise rents to cover the costs of domestic reform, i.e. the costs of electricity, water, refuse collection, sewerage, etc. Escalating rents became the salient feature of township life in the early 1980s.

Government's reform policies became a significant stimulus for the emergence of mass opposition in the African community, and latitude for that opposition to organise. The role of reform in the emergence of mass opposition worked in two ways. First, reform policies gave rise to grievances. These became the stimulus for the formation of new organisations, as well as the fuel for their efforts at mass political mobilisation. Second, reform limited the government's latitude in acting repressively against opposition organisations once they emerged. To ban newly created organisations and to put a blanket restriction on all political expression by the African majority "would have made it impossible to convince the international community of the seriousness of the South African government's intentions" (Price, 1991: 160). Out of these new organisations, the United Democratic Front (UDF) was the most significant.

In the history of African resistance in South Africa, the UDF was a movement of unprecedented pervasiveness and depth. The UDF was a broad coalition of student groups, civic associations, church societies, women's organisations and trade unions. At its peak, it claimed a total membership of two million and an adherence to about 700 affiliates grouped in ten regional clusters and embracing every major centre of population in the country. Its affiliates were ideologically diverse but united only in their opposition to the apartheid government and demand for the universal franchise (Lodge et al., 1991).

The immediate spur to the founding of the UDF was the government's reform proposals in 1982 and 1983 for the reform of the influx control system to control and regulate the presence of Africans in the cities, and the introduction of the new constitution that gave coloured and Indians limited power in a Tricameral Parliament but excluded the African majority. While these proposals were a catalyst for the UDF's birth,

> the actual genesis of the UDF lay in five strands of activity that developed following the banning of black consciousness bodies in 1977. Youth and student groups, trade unions, township civic organisations, and the revival of the nationalist tradition linked to the ANC each contributed in important ways to the UDF's creation.
>
> (Lodge et al., 1991: 35)

Conditions in exile and moving to negotiation

The ANC's external mission, 1960–1983

Immediately after the banning of the ANC and PAC, the organisational base of these resistance movements shifted into exile and while both professed a commitment to end apartheid, competition between them continued. By 1983, however, the fortunes of the PAC would considerably decline, and the ANC would resurge. Any explanation of the ANC's resurgence inside South Africa in the 1980s needs to consider its diplomatic activities in exile. The ANC's exile diplomacy was the responsibility of the "external mission," established by Oliver Tambo on the eve of its banning in 1960. The purpose of the external mission was to function as a foreign mission devoted to fundraising and diplomacy. After the arrest of the internal leadership at Rivonia in mid-1963, the external mission assumed greater responsibility.

The ANC's external mission inherited three key objectives. The first was the physical survival and relocation of the ANC. The difficulty with this was that South Africa was surrounded by colonial territories too economically reliant on South Africa to provide secure bases for banned South African organisations. As a result, the ANC had to relocate beyond the Zambezi River. Second, the external mission assumed responsibility for military decisions. The continuation of the armed struggle was made possible through the alliance with the SACP and the support of the Soviet Union. The third objective was most important: to gain exclusive recognition in the international community as the sole legitimate representative of South Africa's African majority. For this, the ANC equated mobilisation for the struggle against apartheid with supporting the ANC, i.e. if people genuinely opposed apartheid they should support the ANC. To pursue these objectives, the ANC established 43 missions in exile between 1960 and 1983. These missions were organised into three important target areas of diplomacy: Western powers (North America and Western Europe); the Soviet Union (including Eastern Europe); and Africa.

The ANC's diplomacy in Africa was the most complex, and it took the ANC many years to acquire legitimacy. In Africa, the PAC's policy of Pan-Africanism was more appealing to continental leaders. Mandela, who embarked on a continental tour, before his arrest, to garner support for the ANC wrote that the ANC's non-racial policy was often criticised: "In the rest of Africa, most African leaders could understand the views of the PAC better than those of the ANC" (Mandela, 1994: 361). By 1964, the ANC had established diplomatic missions in Algeria, Egypt, Morocco, Tanzania and Zambia, while the PAC had representation in Botswana, Egypt, Tanzania and Zaire. The Organisation of African Unity, the United Nations and the government of Tanzania for many years tried to mediate and manage the tensions between the ANC and PAC. In 1969, for instance, the United Nations General Assembly gave recognition to both the ANC and the PAC as authentic representatives of South Africa's population. And Tanzania housed both the ANC and the PAC (Pfister, 2003: 57).

Five years later, the ANC still shared the privilege of being granted observer status at the United Nations General Assembly and the Special Committee against Apartheid with the PAC. This began to change from the mid-1970s. Five factors are important. First, Zambia's president, Kenneth Kaunda, had for many years lobbied the Organisation of African Unity and the United Nations to recognise the ANC exclusively. Kaunda went to the extent of expelling PAC members from Zambia in 1962 (Gerhart and Glaser, 2010: 152–156). In addition, the ANC was able to establish its headquarters in Lusaka in 1970. Second, the independence of Angola and Mozambique strengthened Kaunda's position and provided further impetus to the ANC's claim to exclusive legitimacy. The MPLA and FRELIMO were not only Marxist-Leninist and part of the Soviet alliance; they were also part of an alliance with the ANC that had been concluded on the Afro-Asian Peoples' Solidarity Organisation Conference in 1969 in the Sudanese capital Khartoum (Pfister, 2003: 55). Third, through a chronic shortage of skilled administrators, persistent internal instability and ill-discipline, the PAC was excluded by the governments of Mozambique and Swaziland (in addition to Zambia). By the end of the 1970s, "the exiled PAC also faced de-recognition by Tanzania, the OAU, and the UN" because of its internal instability (Gerhart and Glaser, 2010: 152). By the beginning of the 1980s, Mozambique, Angola and Zambia became openly hostile to the PAC, and Lesotho began to expel PAC members. Fourth, when a leading Southern African regional organisation was formed in 1974 by Botswana, Tanzania and Zambia, the Front-Line States, to pursue the objective of majority rule in Southern Rhodesia (later Zimbabwe), South West Africa (later Namibia) and South Africa, the governments of Zambia, Angola and Mozambique lobbied for sole recognition of the ANC. While the Front-Line States continued to play the role of mediator in the conflict between the ANC and PAC, the lobbying paid dividends; the ANC was able to establish MK training camps in Angola and Mozambique, while APLA was forbidden to do the same in Botswana and Zimbabwe. This facilitated MK's ability to launch military attacks against South Africa, thereby increasing the ANC's visibility.

Five, the formation of the UDF in 1983 provided the ANC with an important source of internal legitimacy. There are two reasons for this. First, most of the UDF's leaders were drawn from the ranks of 1950s ANC veterans; this leadership had been members of the Congress Alliance and viewed themselves as part of the ANC underground inside the country. Further, a significant number of these leaders "had spent time in jail for ANC or MK-related activities or had joined the ANC whilst in jail" (Seekings, 2000: 312). Second, UDF leaders generally saw themselves as subordinate to the ANC in exile.

Conditions in Southern Africa and pressure for negotiation

Towards the end of 1983, the ANC was subject to international pressure for a negotiated resolution to the South African conflict. The first important source of pressure came from the United States in 1983. As part of the Ronald Reagan's administration's mediation in the Angolan civil war, the United States government sought to raise the profile of their dialogue with the ANC to test their seriousness about negotiation. According to Chester Crocker, the United States Assistant Secretary of State for African Affairs:

> We would use our contacts to focus on the shape of a post-apartheid future, underscoring our conviction that Marxist-Leninist principles were the last thing South Africa needed. Raising the visibility of our ANC contacts would directly confront Pretoria's absurd attempt to dictate who should be on the other side of any future table. . . . Meeting visibly with the ANC would set an example to Pretoria: talking to someone does not mean that you approve of them or agree with them. Placing our weight solidly behind negotiation would be the best way to signal to all parties the alternatives they faced.
>
> (Crocker, 1993: 318)

Crocker sent his senior intelligence staffer, Robert Cabelly, to make contact and meet with the ANC through Thabo Mbeki, Tambo's political secretary. On 7 September 1983, at the United States Information Service office in Lusaka, Cabelly met Mbeki and Sipho Makana, the head of information at the ANC's intelligence department. Makana recalls that the encounter was very blunt: "we don't trust each other but we have to work together." He and Mbeki read it as an attempt by South Africa to get a message to the ANC: "Drop the SACP and the Soviet Union, and we can do business" (Gevisser, 2007: 489). Cabelly insisted that the ANC become part of the "policy reforms in the region," and if this was not done, the ANC would be "driven out of the region" (Shubin, 1999: 209).

Cabelly told Mbeki's biographer, Mark Gevisser, that he reported three primary impressions to Crocker:

> First, that the ANC was in no way a military threat to South Africa; second, that behind the united front of the frontline states, they were all very iffy about the ANC; and third, that Thabo Mbeki was a very sharp guy.
>
> (Gevisser, 2007: 488)

Mbeki and Cabelly kept an open channel of communication, and in the following three years, would meet at least six times in Lusaka, culminating in the first official meeting between the ANC and the United States government in Washington in 1987.

Taken together, two important changing conditions in Southern Africa contributed to the shift towards exploring negotiated solutions for the ANC: the position of MK in Mozambique and resultant pressure from the Front-Line States. The regional strategy of the South African government involved various military and economic policies designed to persuade the countries in the region to expel the ANC from their territories (Simpson, 2006: 207). In 1984, this strategy began to bear fruit. At the same time, MK intelligence officers had warned the ANC leadership on the need to locate the armed struggle within South Africa's borders to overcome MK's dependence on rear bases in neighbouring countries (Pillay, 1989). For MK in 1984, Mozambique was of strategic importance. MK's structures in Mozambique were the most active at the time and were responsible for Natal, the Transvaal and the Cape, therefore handling most MK personnel flowing in and out of South Africa (Simpson, 2009: 207). Because Mozambique could not fight a war on two fronts, i.e. the Zimbabwe-Rhodesian and the South African, it chose to prioritise the immediate Zimbabwean struggle for independence (FRELIMO, 1984). As a result, the ANC adopted three measures to adapt to Mozambique's needs.

First, MK would not transport guerrillas or weapons into South Africa across Mozambique's borders; instead, MK would infiltrate South Africa indirectly through Swaziland (Barrell, 1992). Second, MK would not establish military training camps on Mozambican soil. Third, MK units inside South Africa would not conduct military operations near Mozambique's borders (Simpson, 2009: 316). The ANC's concessions had important consequences; because the Mozambique-Swaziland-South Africa border area became a hive of activity, especially in the post-Soweto exodus where large groups of militant youth crossed the borders, the Swazi and Mozambican governments soon lost their nerve (Rabkin, 1989). As the civil war with Renamo intensified, with the SADF increasing the rate of commando raids into Mozambique, Samora Machel succumbed to pressure; support for MK was replaced by a desire to achieve rapprochement with South Africa.

After an SADF commando raid in May 1983 killing several Mozambicans, an angry Machel told John Nkadimeng, the ANC representative in Mozambique, that it was time the ANC "got its act together and started to make its numbers count" (Simpson, 2006: 209). The number of ANC members permitted to reside in the country was subsequently reduced and steps were taken to reduce the movement of its activists in and out of the country. Under pressure, Machel sought to achieve a rapprochement with South Africa at any cost and in pursuit of improving relations, the Frente de Libertação de Moçambique (FRELIMO) government began a process of negotiation with the South African government, culminating in the signing of the Nkomati Accord on 16 March 1984. The Accord stipulated that "neither country could allow its territory to be used as a springboard for attacks on the other." Essentially, this involved Mozambique agreeing to expel the ANC, and South Africa ceasing its support for Renamo (Simpson, 2006: 209).

Because of the Accord, over 100 MK personnel in Mozambique were expelled. Large numbers crossed the border into Swaziland, taking with them truckloads of arms and ammunition, and entered an ANC infrastructure designed to support between 70 and 80 members in transit (Barrell, 1993: 337). This exodus was exacerbated by a simultaneous intake of larger recruits from South Africa into Swaziland. Raymond Lalla, MK's chief of intelligence in Natal, recalled that "while 100 or so went from Mozambique to Swaziland . . . about 300 to 400 went from South Africa to Swaziland" (Lalla, cited in Simpson, 2006: 210). The cooperation between Swazi and South African security agents compounded the problem; South African agents operated with authority in Swaziland. The sudden influx of large numbers of MK personnel made skirmishes with local security forces, and confrontation with South Africa security agents, inevitable. When an MK assassination squad killed a senior Swazi intelligence officer, ANC structures became "subject to an aggressive conjoint Swazi-South African offensive" (Simpson, 2006: 210). The ensuing Battle of Swaziland took a heavy toll on ANC activists, people with almost a decade of experience in underground work and therefore poised to be promoted to positions of leadership in the future (Pillay, 1989).

The turning point that signalled a shift towards negotiation inside the ANC came during these changes, in the run-up to the Nkomati Accord. The ANC's Lusaka office was concerned about its exclusion from consultations and briefings by the Mozambican government on high-level South Africa-Mozambique ministerial negotiations. Johnny Makhathini, the ANC's chief diplomat, stated that this had made Tambo unusually anxious. In anticipation of the signing of the Accord, the ANC's national working committee called an extended meeting at the end of 1983, to explore scenarios for potential negotiations. The committee commissioned a group chaired by Pallo Jordan, a senior strategist, with a brief to examine various scenarios in the event of negotiations. Jordan reported that negotiations could come about under three circumstances: the outright defeat of the apartheid regime; a stalemate; or a "Patriotic Front dilemma," i.e. the situation of the Zimbabwean Patriotic Front (the coalition of the Zimbabwe African National Union and the Zimbabwean African People's Union) in 1979 when the Front-Line States gave them an ultimatum to go to Lancaster House or get out of their countries. They pointed out that if the ANC was subjected to sufficient political pressure by the Front-Line States, it would need to be well prepared.

In the chaos of the aftermath of the Nkomati Accord, and the ensuing "Battle of Swaziland," the exploration of negotiated solutions began. The regional implications of the Nkomati Accord were discussed at a Front-Line States summit meeting in Arusha, Tanzania, on 29 April 1984. An important shift in favour of a negotiated solution to the South African conflict occurred with Front-Line State leaders. The final communiqué of the summit illustrates this. Front-Line State leaders made it clear their preference for a negotiated solution to the end of apartheid and set preconditions:

> For South Africa, the objective of the Front-Line States and Liberation Movements is the abolition of apartheid by whatever means are necessary. The Leaders present again reiterated their strong preference for apartheid to be ended by peaceful means. This can be achieved only through a process agreed upon in free discussions between the present South African regime and genuine representatives of the people of South Africa who are unrepresented in the present government structure of that country. A prerequisite for any such discussions would be the unconditional release from prison, detention, house arrest or "banning" of Nelson Mandela and all other political leaders. Difficult as this step may be in the eyes of the present South African Government, there is no way to peace in southern Africa except through discussions between the South African Government and the African people of South Africa.

The ANC was identified as principal liberation movement:

> The political and the armed struggles being waged by the peoples of Namibia and South Africa led by SWAPO and ANC respectively, are taking place inside those two countries. The struggle is between the people of Namibia and the occupying power, and between the people of South Africa and the apartheid regime. Therefore, the strategy of the Liberation Movements is that of internal struggle, firmly based on the people's will and determination.
>
> (cited in Gomes, 1984: 144–146)

The Front-Line States summit was important; it put pressure on the ANC to add negotiation into their policy alternatives. This pressure from the Front-Line States was sufficient and the ANC began to explore negotiation possibilities.

Crisis: the popular revolt

Five months after the Front-Line States Summit and as the ANC began exploring negotiation possibilities, an uprising began in the townships of the Vaal Triangle that set into motion a sustained period of popular protest unprecedented in scope and intensity. The uprising and its consequences significantly challenged the authority and legitimacy of the South African government and began the process that would crumble apartheid.

The Vaal uprising

On 3 September 1984 the government began to lose control of the reform process. The uprising that began in the Vaal Triangle was a rejection of reform and was initiated by the UDF-affiliated Vaal Civic Association over the issue of rent increases.

The rent increases had an important context. As discussed, as part of Botha's reforms, legislation was passed to deal with the position of urban Africans, culminating in the Black Local Authorities Act of 1982, which gave more powers to black municipal councils in running township affairs. Revenue for the councils would come from the rent and service charges that would accrue once the council obtained responsibility for the control of housing, as well as special levies on township residents (Price, 1991: 131). This township self-financing regime soon reached a cul-de-sac; rising inflation and the government policy of getting township residents to pay for township upgrade themselves escalated the costs of financially administering townships. Rents were consistently hiked to cover the costs of electricity, water, refuse collection, sewage and the like.

Township residents subsequently held public meetings addressed by various national opposition organisations such as the Azanian People's Organisation, the Azanian Students Organisation and the UDF-affiliated organisations such as the Soweto Civics Association, Congress of South African Students and Vaal Civic Association. Residents resolved not to pay the increases and called on the councillors to resign. When the councillors refused to reduce the increases and meet the demands of the residents, the Vaal Civic Association called for a work stay-away and a school boycott on 3 September. On 3 September 1984, 60 percent of workers stayed away from work and almost all the 93,000 pupils in the Vaal Triangle boycotted classes, solidifying an emerging alliance of residents, trade unions and students. A week-long state of paralysis set in, with a profound impact on the Vaal Triangle's industries and wider regional economy.

When the overwhelmed local councils requested police assistance to restore order, violence followed, and in the next four weeks, the Vaal witnessed pitched battles between residents and students against police, leaving more than 60 people dead, and thousands of arrests and detentions. A phase of general chaos ensued; police and commercial vehicles were stoned, the homes of community councillors were torched and the school boycotts were extended and expanded in geographical reach. New anti-apartheid organisational structures emerged; a Congress of South African Students proposal to trade unions on 27 October led to the formation of the UDF-affiliated Transvaal Regional Stay-away Committee, an alliance of 36 political, community and student organisations and trade unions.

Toward the end of October, the government stepped in to re-establish order; 7,000 SADF soldiers, assisting the South African Police (SAP), conducted Operation Palmiet, a major search-and-arrest operation in the Vaal Triangle. Over 400 people were arrested and detained (SAIRR, 1985: 75). The state's response intensified the uprising. The Transvaal Regional Stay-away Committee called for another two-day stay-away between 4 and 6 November. The call was once again widely heeded; in a massive demonstration of the nature of discontent, 800,000 workers stayed at home, joined by 400,000 pupils from an extended school boycott led by Congress of South African Students. The discontent in the Transvaal townships converged in the November stay-away organised by the

Transvaal Regional Stay-away Committee, when school children, community organisations and trade unions united under the Transvaal Regional Stay-away Committee and expressed their discontent in the largest political stay-away on record (SAIRR, 1985: 6).

The government response to the uprising was two-fold. First, the government declared a partial state of emergency on 21 July 1985. Second, the military intervened again, occupying the streets in force, setting up road blocks, conducting house-to-house searches and maintaining 24-hour patrols (Lodge et al., 1991: 78). Soldiers and policemen were given absolute authority to arrest, interrogate, search homes and confiscate possessions. These powers were used extensively. When the partial state of emergency failed to suppress the uprising, the government declared a second, and general, state of emergency on 12 June 1986. Unlike the first state of emergency, which affected specific magisterial districts, the second affected the whole of South Africa. Applied with an unprecedented harshness that temporarily put a halt to the uprising, it was renewed annually for four years. The detentions which came with this general state of emergency were particularly damaging to the UDF. In the first six months of the general state of emergency, between 20,000 and 30,000 people were detained, and several thousand endured months and years in police cells and prisons. Detentions were countrywide, with the largest numbers recorded being in Soweto and Port Elizabeth.

Operation Zikomo

The ANC initially sought to provide guidance to the township uprising. They sought to "encourage confrontation while moderating expectations":

> [In] our planning, in our thinking, we must proceed from the basis that we inflicted a humiliating defeat on our enemy [through the boycott of coloured and Indian elections]. . . . [As] revolutionaries, as fighters for liberation, [we] must plan how we should continue our offensive, knowing very well that the enemy will, as it must, hit back to stop the emergence and consolidation of the revolutionary situation that Pretoria fears so much.

The ANC called for a campaign to make South Africa ungovernable:

> We must destroy the enemy organs of government. We must render them ineffective and inoperative. . . . In rejecting Botha's regime, we also reject his puppets. There is no reason that we should allow their puppets to control our lives. . . . In every locality and in all parts of our country, we must fight to ensure that we remove the enemy's organs of government.
>
> (Barrell, 1993: 352)

The ANC's opportunity to intervene and reinforce the uprising arrived in mid-1985 with the launch of Operation Zikomo, a large-scale infiltration of MK combatants into South Africa. According to Ronnie Kasrils, the MK chief of intelligence, the purpose of Zikomo was to "inject several hundred combatants as 'shock forces' in the township uprisings." They were to "form a kind of officer class for township militants, providing them with leadership and training" (Kasrils, 1989). However, the ANC's political conditions in exile, i.e. the dismantling of its military structures in Mozambique and the uncertain transitional environment of Swaziland, severely limited its ability to provide tactical guidance to the township revolt. This was compounded by the fact that MK strategists sought to apply prescriptions of military combat work to the revolt. The view developed that MK fighters would form the officer corps of an army to be created by organising and arming the township activists, resulting in a coordinated and sustained uprising (Simpson, 2006: 200).

Ivan Pillay, MK's intelligence chief in Swaziland, told Barrell that the combatants had minimal back-up: "they had maybe . . . R1,000 or R2,000, maybe . . . 12 hand grenades and an AK . . . many of them just being put across the fence and sent home to integrate themselves with the defence committees, street committees etc" (Pillay, 1989). According to Mac Maharaj, a senior ANC and MK strategist, Zikomo was a legacy of the Angolan mutiny the previous year and "represented a belated attempt to accommodate the grievances in the [MK] camps by sending many cadres back home." However, "it quickly degenerated into sending them like cannon fodder, to put it crudely" (Maharaj, 1990).

Several arguments had preceded Zikomo: the lack of underground structures to integrate MK; and the poor quality of political and intelligence briefings guerrillas received before infiltration. From this view, Zikomo was an attempt to compensate for the unpreparedness of the ANC when the Vaal uprising began (Barrell, 1993: 389). Zikomo, however, did have some important short-term effects. As the government lost control over some of the townships, the newly infiltrated guerrillas survived. Consequently, MK activity increased to new levels from June 1985:

> whereas there had been 30 attacks in the five months to May, there were 31 in June alone and 75 more between July and December; a total of 136 attacks for the year, more than double the number in any previous year.

In 1985, "the state killed or captured a mere 31 MK guerrillas, which meant a ratio of three guerrillas captured or killed for each 13 attacks; MK's best year and most favourable casualty rate ever" (Barrell, 1993: 390–391).

However, the ANC was not able to provide tactical direction to the uprising. MK's intelligence officers acknowledge that their role in developing street committees and rent boycotts in the townships in the 1985–1986 period was minimal. Joe Slovo and Ronnie Kasrils acknowledge that the ANC simply picked up on local initiatives made by ordinary residents and internal activists and then, post facto, developed strategies which made sense to them. After the second state of emergency, MK could not spread insurrectionary pressures beyond scattered localities, and therefore could not attenuate security forces to any significant degree (Barrell, 1993).

As the state rolled back the unrest through the second state of emergency, MK's casualty rate rose sharply. Bill Anderson, a senior ANC intelligence officer based in Lusaka, recalled that intelligence communications after losing the eastern front in the post-Nkomati period were established in an ad hoc manner "with infiltrated units only given very brief instructions about potential contacts in the internal underground." Most of these units "soon lost contact with their external handlers upon entry into the country and were left to fend for themselves" (Anderson, 1991: 1). Kasrils estimated that as many as

> 75–80% of those infiltrated in the early 1980s were lost by 1986/87, whether through being killed, captured or having deserted for a variety of reasons ranging from a loss of contact with their external commanders, a shortage of ammunition, or basic disillusionment with the ANC.
>
> (Kasrils, 1990)

Usually, "communications were so poor that the first the forward areas usually heard about the cadres that they deployed was after news of their capture or death was announced in the media" (Simpson, 2006: 203).

Kabwe Conference: talks and negotiations

The importance of the Kabwe Conference should be viewed within this context of early discussions with United States diplomatic envoys over possibilities of a negotiated solution, the Nkomati Accord and the closure of MK's eastern front, the Front-Line States' preference for a negotiated end to apartheid and MK's attempt to reinforce the uprising. These developments presented the ANC with two fundamental choices: (1) to continue the armed struggle with limited possibilities of its success, or (2) to pursue a negotiated settlement. Given that the Kabwe Conference occurred during Operation Zikomo, armed struggle could not be discounted in 1985. The ANC therefore theorised that the two options could be mutually reinforcing: "revolutionary pressures could feed the prospects for negotiations; and, if negotiations started, this might create legal space in which its organisers could advance the prospects for revolutionary confrontation. But realising a symbiotic relationship between them would prove difficult" (Simpson, 2006: 203).

Amid this fluidity, Tambo, who had repeatedly been approached for a meeting by various intermediaries acting for South African business interests, seized the opportunity to make the case for negotiation possibilities. He asked conference delegates "for clearance to meet an unnamed group of 'important people' who wanted to talk to the ANC; the talks, he specified, would not amount to negotiations with the government" (Simpson, 2006: 395). This request for clearance was presented as a tactical shift by Tambo in his political report to the conference. Tambo stated that the ANC could not be against negotiations and a negotiated settlement in principle. The ANC had to place great emphasis on its role as an alternative government of South Africa. This meant that it had to act as a "credible representative of a liberated South Africa." This had tactical and strategic implications:

> It is clear that we have to improve the quality of our diplomacy and therefore the training of our representatives and their staff. We need also to tap and utilise in a better way the intellectual cadres available to us, both inside and outside our country.
>
> (Tambo, 1985: 1)

In other words, the ANC needed to evolve a set of ideas and tactics in preparation for the possibility of a political settlement. Tambo drew a distinction between "talks" and "negotiations." "Talks" were regarded as exploratory exchanges of views, designed to feel out an enemy or, alternatively, to cement understandings with real, temporary or potential alliances (Barrell, 1985: 4). Tambo identified categories of talks. The first comprised talks with ANC-aligned organisations inside South Africa, such as organisations aligned to COSATU and the UDF. The objective here was to build unity with all those who sought to dismantle apartheid and to draw them in as components of an ANC-led assault (Tambo, 1985). The second category comprised talks with non-governmental organisations not aligned to the ANC. These would include business organisations, civil society groups and opposition political parties inside South Africa, such as the Progressive Federal Party. The objective here was to turn them against apartheid.

Negotiations were understood as having a clearly defined framework within which attempts would be made to settle the South African conflict. A range of preconditions applied, the most important being that negotiations should be premised on the agreement to dismantle apartheid, replace it with a democratic political system. This was not negotiable. Other preconditions included the release of political prisoners, the unconditional return of exiles and a climate of political freedoms conducive to negotiations. Talks and negotiations, Tambo continued, were not mutually exclusive but complementary. If the ANC was to negotiate from a position of strength, it had to use talks with non-ANC aligned organisations and constituencies to politically isolate the South African government. Successful talks thus bolstered and strengthened the ANC's negotiation strategy and tactics. The Kabwe Conference endorsed Tambo's case for talks and negotiations and gave its approval for him to proceed to meet the "unnamed group of important people" (Simpson, 2006: 395).

According to Maharaj, Tambo's political report was important: "there was a formal acknowledgement of the primacy of the political in the balance between the political and military components of the struggle" (Maharaj cited in O'Malley, 2007: 234). The implication of this tactical shift was that the political struggle became fundamental and armed struggle had to be integrated into it. Simply put, if apartheid could not be defeated by the armed struggle, then all that remained was the political option with MK support. MK's armed struggle was one element of the political struggle, and not its principle or even necessarily its important vehicle (Maharaj, 1990). Tambo's alternative diplomatic option, i.e. talks, and negotiation represented a potentially more important vehicle.

The Nkomati Accord thus led to the important rethink and shift toward the consideration of negotiation possibilities. The closure of MK's eastern front seriously hampered MK at a time when the ANC needed to reinforce the momentum generated by the uprising. With MK's shortcomings, the momentum could only be sustained through alternative tactics. Tambo's diplomatic alternative was a way out; while it was not military, it was still aimed at fighting apartheid.

The Mandela question

As discussed previously, in 1973, the NP government realised that white South Africans could no longer monopolise central government. As a result, the Theron Commission was set up to examine the constitutional position of coloureds. Following Theron's report in 1976, a cabinet committee proposed a parliament with separate racial chambers, and a council to mediate in matters of mutual concern with ultimate power exercised by the State President. This resulted in the Tricameral Constitution – endorsed by white voters in a referendum in November 1983 and inaugurated in September 1984. The aim was to preserve white minority rule by "[associating] the 2.5 million coloureds with whites to broaden the NP's power base, preventing their surrender to a 'black-power' situation" (Melunsky, 2002: 81).

The Tricameral Constitution was not meant to provide a final solution: it was tailored as a transitional document. Botha made this clear: "We do not know what tomorrow will bring. We are not prophets. This is a step in the dark. We can only proceed into the future with faith" (Botha cited in Lipton, 1985: 53). Excluding Africans from this new constitution raised new questions on African political rights and African political representation in central government. These questions moved centre stage in the constitutional reform debate. Apartheid's basic principle and answer to this question was that African representation took place in the homelands. However, many government officials by 1980 realised that not all Africans would be politically represented inside the homelands. In 1980, for instance, Botha conceded that "urban blacks might gain representation outside the homelands." In opening the Tricameral Parliament, he acknowledged that "black political rights topped government's agenda" (Melunsky, 2002: 82). Botha, however, had no idea how to proceed beyond this point.

As discussed, in February 1983 Botha established the SKK to deal with black constitutional issues. Chaired by Heunis, it was attended by all senior cabinet ministers: F.W. de Klerk, Barend du Plessis, Gerrit Viljoen, Louis le Grange, Pik Botha, Kobie Coetsee and Magnus Malan. SKK met monthly and received inputs from "academics, businessmen and especially, [officials of the department of] Constitutional Development" (Melunsky, 2002: 83). While there was no obvious direction of argument, nor any single paper of special importance, constitutional policy was gradually formulated within SKK and became the point in the political system where pressure for change was generated.

The constitutional reform process that unfolded had some important consequences for South Africa. First, the process shifted the terms of debate in the South African government, providing the framework for apartheid's demise. Botha "forced whites, willingly or not, to embark on a voyage to a new and inevitably much different future" (Melunsky, 2002: 93). The debate was no longer whether apartheid should end but how, i.e. sequences, time spans, and methods. Second, constitutional reform was an attempt to share power while preserving white minority rule, i.e. without losing control. Power-sharing involved granting citizenship to Africans and accepting their permanence in urban areas. Reform, however, did not involve Africans and whites participating in the same structures; it involved African participation in a constitution in which whites would have the final say. Government strategists had no idea how this would be done, but Botha would have been happy if Mandela would be part of the process (Melunsky, 2002: 93). Therefore, Botha favoured negotiations and African participation in central government but only on his terms. Third, the constitutional reform process was rejected, resulting in an uprising that created a crisis of legitimacy. Consequently, the government realised it was running out of options. As constitutional reform failed to acquire the necessary legitimacy, government strategists were "forced to accept that negotiations and constitutional change must include the ANC, pre-eminently Mandela" (Melunsky, 2002: 93). Fourth, the message from constitutional development and SKK was that the "ANC's unbanning and Mandela's release were pre-requisites for meaningful constitutional reform" (Melunsky, 2002: 94). Talking to Mandela became the most important strategy for continuing reform in the face of a legitimacy crisis. The identification of the ANC was important; the events post-1983 (discussed in the previous chapter) showed that the ANC was weak militarily and a moderate organisation.

Approaching Mandela: the logical conclusion of reform

In June 1980, the month the South African parliament passed the Republic of South Africa Constitution Amendment Act, Dr Jannie Roux, then the Deputy Commissioner of Prisons, spoke with Mandela for two and a half hours. Roux reported that "Mandela took strong exception to being called a 'self-confessed communist.'" He

> appeared to see a place for white people in a future South Africa, but not as holders of political power: he had in mind a five-year transition during which they would be accustomed to the transfer of power; but he understood [Roux's] warning that whites would not just capitulate.

He "appeared to have relatively rigid thinking patterns . . . and it is difficult to get him to accept an opposite viewpoint" (Roux cited in Sampson, 1999: 298).

In February 1981, the Department of Justice received another report about Mandela. The report stated that Mandela "had so adjusted himself to prison regulations that he gave the impression of good behaviour, and no contraventions of prison regulations had been recorded against him up to 1976." It further stated that Mandela adopted a "persistent attitude by making repeated representations about conditions, but in a way that no steps can be taken against him." It warned that this was not good behaviour:

> he gives the orders and then withdraws to regard his actions from a distance. Mandela sticks to his chosen course and influences everyone with him not to

> deviate from this. . . . Mandela has in no way changed his position and that imprisonment so far has had no positive effect on him.
>
> (cited in Sampson, 1999: 298–299)

Botha appointed Roux as his director-general in the Office of the State President. The psychological profile of Mandela was for perusal of the Broederbond and the cabinet, and it had a major bearing on Mandela's removal from Robben Island in 1982, along with the Rivonia political prisoners (Bell and Ntsebeza, 2001: 76–77). In October 1981, Botha appointed his Deputy Defence Minister, Kobie Coetsee, as the Minister of Justice and Prisons. On instruction from Botha, his immediate task was to work on a policy for releasing political prisoners.

Botha was not initially concerned with Mandela; his concern was with the imprisonment of Breyten Breytenbach, a dissident Afrikaner poet and ANC supporter. Breytenbach was a member of a prominent Cape National Party family close to Botha, and the twin brother of the legendary SADF soldier Colonel Jan Breytenbach. According to Coetsee, Botha was "unhappy about the security system having dealt with Breyten Breytenbach the way it did . . . and felt that he was dealt with unfairly by the . . . justice system." Jailed in 1975, Botha believed that Breytenbach was simply an idealist "who should be given another chance" (Coetsee, 1995: 1). Coetsee got instruction from Botha to find legal ways of getting Breytenbach out of prison (Coetsee, 1997: 1). The problem was that political prisoners did not qualify for parole or remission of sentence: "I had to tell [Botha] that the policy was . . . not to release political prisoners until the sentence had expired, and in the case of life sentences it meant a life sentence" (Coetsee, 1995: 1). Coetsee told Botha that the only way he could get Breytenbach out of prison was to change government policy regarding the release of political prisoners. Botha simply told him to work on it, as long as Breytenbach got out of prison.

With Botha's support, Coetsee got cabinet approval to change the government's political prisoner release policy: "all of them would be entitled to the same release facilities as other prisoners" (Coetsee, 1999: 1). Most cabinet ministers were in support of this; political prisoners with life sentences were the most problematic for the government and had the greatest influence on younger political prisoners:

> Those who had no prospect of ever being released were the most difficult people in all the prison, and because they were so difficult they were all taken down to Robben Island, which makes Robben Island the most difficult place to manage. They couldn't get staff and personnel . . . to go to Robben Island. So, I said with this we've also got to change, people with the prospect of being released could become model prisoners . . . we should try and arrange for prisoners to be not grouped together and to be confined Robben Island but . . . there must be other institutions to which they can go as well.
>
> (Coetsee, 1995: 2)

The goal of the new release policy was to demystify the Rivonia political prisoners and demobilise Robben Island of radical political prisoners. Coetsee was soon confronted with the "release Mandela" question. Coetsee stated that Botha wanted to release Mandela; he considered Mandela's release "as a given situation but he wanted him released to have him safely deposited where he couldn't cause any more trouble. . . . He wanted him to go to the Transkei" (Coetsee, 1998: 1). Botha did not initially consider Mandela's release as part of a political solution: "[According to Botha] his release was solving the problem of him being in jail" (Coetsee, 1995: 2). Botha saw Mandela as part of the problem; "he wanted him out of jail because imprisoning him was more trouble than it was worth" (Coetsee cited in Waldmeir, 1997: 93).

Coetsee subsequently familiarised himself with Roux's background reports on Mandela. When he asked for further reports, he was given a more detailed analysis from the Department of Prisons, which made specific points:

> A. Mandela is exceptionally motivated and maintains a strong idealistic approach; B. He maintains outstanding personal relations; C. He is manipulative, but nevertheless not tactless or provocative; D. There are no visible signs of bitterness towards whites, although this may be a fine game of bluff on his part; E. He acknowledges his own shortcomings, but nevertheless believes in himself; F. He is a practical and pragmatic thinker who can arrive at a workable solution on a philosophical basis; G. He has a capacity for integrated and creative thought; H. He has an unbelievable memory, to reproduce things in the finest detail; I. He has an unflinching belief in his cause and in the eventual triumph of African nationalism; J. He regards himself as called to the task and this elevates him above the average white who, according to him, has apparently lost his idealism; K. He believes in self-discipline, and continually taking the initiative, to the requisites of success. There exists no doubt that Mandela commands all the qualities to be the Number One black leader in South Africa. His period in prison has caused his psycho-political posture to increase rather than decrease, and with this he now has acquired the characteristic prison-charisma of the contemporary liberation leader.
>
> (cited in Sampson, 1999: 299).

The analysis provided no answer of what to do with such an opponent.

In November 1979, Botha appointed Professor Lukas Daniel ("Niel") Barnard as the head of the Department of National Security (DONS), the successor to the Bureau of State Security (BOSS). In June 1980, DONS was renamed the National Intelligence Service (NIS). At the time, the NIS was a transitional organisation; the intelligence staff at NIS comprised two groups. At the senior level were many old BOSS officials recruited from the ranks of the security police in the 1960s. At lower levels were younger intelligence officers, recruited from universities with degrees in political science, law, psychology and African studies (Swilling and Phillips, 1989: 41). Barnard was of the younger generation and sought to transform NIS from its predecessor BOSS; "[originally] consisting of former security policemen, it subsequently turned itself into an organisation that valued professional, often academic, qualifications" (Seegers, 1996: 250). Professional reviews of individuals included assessments of relevant books read and it was open to civilian influence, the largest part of its budget was spent on research and it recognised the strategic studies qualifications of the University of Pretoria (UP) and Orange Free State (UOFS).

The NIS focused on the long-term resolution of events at a macro level; the NIS spoke the language of causes, consequences and prevention and much of its work involved the gathering, sorting and evaluation of information obtained in the media, the security, public and diplomatic services, and from informants (Seegers, 1996: 50; Swilling and Phillips, 1989: 41). According to Maritz Spaarwater, an NIS official who worked in various senior positions, the NIS "was intellectualised and transformed into the nearest thing the state had to an objective think-tank" (Spaarwater, 2012: 116). Under Barnard, it rapidly gained credibility and respect of senior government officials, especially Botha. The NIS reported to Coetsee.

Barnard states that the NIS took the view from the early 1980s that a negotiated end to apartheid was the only viable solution to the South African conflict:

> [We] were confronted daily with an accurate assessment about the real problems of this country. . . . You see the problems internally, you see the problems with the labour unions, you see the problems with education, you see the problems with socio-economic development, and you see the speeches made by other people. . . . I tried to form an honest assessment based on good and accurate intelligence as to the true problems of this country.
>
> (Barnard, 1998: 1)

Barnard states that his perceptions were shaped by two senior colleagues; Mike Louw and Maritz Spaarwater. Louw was Barnard's deputy and came from the political studies department at UOFS. He had risen through BOSS where he wrote the agency's annual intelligence estimate (Saunders, 2006: 232). When he joined NIS, Louw became the Chief Director of Evaluation and deputy to Barnard. Louw agrees with Barnard's interpretation stating that by the end of the 1970s, the realisation of the permanency of the urban African population had rendered apartheid unworkable:

> The whole idea on which South Africa was built was crumbling. The homelands were failing hopelessly, they were totally corrupt, and billions were pumped into them and would just disappear. Apartheid couldn't work because it wasn't tackled with gusto, and implemented with vision – it was just handouts here and there. . . . We were left without anything to guide the country, except the pragmatic constitutional manoeuvrings of PW Botha.
>
> (Louw, 1995)

Louw had a significant impact on Barnard's thinking:

> Mike Louw was a man who very strongly all the time took the line that there is only one solution for this country and that is to find a political settlement; there is just no other way out. That influenced my thinking to a large extent.
>
> (Barnard, 1998: 1)

Spaarwater was younger than Louw and "had been part of the short-lived radical movement among Afrikaner students in the late 1960s that debated the theological morality of apartheid." He confirms Louw's explanation and points out that "his disillusionment with apartheid had taken root in 1978 when it became clear . . . that NP politicians' claim that government policy would reverse the influx of black people to the cities was nonsense" (Louw cited in Saunders, 2006: 233). He rose to the rank of colonel in MID and was recruited by Louw to the NIS. Spaarwater writes that research output from NIS in the early 1980s gradually inspired a rethink in the higher echelons of the South African government about the country's security situation. This led to the realisation that "the only way out was to proceed to a negotiated settlement." Louw, he writes, was critical to this process: "No one in the intelligence community had a greater influence on bringing this about than Mike Louw, with the strong leadership and support of Niel Barnard, in gaining the confidence of the highest decision-makers" (Spaarwater, 2012: 120). This shift among a handful of NIS strategists coincides with debates and initiatives concerning reforming political prisoner release policy. In this context, Mandela was identified as an important actor (Barnard, 1994).

Fourteen months after the Department of Prisons' final psychological profile of Mandela on Robben Island, Mandela, Walter Sisulu, Govan Mbeki, Andrew Mlangeni and Ahmed Kathrada (the ANC leadership on Robben Island) were transferred to Pollsmoor Prison in April 1982 (Mandela, 1994: 611). Niel Barnard stated the intention: "One of the critical issues at the start of the '80s, when I was at the NIS, was we should find a way of almost demystifying this man [Mandela]. . . . How should we defuse a very critical and difficult situation?" (Barnard, 1999). The government began to use Mandela's isolation to investigate his views on South Africa's political future. This was done by authorising visits by influential personalities.

In August 1984, one month after the beginning of the Vaal uprising, Mandela was visited by a journalist, Benjamin Pogrund of the Rand Daily Mail whom he hadn't seen in 20 years. In October 1984, he was visited by Professor van der Merwe from the University of Cape Town who had been trying to broker peace between the government and the ANC. In late 1984 and early 1985, he was visited by Lord Nicholas Bethell, a member of the British House of Lords, and Professor Samuel Dash, from Georgetown University's law faculty. Mandela and Lord Bethell discussed the armed struggle and Mandela explained that it was up to the government to renounce violence (Mandela, 1994: 619). In his discussions with Professor Dash, Mandela laid out what he saw the minimum for a future non-racial South Africa: "a unitary state without homelands, non-racial elections for the central Parliament and one-person one-vote" (Mandela, 1994: 620).

The township uprising had important implications for constitutional reform. In January 1985, SKK persuaded Botha to announce at the opening of parliament that "Africans permanently resident in South Africa could not forever be politically represented in homeland structures." Urban Africans

> were to have the right to political participation and a say [inspraak] in the higher levels. . . . Consequently, structures must be developed for black

> communities outside national states [i.e. in non-independent homelands] whereby they can enjoy self-determination over their own affairs up to the highest level.
>
> (cited in Melunsky, 2002: 84)

Botha proposed an open-ended non-statutory black negotiation forum. He stated that "existing mechanisms for negotiation must be improved and expected all 'responsible' black leaders to participate." Heunis elaborated that "anyone could participate, and the only qualification was renouncing violence" (cited in Melunsky, 2002: 84). Negotiation meant negotiating structures for urban African representation outside non-independent homelands, and within central government. It did not mean negotiating the end of apartheid; it meant negotiating the reform of apartheid.

Following from this, while on a European tour at the beginning of January 1985 Botha had been encouraged by German leader Franz-Josef Strauss, the Bavarian Christian-Socialist, to offer to release Mandela if he would renounce all violence. Botha presented this formula to the cabinet but was warned by Coetsee and Louis le Grange, the Minister of Law and Order, that Mandela would not give up his strongest bargaining chip prematurely (Sampson, 1999: 335). However, with the support of the rest of the cabinet, Botha further told parliament that he was offering Mandela his freedom provided he "unconditionally rejected violence as a political instrument" (Sparks, 1994: 49). Publicly challenging Mandela, he concluded that it was therefore "not the South African government which now stands in the way of Mr Mandela's freedom. It is he himself" (cited in Mandela, 1994: 620–621).

Mandela, determined to insert himself into the political process, prepared a statement which rejected the offer but kept open the option of negotiation. The statement was read out at a mass rally in Jabulani Stadium, Soweto:

> I am surprised at the conditions that the government wants to impose on me. . . . It is only . . . when all other forms of resistance were no longer open to us, that we turned to armed struggle. . . . Let [Botha] renounce violence. Let him say that he will dismantle apartheid. Let him unban . . . the African National Congress. Let him free all who have been imprisoned, banished or exiled for their opposition to apartheid. Let him guarantee free political activity so that people may decide who will govern them. . . . Only free men can negotiate. Prisoners cannot enter into contracts. . . . I cannot give any undertaking at a time when I and you, the people, are not free.
>
> (Mandela, 1994: 622–623)

To Botha's formula, "Mandela in exchange for non-violence," Mandela responded, "legality in exchange for non-violence" and Botha's gambit became an albatross. Realising the deadlock, Coetsee was summoned to the President's office and Botha told him: "You know we have painted ourselves in a corner. Can you get us out?" (Coetsee, 1999).

Concluding remarks

Therefore, on the eve of the Vaal uprising, an event that would produce an organic crisis, the main actors in the South African conflict were the South African government, on the one hand, and a collection of opposition organisations on the other, based inside South Africa and internationally. The central issue of the conflict was white minority rule, and the NP government's system of apartheid (in its various formulations) was central for the implementation of white minority rule. The NP government in 1983 under PW Botha should be understood within the context of the changes in the 1970s. The NP government realised that they could not slow the pace of African urbanisation. Separate development was not going to achieve the goal of reversing African urban migration. After the Soweto uprising, leading Afrikaners began to question the ethical basis of apartheid. As a result, PW Botha reached three conclusions: (1) classic apartheid was impracticable; (2) Afrikaner political and social isolation could not work; and (3) a political formula for urban Africans had to be found. The goal, however, was still the same: the preservation of white minority rule. Given the changes of the 1970s, an alternative framework had to be found to maintain this goal. Constitutional reform, the Republic of South Africa Constitution Act of 1983, the Black Local Authorities Act of 1982 and accompanying legislation, was the development of this alternative framework. Thus, the NP government in 1983 was undergoing reform.

In 1983, there were two anti-apartheid fronts. Externally there was the ANC, PAC and an important number of international solidarity anti-apartheid organisations covering the broad spectrum of international politics. This external front also included governments and regional and international organisations. By 1983, the ANC had become a prominent anti-apartheid organisation, surpassing the PAC. It by no means, however, was the solely recognised organisation. Internally there was an abundance of civil society-based organisations bound together by a commitment to social and political equality, and the universal franchise. The most prominent were those under the umbrella of the UDF which had important historical ties to the 1950s Congress Movement. In this anti-apartheid organisational mosaic, the historical ties between the ANC and the UDF, as discussed, were older and stronger. This gave the ANC a powerful sense of historical legitimacy.

Thus, in 1983, neither the NP government nor the ANC were on a pain-producing path. Both parties did not perceive the conflict to be a hurting stalemate and there was no mediator in sight to deflect the parties from their unilateral positions into a joint bilateral solution. An aborted pre-negotiation initiative in 1979 confirms this absence of a pain-producing path. On 30 and 31 October 1979, Chief Mangosuthu Buthelezi, the chief minister of the KwaZulu Bantustan and leader of Inkatha, brought an official delegation to London to meet Tambo and senior ANC leaders. According to Thabo Mbeki, the ANC's propaganda chief and later chief diplomat, the South African government had sent a message through Buthelezi on possibilities of opening a communication channel, but the ANC was not ready to listen. Tambo's response to Buthelezi had been curt: "What has PW done to suggest that he's worth seeing?" (Gevisser, 2007: 492–493).

Bibliography

Barrell, H. 1985. "ANC and Business: The Tactics of Talks," *Work in Progress* 39, October.

Barrell, H. 1992. "The Turn to the Masses: The African National Congress Strategic Review of 1978–1979," *Journal of Southern African Studies* 18(1): 64–92.

Barrell, H. 1993. *Conscripts to Their Age: African National Congress Operational Strategy, 1976–1986* (Doctoral Dissertation). Oxford: University of Oxford.

Bell, T. and D. Ntsebeza. 2001. *Unfinished Business: South Africa, Apartheid and Truth*. Cape Town: Redworks.

Carter, G. and T. Karis. 1971. *From Protest to Challenge, Volume 1*. Hoover: Stanford.

Crocker, C. 1993. *High Noon in Southern Africa: Making Peace in a Rough Neighbourhood*. Johannesburg: Jonathan Ball.

Davenport, T. 1970. "The Triumph of Colonel Stallard: The Transformation of the Natives (Urban Areas) Act Between 1923 and 1937," *South African Historical Journal* 2(1): 77–96.

Eidelberg, P. 1997. "South African Apartheid: The Homeland-Township Nexus, 1948–1986," *South African Historical Journal* 36(1): 88–112.

Ellis, S. 2012. *External Mission: The ANC in Exile, 1960–1990*. Johannesburg: Jonathan Ball.

Ellis, S. and T. Sechaba. 1992. *Comrades Against Apartheid: The ANC and the South African Communist Party in Exile*. London: James Currey.

Final Communiqué, Front-Line States Summit Meeting, Arusha, Tanzania, 29 April 1984 cited in Alves Gomes, "Southern Africa 1984," *Review of African Political Economy* 29(1984): 144–146.

Fraternal Message from the African National Congress to the FRELIMO Party, 31 January 1984. Folder 54, Part 3, A2675 Karis-Gerhart Collection, Historical Papers, University of the Witwatersrand.

Gerhart, G. and C. Glaser. 2010. *From Protest to Challenge: A Documentary History of African Politics in South Africa, 1882–1990, Volume 6: Challenge and Victory 1980–1990*. Bloomington: Indiana University Press.

Gevisser, M. 2007. *Thabo Mbeki: The Dream Deferred*. Johannesburg: Jonathan Ball.

Giliomee, H. 1972. *The Parting of the Ways: South African Politics 1976–82*. Cape Town: David Philip.

Giliomee, H. 1979. "The Afrikaner Economic Advance," in H. Giliomee and H. Adam, eds. *Ethnic Power Mobilised*. New Haven: Yale University Press.

Giliomee, H. 2012. *The Last Afrikaner Leaders: A Supreme Test of Power*. Cape Town: Tafelberg.

Giliomee, H. and L. Schlemmer. 1989. *From Apartheid to Nation-Building: Contemporary South African Debates*. Cape Town: Oxford University Press.

Johns, S. and R. Davis. 1991. *Mandela, Tambo and the African National Congress: The Struggle Against Apartheid 1948–1990, A Documentary Survey*. Oxford: Oxford University Press.

Lipton, M. 1985. *Capitalism and Apartheid: South Africa 1910–1986*. Aldershot: Wildwood House.

Lodge, T. 1983. *Black Politics in South Africa Since 1945*. Johannesburg: Ravan Press.

Lodge, T., B. Nasson, S. Mufson, K. Shubane and N. Sithole. 1991. *All, Here and Now: Black Politics in South Africa in the 1980s*. Cape Town: David Philip.

Mandela, N. 1994. *Long Walk to Freedom*. Edinburgh: Little, Brown and Company.

Maylam, P. 1990. "The Rise and Decline of Urban Apartheid in South Africa," *African Affairs* 89(354): 57–84.
Melunsky, J. 2002. *The Rejection of Silence and Desolation: Explaining Political Transition in Modern South Africa* (Doctoral Dissertation). London: School of Oriental and African Studies.
Norval, A. 1996. *Deconstructing Apartheid Discourse*. London: Verso.
O'Malley, P. 2007. *Shades of Difference: Mac Maharaj and the Struggle for South Africa*. New York: Penguin Books.
Pfister, R. 2003. "Gateway to International Victory: The Diplomacy of the African National Congress in Africa, 1960–1990," *Journal of Modern African Studies* 41(1): 51–73.
Posel, D. 1991. *The Making of Apartheid, 1948–1961: Conflict and Compromise*. Oxford: Oxford University Press.
Pottinger, B. 1988. *The Imperial Presidency: PW Botha the First 10 Years*. Johannesburg: Southern Book Publishers.
Price, R. 1980. "The Meaning of Government-Led Reform," in R. Price and C. Rosberg, eds. *The Apartheid Regime*. Berkeley: Institute of International Studies.
Price, R. 1991. *The Apartheid State in Crisis: Political Transformation in South Africa 1975–1990*. New York: Oxford University Press.
Report of the Native Laws Commission 1946–48, Department of Native Affairs, Union of South Africa, Pretoria 1948, UG No. 28–1948 (Chair: Fagan): [Fagan Report].
Republic of South Africa, Report of the Commission of Inquiry into the Legislation Affecting the Utilisation of Manpower [Riekert Commission Report]. Pretoria: Government Printer, 1979.
Sampson, A. 1999. *Mandela: The Authorised Biography*. London: Harper Collins Publishers.
Saunders, J. 2006. *Apartheid's Friends: The Rise and Fall of South Africa's Secret Service*. London: John Murray.
Schrire, R. 1991. *Adapt or Die: The End of White Politics in South Africa*. London: Hurst and Co.
Seegers, A. 1996. *The Military in the Making of Modern South Africa*. London: Tauris Academic Studies.
Seekings, J. 1988. "The Origins of Political Mobilisation in the PWV Townships, 1980–1984," in W. Cobbett and R. Cohen, eds. *Popular Struggles in South Africa*. London: James Currey.
Seekings, J. 2000. *The UDF: A History of the United Democratic Front in South Africa 1983–1991*. Cape Town: David Philip Publishers.
Shubin, V. 1999. *ANC: A View From Moscow*. Belville: Mayibuye.
Simpson, T. 2006. *The People's War of Umkhonto We Sizwe, 1961–1990* (Doctoral Dissertation). London: University of London.
Simpson, T. 2009. "The Making (and Remaking) of a Revolutionary Plan: Strategic Dilemmas of the ANC's Armed Struggle, 1974–1978," *Social Dynamics* 35(2): 316–341.
Smuts, J. 1942. "The Basis of Trusteeship in African Native Policy." An address delivered under the auspices of the South African Institute of Race Relations in City Hall, Cape Town, 21 January 1942. Johannesburg: South Africa Institute of Race Relations.
South African Institute of Race Relations. 1985. *Race Relations Survey, 1984*. Johannesburg: Institute of Race Relations.
Spaarwater, M. 2012. *A Spook's Progress: From Making War to Making Peace*. Cape Town: Zebra Press.

Sparks, A. 1994. *Tomorrow Is Another Country: The Inside Story of South Africa's Negotiated Revolution*. Sandton: Struik Book Distributors.

Swilling, M. and M. Phillips. 1989. "The Powers of the Thunderbird: Decision-making Structures and Policy Strategies in the South African State," in *South Africa at the End of the Eighties*. Johannesburg: Centre for Policy Studies.

Tambo, O. 1985. Political Report on the National Executive Committee to the National Consultative Conference of the African National Congress, 17 June 1985, Kabwe, Zambia.

Transcript of Bill Anderson interview by Howard Barrell, 8 April 1991, Folder 1 Part 1, Karis-Gerhart Collection, Historical Papers, University of the Witwatersrand.

Transcript of Ivan Pillay interview by Howard Barrell, 20 July 1989, Folder 31, Part 1 Karis-Gerhart Collection, Historical Papers, University of the Witwatersrand.

Transcript of Ivan Pillay interview by Howard Barrell, 23 July 1989, Folder 31, Part 1 Karis-Gerhart Collection, Historical Papers, University of the Witwatersrand.

Transcript of Kobie Coetsee interview by Patti Waldmeir, 3 March 1995. Giliommee Papers BC 1070, Manuscripts and Archives Department, University of Cape Town.

Transcript of Kobie Coetsee interview with Padraig O'Malley, 26 September 1997.

Transcript of Kobie Coetsee interview with Padraig O'Malley, 5 September 1998.

Transcript of Kobie Coetsee interview with John Carlin, 25 May 1999a.

Transcript of Kobie Coetsee interview with Padraig O'Malley, 6 November 1999b.

Transcript of Mike Louw interview by Patti Waldmeir. Giliommee Papers BC 1070, Manuscripts and Archives Department, University of Cape Town.

Transcript of Mac Maharaj interview with Howard Barrell, 20 November 1990a, Folder 18 Part 1Karis-Gerhart Collection, Historical Papers, University of the Witwatersrand.

Transcript of Mac Maharaj interview by Howard Barrell, 30 November 1990b, Folder 18, Part 1 Karis-Gerhart Collection, Historical Papers, University of the Witwatersrand.

Transcript of Niel Barnard interview by Patti Waldmeir, 25 November 1994. Giliommee Papers BC 1070, Manuscripts and Archives Department, University of Cape Town.

Transcript of Niel Barnard interview with Padraig O'Malley, 17 September 1998.

Transcript of Niel Barnard interview with John Carlin, 25 May 1999.

Transcript of Ronnie Kasrils interview with Howard Barrell, 19 August 1989, Folder 14, Part 1 Karis-Gerhart Collection, Historical Papers, University of the Witwatersrand.

Transcript of Ronnie Kasrils interview with Howard Barrell, 13 September 1990, Folder 14, Part 1 Karis-Gerhart Collection, Historical Papers, University of the Witwatersrand.

Transcript of Sue Rabkin interview by Howard Barrell, 7 July 1989, Folder 32, Part 1 Karis-Gerhart Collection, Historical Papers, University of the Witwatersrand.

Turok, B. 2003. *Nothing But the Truth: Behind the ANC's Struggle Politics*. Johannesburg: Jonathan Ball.

Welsh, D. 1994. "The Executive and the African Population: 1948 to the Present," in R. Schrire, ed. *Malan to De Klerk: Leadership in the Apartheid State*. London: Hurst and Co.

4 Getting to the table

The mission of the eminent persons group

By 1985, the apartheid regime was engulfed in an organic crisis. The government was facing a popular uprising, and a partial state of emergency was imposed. Internationally, the country's growing isolation was evident in arms embargoes and cultural and sport boycotts. In October that year, the Commonwealth held a Commonwealth Heads of Government Meeting (CHOGM) in the Bahamas. The overriding issue was apartheid and the crisis it had created. The Commonwealth meeting established an eminent person's group (EPG) to embark on a mediation effort to encourage dialogue towards an establishment of a non-racial and representative government. To understand the nature of this effort, i.e. the EPG's objectives, and their perceptions of the conflict and the parties within it, it is important to trace the evolution of the South African question in the Commonwealth. This is important; the South African government did not have the political interest to accept the EPG's mediation. Yet the EPG's resolving formula proved to be prophetic.

The Commonwealth and the South African question

The modern Commonwealth has its origins in the post-war era. In this period, a special formula was devised to allow decolonised countries, i.e. India and Pakistan (1947), Ceylon (1948) and Malaya (1957), to join what was previously an old boys club for the white-ruled British Dominions. While Britain was initially reluctant to allow the new republics to join the organisation, they soon begun to see Indian and Pakistan membership as a counter-balance during the Cold War. British Prime Minister Clement Attlee sought closer integration with the old colonies in order to "revive the broken post-war British economy, maintain its defence capabilities and to continue to project world-wide influence" (Dubow, 2017: 292). Attlee told the House of Commons in 1948 that Britain was "not solely a European power but a member of a great Commonwealth and empire" (cited in Dubow, 2017: 292). India, the largest of the newly independent countries, decided to remain in the organisation less for nostalgic reasons, and more for pragmatic reasoning. India's prime minister, Jawaharlal Nehru, sought to "refashion the Commonwealth as a postcolonial institution and as a base for its own independent power" (Dubow, 2017: 292).

The 1949 Declaration of London eliminated allegiance to the crown as a condition for Commonwealth membership. This led to the emergence of a multiracial Commonwealth, signalling an important departure from previous arrangements between Britain and the white dominions. Commonwealth heads of government meetings (CHOGM) were no longer akin to cabinet meetings at number 10 Downing Street; it became a policy-making body with economic and security arrangements baked in (Dubow, 2017: 293).

The expansion of the Commonwealth membership with newly independent African states in the 1960s, and the accompanying emergence of an Afro-Asian bloc, also witnessed the reconfiguration of the international system in the United Nations. Ghana joined India in the Initiative of Five as founding members of the Non-Aligned Movement (NAM) in Belgrade in 1960, a multilateral organisation that sought to bridge the gap between the developed and developing world, define an independent line in international affairs and a commitment to the struggle against imperialism, colonialism and racism. By the late 1970s, there was a remarkable similarity of membership of the Commonwealth and NAM: "twenty-two nations within the larger organisation of eighty-seven" (Onslow, 2015: 1061). Within these changes, Commonwealth politics changed; they now were typified by balancing between the economic interests of Britain and the conflicting political interests of her former colonies, particularly in regards the demands from many in the Commonwealth to do something about the white minority regimes of southern Africa. Singapore's long serving prime minister, Lee Kuan Yew, recollects that Rhodesia and apartheid occupied considerable time and took centre stage at every Commonwealth conference (Lee, 2000: 363).

The problem of South Africa

In the 1950s, the Commonwealth was a welcome old boys club for South Africa. In 1956, Gwendolen Carter, a political scientist who wrote extensively on South Africa, concluded that:

> [the Commonwealth] remains the one international organization in which South Africa is still welcome; its membership therein, too, has been a major reason why the older Commonwealth countries have been reluctant to join in the chorus of censure levied at South Africa in the United Nations over its policies towards South West Africa, the Indians in South Africa and apartheid.
>
> (Carter, 1956: 135)

Newly independent India and Ghana were initially ambivalent about South Africa. While Kwame Nkrumah condemned apartheid, he also pledged that Ghana would continue to trade with South Africa and receive its technical assistance. Britain was also determined to keep South Africa within the Commonwealth fold. By 1960, Britain had extensive economic interests in South Africa: in 1960, Britain had invested £900 million in the country; exports to South Africa accounted for than £150 million annually; South Africa was the United Kingdom's (UK) fifth most important market for good exports; £200 million worth of South African gold marketed each year in London provided valuable support for the sterling; and Britain supplied 41 percent of new motor vehicles registered in South Africa (Dubow, 2017: 295). Therefore, unlike the United Nations whose forums were increasingly hostile to South Africa's domestic politics, the Commonwealth "remained a relatively protected space from which to observe and participate in international affairs." Its internal affairs "were conducted with greater decorum and with less public scrutiny than was the case of the UN general assembly" (Dubow, 2017: 295).

The turning point comes in 1960 with a remarkable concurrence of events. At the beginning of 1960, South Africa's Prime Minister Hendrik Verwoerd took a gamble and held a referendum on the country becoming a republic. Held in October that year, white South Africa voted in favour of republican status. The problem with this was that according to the formula set by India and Pakistan for Commonwealth membership, former British colonies that became republics had to reapply for membership of the Commonwealth (Taylor, 2000: 58). This inevitably raised the question of South Africa's application to join as a republic, and given the country's controversial domestic politics, newly independent African countries took aim. This matter came to a head at the 1961 Commonwealth prime ministers conference in London. The opening salvo was fired by Julius Nyerere who published in a letter in *The Observer* stating that an independent Tanganyika would not join the Commonwealth if South Africa was a member. While Britain, New Zealand and Australia sought to keep the agenda focused on constitutional questions, India entered the fray and developed a strategy that sought to use the Commonwealth to change apartheid's policies and practices (Dubow, 2017: 298). Nehru argued that unless the Commonwealth publicly and forthrightly denounced apartheid, the organisation would be imperilled (Dubow, 2017: 298). Pressure was mounted with Nigeria and Ceylon questioning whether apartheid was consistent with the basic ideals of the Commonwealth (Hyam and Henshaw, 2003: 264–269; Miller, 1961: 61; Dubow, 2017: 298). While Britain did everything possible to avert South Africa's exit, seeking desperately to find a formula, the point of no return was reached when the South African prime minister was willing to countenance a group statement identifying apartheid as "inconsistent with the basic ideals on which the unity and influence of the Commonwealth rest," coupled with his refusal to accept the possibility of black Commonwealth diplomats in Pretoria (Dubow, 2017: 298). In the face of mounting pressure from India and African countries, Verwoerd withdrew the application to join as a republic. This however did not end Britain's relationship with apartheid. British Prime Minister Harold Macmillan reassured South Africa that

> withdrawal would not in any way affect the substance of Anglo-South African relations; that in particular, the benefits which the National Party regime received from membership in the Sterling Area and the Preference Area and Simons Town Agreements would remain essentially intact.
>
> (Berridge, 1981: 127)

The Commonwealth post-South Africa's departure

After South Africa's departure, the Commonwealth underwent transformation. Seeking a new mission in the context of a new membership body, the Commonwealth began to settle on the idea that it served as a bridge between developed and developing countries. This implied "operating on a global scale as an intergovernmental agency geared to development and committed to greater economic equality between North and South" (Dubow, 2017: 300). With this came a new discourse on multiculturalism and non-racialism. Britain's colonial secretary Iain Macleod portrayed the Commonwealth as a family, stating his belief "in the brotherhood of man – men of all races, of all colours, of all creeds." Guy Arnold also maintained that South Africa's departure meant that the Commonwealth "had finally decided that it would uphold the principle of multiracial equality" (Dubow, 2017: 300). Because of this new evolving role, South Africa's departure was not enough for the organisation; Commonwealth membership repeatedly involved itself in the apartheid, Rhodesian and Namibian questions. South Africa's domestic politics were a principled and moral issue. The preoccupation with apartheid South Africa spawned a great irony; the organisation's modern development came to be influenced more by its most celebrated outsider than by any country within its fold (Vale and Black, 1994: 5).

Events took a turn when Ian Smith's regime in Rhodesia unilaterally declared independence (UDI) from Britain. Because Rhodesia never legally ceased being a colonial possession of Britain, many Commonwealth members looked towards London to solve the dilemma. When Britain appeared reluctant by constraining the imposition of sanctions on Smith's government, the perception was created that London was sympathetic towards the regime. This set Britain on a collision course with members of the Commonwealth who began to use the Rhodesian issue to attack Britain. As events unfolded, Nigeria's prime minister, Tafawa Balewa, called a Commonwealth prime ministers conference in 1966 to discuss Rhodesia's UDI. It was in this meeting that the Rhodesian issue led to a divisive debate within the Commonwealth. At issue was what appropriate action should be taken as a result of the unlawful declaration. Divisions emerged between Britain and most of the Commonwealth membership. African members demanded stronger action and punitive sanctions against Rhodesia, and a far more hard-line approach. By contrast, Britain argued for a non-confrontational approach. Zambia's Kenneth Kaunda threatened to take Zambia out of the Commonwealth in 1966, and even "to seek Britain's expulsion, in protest at Harold Wilson's failure to bring Smith to heel" (Dubow, 2017: 300–301). Uganda's Prime Minister Milton Obote went further and suggested that Britain was reluctant to bring Smith to heel or to have UN sanctions "because of a diabolical British plot to give Ian Smith time to consolidate his regime" (Lee, 2000: 353). Prime Minister Lee of Singapore believed that Britain had to "buy time for its economic interests in South Africa and Rhodesia" and Wilson was thus faced with the problem of going against domestic opinion (Lee, 2000: 354).

The Lagos meeting set the tone of the balance of forces in dealing with South Africa. Britain would frequently make the case for non-confrontational approaches to protect its commercial interests in southern Africa. On the other hand, most Commonwealth members favoured a more vigorous and hard-line approach. In a mediating role, Canada sought to preserve the status quo "whilst appearing to be sympathetic to demands for stronger action" (Taylor, 2000: 60). Dubow writes that it was tensions in the Commonwealth over the issue in Rhodesia that help explain the failure to convene a heads of government meeting in 1967–1968 (Dubow, 2017: 300). Gradually, Britain's position served to delegitimise London in the eyes of many Commonwealth members, especially at CHOGMs (Taylor, 2000).

In the 1970s, the Commonwealth's autonomy and identity in the international system gathered cogency and importance. This was mainly because of the emergence and coming of age of a large charismatic group of post-independence leaders. These included Lee Kuan Yew (Singapore), Pierre Trudeau (Canada), Julius Nyerere (Tanzania), Kenneth Kaunda (Zambia), Indira Gandhi (India), Malcolm Fraser (Australia) and Michael Manly (Jamaica) (Onslow, 2015: 1067). They were later joined by Rajiv Gandhi (India), Bob Hawke (Australia), Robert Mugabe (Zimbabwe), Brian Mulroney (Canada) and Margaret Thatcher (Britain). In this era of elite politics, characterised by an emergent personal network of heads of state (who had played significant individual roles in their respective nation's independence) Commonwealth structures were transformed; "personal contact and friendships engendered that critical but intangible element of 'trust' in international diplomacy which provided the continuing glue for the Commonwealth as an active association" (Onslow, 2015: 1067).

The South African question comes into refocus in 1971. Concerned about an alleged Soviet naval build-up in the Indian ocean, Britain renewed military sales to South Africa. This matter was complicated; in 1967, Wilson had bowed to pressure and announced that Britain would no longer supply arms to South Africa "even if contracts existed or the material needed was for the maintenance of equipment which had previously been supplied from Britain" (Ziegler, 2010: 261). The matter was further complicated by the existence of the Simon Town Agreement under which Britain and South Africa shared naval defence responsibilities of the South Atlantic and Indian Oceans against Communist threats. Edward Heath, Britain's prime minister in 1970, never believed in the utility of sanctions and boycotts; "his instinctive belief was that boycotts and sanctions would merely reinforce the intransigence of the South African government" (Ziegler, 2010: 261). He further believed that to continue the arms embargo to South Africa was both politically unwise and legally unjustifiable. Consequently, arms sales to South Africa were resumed soon after he assumed the premiership in 1970.

The consequence was a major outcry from other African countries. Tanzania, Uganda and Zambia immediately threatened to leave the Commonwealth over Heath's decision (Ziegler, 2010: 262). Further, the Archbishop of Canterbury told Heath that "99 out of the 110 bishops gathered at Lambeth had asked him to express disquiet at the arms sale" (Ziegler, 2010: 262). On the Rhodesian question, Heath similarly inclined towards the views of his right wing; Heath "did not think that blacks were ready to govern themselves and viewed with distaste and alarm the activities of those who were in favour of somehow coercing Ian Smith's government to surrender" (Ziegler, 2010: 263).

These views on Southern Africa put him at odds with his Commonwealth peers. It became clear that in the run-up to the upcoming Commonwealth conference to be held in Singapore in January 1971, the issue of South Africa's arms sales and Rhodesian independence would dominate the agenda. The Singapore conference would turn out to be a watershed. Lee Kuan Yew, the host of the conference, writes that prior to the conference he had agreed with Heath that the issue of arms to South Africa would be treated as a separate item on the agenda, and that a study group would consider the issue and report its findings to the secretary-general. Despite the attempt at damage control with Prime Minister Lee, the reality was worse than he had imagined possible. According to Lee, Heath was simply not comfortable in a Third World multicultural setting:

> It was his first experience of such a gathering. The African leaders set out to make him feel isolated. A little shy and guarded, he was different from Harold Wilson with his pipe-puffing bonhomie. Heath appeared stiff and ill at ease, spoke with a strong Oxford accent, and bristled when provoked.
>
> (Lee, 2000: 359)

The conference revealed the stark division in the Commonwealth over the South African question. The conflicting positions are illustrated by the arguments of Nyerere and Heath. Nyerere's view would later emerge as the Commonwealth line on South Africa. Nyerere's position was that if the Commonwealth was not opposed to racism, then they had "no business sitting down together in an association which consists of representatives of all racial groups in the world" (Nyerere, 1971: 1). African countries, he pointed out, have "absolute hostility to the South African regime" as it denied the humanity of Africans "on grounds of characteristics that we share." African governments were thus not only determined that apartheid's leaders be condemned; they wanted to work towards a South Africa "governed on the principles of humanity with the equality of every citizen recognised regardless of race or colour" (Nyerere, 1971: 3). To this end, Britain, which bore responsibility to the problems of South Africa, had "a special responsibility in this matter" (Nyerere, 1971: 4). Britain's actions however were a deviation from their own commitment since 1955. Nyerere's position was not to dictate to Britain what her national interests should be; it was rather to ask her to look for other means of solving the problem she was faced with considering the policy of apartheid.

Lee's observation was that Nyerere had sized up Heath and unlike Kaunda or Obote had decided not to preach to him, giving him an effective argument on a high moral plane. Heath explained that the issues of apartheid and the sale of arms were two separate questions and that Britain "considered it necessary to retain [Britain's] right to use facilities granted under the Simons Town Agreements" (Heath cited in Ziegler, 2010). Thus, the equipment to South Africa was a matter of defence policy and had nothing to do with apartheid:

> Britain depended on the free movement of goods and the freedom of the seas. Half its oil supplies and a quarter of its trade passed through the sea route around the Cape. The Soviet Union posed a maritime threat.
>
> (Lee, 2000: 360–361)

These tensions, however, helped keep the Commonwealth intact as opposed to tearing it apart. While it was reinvigorated with a sense of moral purpose, divisions between Britain and most of the membership over the South African question remained. The Singapore meeting had important consequences that defined the way forward for the southern African question. The first part of the resultant Singapore Communiqué noted that the tensions in southern Africa "were likely to increase rather than decrease unless there were fundamental changes in the conditions now prevailing" (Singapore Communiqué, 1971: 1). The Communiqué, however, did not resolve as to how these changes should occur. All that was suggested was to deal specifically with the issues of maritime security in the South Atlantic and Indian Ocean, and arms sales to South Africa by means of a "a Study Group, consisting of representatives of Australia, Britain, Canada, India, Jamaica, Kenya, Malaysia and Nigeria, with instructions to consider the question further and report to them through the Secretary-General as soon as possible" (Singapore Communiqué, 1971: 1).

The important outcome of the conference was the Declaration of Commonwealth Principles which recognised racial prejudice as "a dangerous sickness threatening the healthy development of the human race and racial discrimination as an unmitigated evil of society" (Singapore Declaration, 1971: 1). The Declaration further stated that "no country will afford assistance to regimes which practice racial discrimination which in its own judgment directly contributes to the pursuit or consolidation of this evil policy" (Singapore Declaration, 1971: 1). Dubow and McIntyre observed that this wording in opposition to racism was notably tougher than that of the other principles, and were articulated as beliefs or convictions (Dubow, 2017: 301; McIntyre, 1991: 87). This was the first attempt to define a clear set of principles to unite the Commonwealth (Murphy, 2011: 272).

The era from Singapore is where the principles and values of racial equality were affirmed and refined, where apartheid South Africa stood out as anathema (Dubow, 2017: 301; Srinivason, 1998: 624–627). Observers of the time point out at the significance of the Gleneagles Agreement on Apartheid and Sport of 1977, the threatened boycott of the 1978 Edmonton Commonwealth Games, and the 1979 Lusaka Declaration on Racism and Racial Prejudice were a consequence of the Singapore moment. Taylor (2000: 61) however cautions the importance of these boycotts; though they were successful in helping to isolate South Africa, boycotts were frequently broken, and Commonwealth consensus only emerged out of symbolic boycotts. Further, the organisation was extremely divided and ineffective when it came to economic issues such as sanctions.

The power-brokers: the road to the Nassau CHOGM

A major turning point happened with the ascension of Shridath "Sonny" Ramphal as secretary-general at the Kingston CHOGM in 1975. Ramphal was the former attorney-general and foreign minister of Guyana, and had risen to prominence in the politics of the NAM in the early 1970s. Ramphal brought "a charisma and intellectual vigour to the post of secretary-general, as well as a particular outlook to his new position as a policy initiator in coordination with heads, rather than simply responding to their instruction" (Onslow, 2015: 1069). This approach produced dynamism in Commonwealth diplomacy during this period. Onslow writes that Ramphal was a departure from most leaders of the organisation. First, Ramphal was an activist secretary-general and "occupied prominent positions on major international commissions of enquiry on social justice and climate change." Second, Ramphal's tenure was characterised by elite politics and the important role played by heads of government, combined with the strong influence of non-alignment amongst key international leaders. Third, Ramphal "relied heavily on personal diplomacy and the telephone" to get things done (Onslow, 2015: 1069). Ramphal's tenure was thus characterised by personal contact, the longevity of leadership and trust. This was augmented by Ramphal's personal networks; Ramphal had important networks in the senior echelons of the anti-apartheid movement, both moderates and radical nationalists alike. Mayall (2010: 18) writes that Commonwealth foreign policy activism on Rhodesia, and then South Africa, in which Ramphal took the lead, was the organisation's "grand strategy," or the closest it came to ever having one.

Throughout the period that Ramphal was the secretary-general, Africa was top of the agenda; the focus was first on white minority rule in Rhodesia and then on the end of white rule in South Africa. Margaret Thatcher, who was the British prime minister during this period, always tended to lean towards the South African government position, and this was sustained by her husband Denis who "was instinctively to the right of her and had many longstanding and close business associations with South Africa" (Ingram, 2008: 781). The dynamic between Ramphal and Thatcher would govern Commonwealth politics for over a decade. When Ramphal walked into the courtyard of the Commonwealth secretariat headquarters, he was a "seasoned practitioner in the international effort to mobilise world opinion against the entrenchment of racism in southern Africa" (Robertson, 2008: 42). One of his first acts was to warn leaders that regional conflicts in southern Africa could no longer be contained and argued for the peaceful resolution of these conflicts (Robertson, 2008: 45).

After the Rhodesian political settlement, with this issue finally coming off the Commonwealth agenda, the South African issue dominated CHOGM discussions for the rest of the decade (Ingram, 2008: 784). Thatcher's appeasement of the apartheid government differed sharply from Ramphal's approach that saw the Commonwealth as "the vanguard of the final push against apartheid" (Ingram, 2008: 784). Ramphal sought to universalise the problem of apartheid:

> [apartheid is] not just the South African problem; it is the Rhodesian problem; it is the African problem they make inevitable, and the world racial problem they exacerbate. But most of all, for the West, it is a national problem, a

> domestic problem, a personal problem, a problem of the quality of Western principles and Western values.
>
> (cited in Dubow, 2017: 302)

To be anti-apartheid was to apply pressure on South Africa, and this became central to the Commonwealth's self-image and legitimacy. The Commonwealth's foreign policy initiatives on South Africa became its most important strategic focus, with pressure for sanctions a major priority (Onslow, 2015: 1050). By contrast, Thatcher argued otherwise, and in doing so, dug in her heels. While she was happy to go along with the repeated condemnation of apartheid, the imposition and toughening of sanctions was another matter:

> Admitted that fundamental changes must be made in South Africa's system, the question was of how best to achieve them. It seemed to me that the worst approach was to isolate South Africa further. Indeed, the isolation had already gone too far, contributing to an inflexible siege mentality among the governing Afrikaner class. It was absurd to believe that they would be prepared to relinquish power suddenly or without acceptable safeguards.
>
> (Thatcher, 1993: 513)

As the South African issue became central to the Commonwealth, Thatcher and Britain became more isolated on the sanctions issue. Just before the 1981 CHOGM in Melbourne, Ramphal said in a speech in London that "it is not possible to be an ally of South Africa and a friend of Africa. No one must then be surprised if Africa chooses other friends" (cited in Ingram, 2008: 785). At the 1983 CHOGM in Delhi, Ramphal was elected for a third term. While Thatcher supported his re-election, she was more than ever at odds with almost all her other Commonwealth colleagues. While all agreed on the immediate issue at the time, i.e. the withdrawal of South African troops from Angola and the independence of Namibia, they continued to disagree over the imposition of economic sanctions against South Africa.

The mediators: the 1985 Nassau CHOGM

The 1985 CHOGM in the Bahamas should be understood within the context of the Commonwealth's political agenda increasingly focused on South Africa and led by an activist secretary-general who took a firm line against apartheid. The rising tide of revolt and state repression that filled South Africa's streets from 1984 was a major turning point. The uprising not only filled the world's television screens; it provoked international opinion to a new pitch of indignation. Subsequently, new anti-apartheid organisations sprang up in Western Europe and North America and old ones "attracted new activists as universities, churches, corporate boardrooms, city councils, and national parliaments became the scene of roiling debates over disinvestment, boycotts and sanctions" (Gerhart and Glaser, 2010: 145).

The upcoming CHOGM meeting in Nassau in October 1985 invariably concentrated on South Africa. In the run-up to the meeting, opposing sides of the South Africa divide began preparing for a showdown. Thatcher held a seminar at Chequers to clarify British thinking on South Africa. The British government agreed that the South African situation was a crisis:

> On the one hand the reform process in South Africa has ground to a halt; the constitutional reforms had proved a dead end because they did not involve even moderate middle-class blacks. On the other, the European Community was moving towards imposing sanctions.
>
> (Thatcher, 1993: 515)

Britain's position in the run-up to the meeting was to try to slow down the rush towards impending sanctions, and "to try to bring about negotiations between the South African government and representatives of the black population" (Thatcher, 1993: 516). On the other hand, and in his pre-CHOGM biennial report, Ramphal appealed to Commonwealth heads that the Commonwealth had an honourable record in the campaign to end apartheid (Ramphal, 2014: 425). He further stated that the rising tide of anger within South Africa and rising demand for economic sanctions externally must be sustained, and that it should be unthinkable that any Commonwealth country should offer comfort to South Africa (Ramphal, 2014: 426).

The mediator's objective: the Commonwealth Accord on Southern Africa

The main issue discussed at Nassau was South Africa's domestic and regional policies, and the implementation of sanctions. At stake was a showdown between Britain and the rest of the Commonwealth member states who believed that some form of punitive measures should be imposed on South Africa to force substantive changes regarding apartheid. Britain was virtually isolated on the sanctions issue. However, that Britain saw the sanctions as counterproductive in no way means they were averse to a solution to the South African question. In a July speech to the Royal Commonwealth Society, Britain's foreign secretary, Sir Geoffrey Howe, announced a six-point plan of urgent action to create a climate of confidence for effective dialogue: the unconditional release of Nelson Mandela and other acknowledged political leaders; an end to forced removals; an end to detention without trial; an early end to the state of emergency; the progressive abolition of discriminatory legislation; and the adoption of a commitment to some form of common citizenship for all South Africans (SAIIA, 1985: 8).

The major difference was less about whether dialogue was needed and more about whether sanctions were the necessary path to peace. Ramphal's role was to steer the summit into proposals that both sides would find tolerable and accept. Four leaders assisted Ramphal towards this end: Bob Hawke, Brian Mulroney, Rajiv Gandhi and Kenneth Kaunda. These leaders would engage Thatcher with compromise proposals which were frequently turned down because they contained sanctions. It was not until the leaders' retreat at Lyford Cray that Ramphal's group were able to debate Thatcher and work out a compromise package of measures that would be adopted by Commonwealth countries. According to this package, certain measures would be taken against South Africa before the six months' deadline, and these were to be followed by further measures after this period if South Africa failed to implement substantial domestic reforms and enter credible negotiations with representatives of black South African leaders within six months.

The summit adopted the Commonwealth Accord on Southern Africa, otherwise known as the Nassau Accord. The Accord called on the South African government to:

a) declare that the system of apartheid will be dismantled, and specific and meaningful action taken in fulfilment of that intent;
b) terminate the existing state of emergency;
c) release immediately and unconditionally Nelson Mandela and all others imprisoned and detained for their political opposition to apartheid;
d) establish political freedom and specifically lift the existing ban on the African National Congress and other political parties;
e) initiate, in the context of a suspension of violence on all sides, a process of dialogue across lines of colour, politics and religion, with a view of establishing a non-racial representative government.

(Commonwealth Accord, 1986: 142)

To this end, a small group of eminent persons would be established "to encourage through all practicable ways the evolution of that necessary process of political dialogue" (Commonwealth Accord, 1986: 143). This group of eminent persons would be appointed and assisted in their tasks by the leaders of Australia, Britain, the Bahamas, Canada, India, Zambia, Zimbabwe and Ramphal, i.e. the so-called contact group. This group would develop the modalities of this effort to assist the process of dialogue. The Commonwealth also agreed on a programme of actions: the "strictest enforcement of the mandatory arms embargo against South Africa; to discourage sporting contacts; and to adopt a number of economic measures against South Africa" (these included a ban on all new government loans; a readiness to take unilateral action to preclude the import of Krugerrands; no government funding for trade missions to South Africa; a ban on the sale or export of computer equipment capable of use by South African security forces; a ban on new contracts for the sale and export of nuclear technology to South Africa; a ban on the sale and export of oil to South and paramilitary equipment; and an embargo on all military cooperation, and discouragement of all cultural and scientific events, except where these contribute towards the ending of apartheid or have no possible role in promoting it) (Commonwealth Accord, 1986).

The next challenge was on the composition of the mission. Thatcher wanted her foreign and Commonwealth secretary, Sir Geoffrey Howe, to lead the group. Ramphal wanted it to be composed of envoys who would be acting in their personal capacity. Thatcher gave way in the end and nominated Lord Barber, the chairman of Standard Chartered Bank, as the British member of the group. Kaunda and Mugabe proposed General Olusegun Obasanjo, the former head of the Nigerian military government between 1976 and 1979. Notwithstanding his background as a military ruler, Obasanjo was a gifted conciliator and internationalist who enjoyed unusual international support in both Africa and the West, and was thus acceptable to all in the Commonwealth, including Thatcher. Obasanjo was appointed as co-chairman of the group, and he would perform this task with Malcolm Fraser, the former Australian prime minister. Other members of the group included Dame Nita Barrow (a Barbados civil society activist), John Malecela (Tanzania's foreign minister), Swaran Singh (India's foreign minister) and Canadian Archbishop Ted Scott.

Before the mission embarked, Thatcher wrote confidentially to President Botha. She gave him an account of the Commonwealth summit, reporting that the South African debate "was a highly unpleasant and bitter one; and there is no doubt that the issue of sanctions will go away, despite my success in preventing the Commonwealth from adopting them at this meeting" (cited in Mole, 2012: 255). The main objective of that meeting, she continued, "was to secure Commonwealth backing for dialogue between the South African government and representatives of the black community in the context of a suspension of violence by all sides." She urged Botha to receive the EPG and allow it to do its work: "I am under no illusion that much of what it will say and do will be distasteful to you . . . but the alternative of refusing – to see the EPG – would be much more damaging" (cited in Mole, 2012: 255).

The letter to Thatcher proved to be significant; ever since leaving the Commonwealth in 1961, South Africa was very distrustful of the organisation. According to Pik Botha, the South African foreign minister, the first reaction from the South African government when they received news of the Nassau decision was negative: "They [are] not welcome here. They [are] an ill-assorted organisation; Useless Commonwealth, they kicked us out in 1961!" (Botha, 2012: 2). Thatcher's intervention persuaded the South African government to accept the EPG. Pik Botha further makes this point: "PW [Botha] had great respect for Thatcher. Of all the leaders over the world, she was the one whom he felt was not in favour of crushing the National Party" (Botha, 2012: 2). Thus, according to Botha, had it not been for Thatcher's intervention, the South African government would not have accepted the EPG mission.

Into the eye of the storm: the eve of the EPG mission

It is important to briefly describe the environment into which the EPG entered South Africa. As discussed in Chapter 3, while on a European tour at the beginning of January 1985 Botha had been encouraged by a group of German leaders, Franz-Josef Strauss, the Bavarian Christian-Socialist, to offer to release Mandela if he would renounce all violence. Botha presented this formula to the cabinet but was warned by Coetsee and Louis le Grange, the Minister of Law and Order, that

Mandela would not give up his strongest bargaining chip prematurely. However, with the support of the rest of the cabinet, Botha further told parliament that he was offering Mandela his freedom provided he "unconditionally rejected violence as a political instrument" (Sparks, 1994: 49). To Botha's formula, "Mandela in exchange for non-violence," Mandela responded, "legality in exchange for non-violence" and Botha's gambit became an albatross.

A chain of important events followed this interaction. In April 1985, Stoffel van der Merwe, a cabinet minister, wrote in a booklet titled "And What about the Black People?" that separate development could not work. He admitted that attempts at expelling blacks from urban areas "had failed, that it was a mistake to force blacks in urban areas to accept citizenship of independent homelands and maintained the situation in which blacks lived in one area and voted in another was ineffective and meaningless." He proposed "including all South Africans in a common political system, though not necessarily within the same structures" (Melunsky, 2002: 85). The booklet confirmed that the government accepted that urban Africans were permanent residents in "white" South Africa with legitimate claims for political representation. However, no detail was provided how this would be achieved, "save for rejecting a fourth parliamentary chamber, and confirming that future dispensations would be group-based" (Melunsky, 2002: 85).

In August 1985, at the NP Natal Congress (in a speech that would become known as the Rubicon speech), Botha declared that South Africa was one country:

> Should any of the Black National States therefore prefer not to accept independence, such states or communities will remain a part of the South African nation, are South African citizens and should be accommodated within political institutions within the boundaries of the Republic of South Africa.
>
> (cited in Schrire, 1991: Appendix A)

Botha announced that Africans "needed a forum to represent themselves in future negotiations and would be included in government." Additionally, Botha admitted that "influx control was out-dated and costly" (Melunsky, 2002: 85). In September 1985, Botha accepted that some Africans who lived and worked permanently inside South African could be granted citizenship:

> We must consequently accept the South African citizenship of those black persons who lost their citizenship because of the independence of Transkei, Bophuthatswana, Venda and Ciskei but who permanently reside in South Africa.
>
> (cited in Pottinger, 1988: 131)

This was Botha's crucial concession as voting rights follow from citizenship rights. Exactly who qualified remained unclear. It was even more unclear "how African participation would be exercised beyond government's commitment to groups, its belief that the country was made up of minorities, that there should be community self-determination, and that no one group should dominate" (Melunsky, 2002: 87–88).

This was the political climate in which Mandela requested a meeting with Coetsee to discuss talks between the government and the ANC, and the period after the Commonwealth summit in the Bahamas. Although Coetsee did not respond, the opportunity came in December 1985 when a routine medical examination diagnosed Mandela with an enlarged prostate gland that required surgery. Mandela's hospitalisation provided the opportunity for Coetsee. He arrived at Mandela's side unannounced. He told Sparks that he was immediately impressed by Mandela. For his part, Mandela was surprised but recognised the government was extending an olive branch: "I was amazed. The government, in its slow and tentative way, was reckoning that they had to come to some accommodation with the ANC. Coetsee's visit was an olive branch" (Mandela, 1994: 624).

Although no substantive political discussions occurred, the government signalled its intent. Mandela told Sparks: "at one point he said to me 'I am interested in your being put in a situation between prison and freedom'" (cited in Sparks, 1994: 25). Coetsee assigned Mandela a new cell, away from his colleagues in order to create the environment for commencing talks (Melunsky, 2002: 142). Coetsee received instruction from Botha:

> We got the green light from Mr Botha that we could start talking to Mr Mandela in general. Just [keep] in mind that at the time it was the department of prisons mostly taking initiatives. We weren't constitutionally equipped, we weren't mandated, that's why Mr Botha also decided to form a committee a little bit later. But it was to have access to Mr Mandela, and put him in a position where he could have the opportunity to impose his views, which he did . . . I got the impression that he decided to use the opportunity and he interpreted it correctly, that it is something very special being designed.
>
> (Coetsee, 1999: 1)

Mandela's second isolation achieved the government's desired results. According to Mandela, he came to the realisation that the time had come to begin discussions with the government:

> I had concluded that the time had come when the struggle could best be pushed forward through negotiations. If we did not start a dialogue soon, both sides would soon be plunged into a dark night of oppression, violence and war. My solitude would give me an opportunity to take the first steps in that direction, without the kind of scrutiny that might destroy such efforts.
>
> (Mandela, 1994: 625–626)

At the same time, Botha continued to give concessions as a way of legitimising constitutional reform. In the same month Botha formally proposed a National Statutory Council to "plan and prepare a constitutional dispensation which provides participation by all South African citizens in the processes of government," and to grant Africans a voice in government "on an interim basis" (Schrire, 1991: 103). However, despite Botha's efforts, no black African leader, even those closely associated with the government, supported the NSC. Buthelezi refused to participate unless Mandela was released (Melunsky, 2002: 88).

Therefore, at the point where the EPG arrives in South Africa, the government had reached a cul-de-sac; despite Botha's concessions, no African leader, even those closely associated with the government, was in full support of these constitutional reform initiatives. Botha expresses this in his private papers: "we are rapidly reaching the stage at which we have to say how far we are prepared to go" (cited in Melunsky, 2002: 104).

The mission of the eminent persons group

The operational principles

The EPG held its first meeting at Marlborough House, London, on 12–13 December 1985, the month that Coetsee approached Mandela. The group was aware of the limitations of their mission; once established they had six months, and at the end of the six months, the seven heads of government would then consider further measures. The group's mandate was also limited to the task for facilitating a process of dialogue for change:

> for ending apartheid and establishing a genuine non-racial democracy in South Africa. It would be those involved in that process – the representatives of all the people of South Africa – to determine the forms of change; it was not our function to prescribe what form a political settlement might take.
>
> (EPG Report, 1986: 20)

The group was also entering a hostile political environment; suspicions from both sides of the conflict questioned the EPG's motives and intentions. According to Thabo Mbeki's biographer, the ANC was instinctively hostile to the initiative, "seeing it – as Tambo later told an NEC meeting – 'as a way of buying Botha a way out of a tight corner'" (Gevisser, 2007: 534). The ANC also perceived the group as a product of the British government to delay sanctions. As for the government, the chief of South Africa's secret service, Neil Barnard, saw it as an attempt to meddle in matters that didn't concern them:

> we took a very strong line, that the future through negotiations will be negotiated by South Africans alone and between South Africans alone. We were not interested in brokers and facilitators and United Nations and Commonwealth and Europe and anybody else. . . . I have a deep distrust of any third party . . . I didn't trust facilitators, I don't trust anybody from the outside because in the end facilitators never know . . . the deep emotions and problems you are struggling through.
>
> (Barnard, 1998: 2)

In order to overcome these perceptions and build confidence, the EPG agreed on four operational principles. First, they would work quietly and in non-public ways, i.e. they would not make any public comment. Second, they would be non-confrontational in their approach. This meant that even when severely provoked, they would always maintain an atmosphere of cordiality. Third, they chose not to always function as a group. They subdivided to make simultaneous visits and shared the tasks of briefing heads of government of neighbouring countries. Fourth, to gain access to all the principal parties and demonstrate independence, the EPG chose to travel alone without any government security personnel. This enabled them to move extensively around the country, with freedom of access to all those they met, making it possible to consult widely.

At the group's second meeting on 12–13 February 1986, the group finalised agreements for the visit of three of its number to South Africa the following week.

Preliminary visit to South Africa (undertaken by Mr Malcolm Fraser, General Olusegun Obasanjo and Dame Nita Barrow)

On 16 February 1986, Obasanjo, Fraser and Barrow arrived in Cape Town as the advance party to explore possibilities for negotiation. Their schedule was heavy; between Monday 17 February and Saturday 22 February they held conversations and meetings with leaders from across the political spectrum – cabinet ministers, prominent members of the internal anti-apartheid movement, churchmen and members of the political opposition inside parliament. The key objective was to test the government's willingness to enter dialogue and open the way for negotiations with the ANC. To this end, discussions with Mandela would be essential: The Commonwealth had recognised that the Mandela question was essential for any political settlement in South Africa.

On 21 February, Obasanjo was permitted to see Mandela on Robben Island in order to discuss the nature of the EPG's brief, and as a preliminary discussion in preparation for his meeting with the full group. Obasanjo was joined by Coetsee and Lieutenant-General W.H. Willemse. While many questions and issues were raised at the meeting, three were important: Mandela's ideological disposition (i.e. whether he was a Communist and what a future South Africa under the ANC would look like); the issue of violence; and negotiation possibilities. Mandela explained that he was a nationalist and not a communist, and since nationalists came in every hue and colour, he was a committed to a non-racial society that embodied the principles of human rights and democracy (Mandela, 1994). Mandela believed that violence could never be the ultimate solution to the South African conflict; however, he added, he was not ready to renounce violence until such time that the government removed troops from the township. Only if such steps were taken could the ANC begin a discussion on suspending the armed struggle. Mandela stated that the time had come for negotiations and that many of the problems between the government and the ANC stemmed from a lack of communication.

Obasanjo was struck by Mandela's physical authority, commanding presence and intellect. He later recalled:

> For me, that first contact was an encounter never to be forgotten. I saw in Nelson Mandela a South African indeed an African and a world leader of no

> mean order. He towered physically and metaphorically above all the leaders we met inside South Africa. His intellect, perception and vision did not appear to have been dimmed by years of isolation and solitude, if anything, they seemed to have been focused and sharpened. In thought and perception, he was freer than his gaolers who were encapsulated and imprisoned in thought, vision and perception!!!
>
> (cited in Iliffe, 2011: 122)

Visit to Lesotho, Botswana, Zimbabwe, Zambia and Angola

Following this preliminary visit, five members of the group (Barber, Malecela, Scott, Barrow and Fraser) visited Botswana, Lesotho and Zimbabwe before proceeding to Zambia. In Zambia they met President Kaunda and Tambo. Here they were joined by Singh, Obasanjo and Ramphal. Before flying back to South Africa, they held talks with President Dos Santos of Angola. The important meeting was with the ANC in Lusaka. Close contacts had already been established with Mbeki. The ANC however was sceptical, and Mbeki had to persuade Tambo that the ANC needed to work with the EPG (Gevisser, 2007: 534). The EPG held consultations with Tambo, Mbeki and members of the ANC executive. The ANC told the EPG that their immediate reaction to the formation of the group was one of disappointment; they had hoped that the Nassau Accord would have led to an increase in international pressure on South Africa through sanctions. Instead, they felt the establishment of the group had relieved pressure on the South African government. The ANC believed in the peaceful resolution to the South African conflict and this they believed would be possible if the government took immediately the steps elaborated in the Nassau Accord. These, the ANC further stated, "coincided with what the people of South Africa had been demanding for many years" (EPG Report, 1986: 86).

The EPG questioned the ANC particularly about the possibility of the suspension of violence on both sides leading towards cessation. The ANC's response was that "it was important to understand the nature of violence, how it came about, who started it, and how others reacted." Violence in South Africa, they continued, was the result of the apartheid system "which needed guns, arrests and prisons to maintain it." The ANC for many years used non-violence in response but at some point, they were left with no alternative but to employ violence. Therefore, for the ANC, "violence would abate if the system was dismantled [and] this would open for a cessation of violence on both sides." The Nassau Accord was essential for the ANC:

> If the conditions set out in the Nassau Accord were fulfilled by the South African government and if there were seen to be prospects for resolving fundamental issues within a short period, it would go a long way in demonstrating that there was no need for violence and help to reduce the level of the armed struggle. *It was conceivable that the struggle could be called off altogether.*
>
> (EPG Report, 1986: 88; emphasis mine)

First visit of the full EPG to South Africa

At the beginning of March 1986, the EPG's four additional members – Lord Barber, John Malecela, Edward Scott and Swaran Singh – joined the three on a full-scale visit to South Africa. As per their brief, they made no public statements but consulted the widest range of opinion. The task was to get an accurate reading of the political mood in the country. Below are the political positions of the relevant sectors of the society.

On 12 March 1986, the full EPG met Mandela at Pollsmoor Prison. The EPG took five main points from this meeting. First, the EPG found no differences between the views of the ANC and Mandela. Second, Mandela stressed his desire for reconciliation "across the divide of colour" and "pledged himself anew to work for a multiracial society in which all would have a secure place." Third, Mandela stressed that his political beliefs were shaped by the Freedom Charter that emphasised

> the necessity for the unity and political emancipation of all Africans in the land of their birth; the need for a multiracial society, free from any kind of racial, religious or political discrimination; the paramountcy of democratic principles and political and human rights; and equality of opportunity.

Fourth, the ANC was driven to armed struggle with great reluctance and in the absence of any other alternative to the violence of the apartheid system. And fifth, he welcomes the Commonwealth initiative and wanted to assist (EPG Report, 1986: 68–70).

Mandela then put forward a concrete proposal. He stated that circumstances needed to be created in which the government and the ANC could talk. One avenue toward this is if positive responses of the ANC and government could be synchronised – "the government withdrawing the army and the police from the townships and taking other agreed steps, while the ANC, agreed, at the same time, to a suspension of violence and to negotiations." Mandela accepted that his release would not be enough to de-escalate violence: "[the ANC] would have to take on the active role of persuading people to call off violent activities and to respect the negotiating process" (EPG Report, 1986: 72).

The EPG found Mandela a unifying, commanding and popular leader, who was an essential and heroic figure to any political settlement in South Africa. The saw his freedom as "a key component in any hope for a peaceful resolution" to the conflict (EPG Report, 1986: 73).

The group met senior members of the South African government on the 3rd, 4th and 12th of March. These included senior cabinet ministers such as Heunis, du Plessis, Pik Botha, Gerrit Viljoen, F.W. de Klerk and President Botha. The position of the government was summarised in a paper handed to the EPG by a senior cabinet minister which read as follows:

> It is the conviction of the Government that any future constitutional dispensation providing for participation by all South African citizens should be the

result of negotiations with the leaders of all communities. The Government will not prescribe who may represent black communities in negotiations on a new constitution for South Africa. The only condition is that those who participate in the discussions and negotiations should forswear violence as a means of achieving political objectives. The agenda for political reform is open. In the process of negotiation, the Government will not prescribe and will not demand. Give and take will be the guiding principle. On the part of the Government, negotiations will be based on the following premises:

- The principle of a united South Africa, one citizenship and a universal franchise with democratic structures;
- Political participation of all communities at all levels on matters of national concern;
- Co-responsibility and power-sharing between these communities on matters of national concern;
- The devolution of power as far as possible;
- The protection of minority rights, without one group dominating the other;
- The sovereignty of the law as the basis for the protection of the fundamental rights of individuals as well as groups;
- Equality before the law; and
- The protection of human dignity, life, liberty and property for all, regardless of colour, race, creed or religion.

(EPG Report, 1986: 80–81)

The government also confirmed that they would review the situation of political prisoners as violence receded and that they were committed to peace. The key question, according to the government, was not whether there was going to be power-sharing but in what manner. In the government's thinking, change was understood within the context of their reform programme.

The EPG also had discussions with the UDF, COSATU, the Progressive Federal Party, homeland leaders, the business community and churches. They were struck by the desire of most South Africans for a non-violent negotiated settlement. The EPG concluded that from the consultations it was clear that the onus was on the government, as wielders of the instruments of coercion, to introduce a climate conducive to negotiations. They also concluded that the reforms introduced thus far were insufficient, and that a "clear and unequivocal statement of intent from the government to introduce positive confidence-building measures and actions would go a long way to restoring people's faith" (EPG Report, 1986: 100).

The possible negotiating concept

After these consultations, the group was satisfied that sufficient ground existed based on which a negotiated solution could be attempted: "no serious person we met was interested in a fight to the finish; all favoured negotiations and peaceful solutions" (EPG Report, 1986: 101). The EPG also concluded that a lack of confidence and credibility were the major obstacles to violence, the government's reform programme would not end apartheid, the initiative for progress rested with the government and that a special role devolved upon the ANC. Based on these conclusions, the EPG put forward a package of proposals to the government which they believed would enable negotiations to commence. Further, several elements had to be encompassed in these proposals.

First related to the negotiating agenda (i.e. what the negotiations were to be about), there was the need for the government "to make a firmer and more categorical statement of intent" (EPG Report, 1986: 102). Second, there needed to be confidence-building measures to demonstrate the government's good faith, i.e. the release of political prisoners to create a new political climate. Third they had to link the release of political prisoners with the initiation of a political process. Fourth, there would need to be a moratorium on violence by both the government and the ANC. And fifth, there would need to be synchronisation, i.e. there had to be prior agreement by both sides to act simultaneously in fulfilment of their commitment (EPG Report, 1986: 103).

On this basis, the EPG developed a "Possible Negotiating Concept" that embodied a "package approach." The text read as follows:

> The South African Government has declared its commitment to dismantling the system of apartheid, to ending racial discrimination and to broad based negotiations leading to new constitutional arrangements for power sharing by all the people of South Africa. In the light of preliminary and yet incomplete discussions with representatives of various organisations and groups, within and outside South Africa, we believe that in the context of specific and meaningful steps being taken towards ending apartheid, the following additional action might ensure negotiations and a break in the cycle of violence.

On the part of the Government:

a Removal of military from townships, providing for freedom of assembly and discussion and suspension of detention without trial.
b The release of Nelson Mandela and other political prisoners and detainees.
c The unbanning of the ANC and PAC and the permitting of normal political activity.

On the part of the ANC and others: Entering negotiations and suspending violence.

It is our view that simultaneous announcement incorporating these ideas might be negotiated if the Government were to be interested in pursuing this broad approach.

In the light of the Government's indication to us that it:

i is not in principle against the release of Mr Nelson Mandela and similar prisoners

ii is not opposed in principle to the unbanning of any organisations
iii is prepared to enter negotiations with the acknowledged leaders of the people of South Africa
iv is committed to the removal of discrimination, not only from the statute books but also from South African society as a whole
v is committed to the ending of white domination
vi will not prescribe who may represent black communities in negotiations on a new constitution for South Africa
vii is prepared to negotiate an open agenda.

The South African Government may wish to give serious consideration to the approach outlined in this note.

The concept was communicated to Chris Heunis and Pik Botha via letters dated 13 March. Pik Botha replied to the EPG on 24 April. There are two important items in Botha's response. The first is with regards to the release of political prisoners: Botha writes that key to the release of political prisoners, the withdrawal of security forces from townships and lifting of the ban on the ANC and PAC is a suspension of violence. The question then is how this could be put into effect. The second issue is with regards to the "specific and meaningful steps to be taken towards ending apartheid" as outlined in the Possible Negotiating Concept. Botha argued that the government had in fact already taken these specific and meaningful steps:

> In line with this commitment the State President announced in Parliament on Friday 18 April 1986, that no further charges would be preferred in terms of the existing legislation [i.e. influx control and pass laws]; that people who have been convicted in terms of this legislation would be released forthwith, and that those who are being detained pending trial would likewise be released. The Government proposed to repeal or amend no fewer than 34 Acts and Proclamations to ensure that the movement of people will not be subject to discrimination on the grounds of colour or race.
>
> (Botha cited in EPG Report, 1986: 106)

These reform measures, Botha continued, were testimony to the government's acceptance that there would no longer be forced removals in pursuit of apartheid. Therefore, Botha concluded, the government was satisfied that they had made such specific and meaningful steps in line with the Possible Negotiating Concept, and that these "should be matched by corresponding responses" from the ANC (Botha cited in EPG Report, 1986: 107). The EPG was encouraged by the contents and tone of the government's response. More significantly, the government had made an important concession; instead of demanding the renunciation of violence as a precondition for talks, the government was now prepared for a suspension of violence. The EPG believed significant progress was being made towards getting to the table.

Second visit by the EPG to South Africa

The EPG resumed discussions in May. Their first meeting was with Pik Botha on 13 May. According to the EPG, this meeting suggested a hardening of the government's position towards the ANC on the basis of which it would be prepared to negotiate; "instead of dealing with specific elements in the concept and the 'modalities' of its implementation, [Botha] raised a number of entirely new issues" (EPG Report, 1986: 110–111). There were two items of contention. First, the government was no longer certain about the intentions of Mandela. Mrs Winnie Mandela had a made a statement that the ANC was not interested in negotiations but only a transfer of power, and the government believed that this was a true reflection of Mandela's own thinking. Second, the government felt that they could not take any significant steps towards negotiations unless these were preceded by tangible and visible evidence of a de-escalation of violence (EPG Report, 1986: 110).

After consultations with Coetsee, the EPG met Mandela again a few days later to brief Mandela. Mandela had no difficulty in accepting the negotiating concept as a starting point. He confirmed his desire "to see violence end and to see peaceful conditions prevail so that fruitful discussions could be held." His release however would not be enough: "it would also be necessary to ensure that he and his colleagues could move freely around the country using their persuasive powers to create a condition of calm in which the agreed negotiation process could begin" (EPG Report, 1986: 112).

The EPG put these proposition to Pik Botha. The government had not accepted the negotiating concept, nor had they rejected it. Botha raised what he perceived were the major problems of the negotiating concept. First, the government did not see itself as dealing with specifically with the ANC; there were many parties opposed to the government and all had to be involved in any future negotiations. Second, detention without trial was necessary for the government to control lawlessness and disorder. Third, Botha questioned the term suspension of violence as it appeared in the concept and Accord; "the government's understanding was that this meant a cessation, an end for all time" (EPG Report, 1986: 114). Botha emphasised that he saw no point in violence as a negotiated solution was inevitable.

The EPG subsequently travelled to Lusaka to brief the ANC. Tambo stated that the ANC was in support of the concept in so far as it corresponded to the principles and requirements of the Nassau Accord. The ANC, Tambo further stated, had no objection to negotiations but their main concern was regarding the intentions of the government – they needed to demonstrate good faith. Tambo affirmed that the ANC and the EPG had a common interest in ending apartheid, and the ANC "appreciated that the concept contained within it that position" (EPG Report, 1986: 116). The ANC asked for ten days to consult before giving a firm answer. When the group returned to South Africa, they consulted the leadership of COSATU, the UDF and AZAPO. They responded with keen interest and asked for time to conduct consultations. The following day the EPG was to meet members of the cabinet constitutional committee (SKK). The government had still neither accepted or rejected the concept. Early that morning, however, news reached the EPG that units of the South African Defence Force (SADF) had earlier attacked three neighbouring Commonwealth countries – Botswana, Zambia and Zimbabwe. The EPG felt that such action against Commonwealth governments who were instrumental in setting up the EPG mission cast serious doubt on the genuineness of the government's attitude towards a negotiated settlement.

The final meeting with SKK took place on the eve of the EPG's departure. Heunis reiterated the views of the government: the EPG was welcome provided it did not represent external interferences in the country's domestic affairs; and the government was not just a negotiating party, it represented the state and institutions of state would have to endorse any proposals emerging from negotiations. The sticking point for the government was the pre-requisites for the opening of negotiations. The essential precondition for the government was the renunciation of violence, specifically by the ANC. Heunis stated that the phrase "suspension" of violence, used in the first letter of the president to the group, "had to be interpreted not in the temporary sense, but as a public commitment to reject violence as a means of attaining political goals." Parties at the negotiating table "would have to subscribe to such a commitment" (EPG Report, 1986: 119). The government's reassertion of its demand for a one-sided "renunciation" of violence was reverting to its original position. The EPG urged the committee to deliberate on the concept. For the EPG however, the attacks on the Commonwealth countries were significant: "it is all too plain that, while talking to the group about negotiations and peaceful solutions, the Government had been planning these armed attacks" (EPG Report, 1986: 120). The government later rejected the negotiating concept.

On return to London, the group's next task was to report its findings to the Commonwealth. The group concluded that in rejecting the concept, South Africa was not yet ready to negotiate genuinely the establishment of a non-racial and representative government in South Africa (Mole, 2012: 258). In recommending further economic measures, the group concluded:

> The question from Heads of Government is in our view clear. It is not whether such measures will compel change; it is already the case that their absence and Pretoria's belief that they need not be feared defers change. Is the Commonwealth to stand by and allow the cycle of violence to spiral? Or will it take concerted action of an effective kind? Such action may offer the last opportunity to avert what could be the worst bloodbath since the Second World War.
>
> (EPG Report, 1986: 141)

Seven Commonwealth leaders gathered at Marlborough House to consider the EPG report. Chaired by Sir Lynden Pindling, of the Bahamas, those present included Rajiv Gandhi, Bob Hawke, Kenneth Kaunda, Robert Mugabe, Brian Mulroney and Margaret Thatcher. They were joined by Sonny Ramphal. Leaders were mindful of "the overwhelming concern of the Nassau CHOGM . . . that there should be further speedy and effective economic action against the regime, in the absence of adequate progress by the South African government in dismantling apartheid and finding a negotiated solution" (Mole, 2012: 259). At the end of the meeting, six of the leaders agreed on a package of 11 sanctions against the apartheid regime. These included those envisaged at the Nassau summit, as well as number of additional ones including a ban on both air travel and investments, as well as a bar on agricultural imports and the promotion of South African tourism. Bank loans to South African companies were banned as well as imports of coal, iron, steel and uranium from the country. Consular facilities were also withdrawn under the agreement. Britain stood aside from the agreed sanctions but announced more limited measures offering a "voluntary ban" on investment in South Africa and tourism promotion.

Within a few days, the United States government voted by a large majority a package of sanctions (including those adopted in London). The imposition of sanctions by the European Community, the Nordic countries and Japan followed.

Outcome of the mediation: basic points of negotiation

In the EPG's own admission, their mission was a failure, i.e. there were no such prospects for the initiation of dialogue (EPG, 1986: 125). On the part of the government, discussions with the EPG floundered on the issue as to whether the ANC should merely suspend violence or terminate it. Many years later Pik Botha told Sue Onslow that "if suspending violence meant only discontinuing violence for as long as negotiations continued, then the threat of a resumption of violence would become a bargaining counter. In other words: 'Keep talking . . . or else'" (Botha, 2012: 4). As for the ANC, Pallo Jordan argued that the proposal was the "instrument of the enemy," i.e. an attempt to get them to agree to the termination of violence to buy the government time (Gevisser, 2007: 534). As for the EPG, they felt that it was unreasonable for the government to ask the ANC to permanently terminate the armed struggle:

> To ask the ANC or other parties, all of them far weaker than the government, to renounce violence for all time here and now would be to put them in a position of having to rely absolutely on the government's intentions and determination to press through the process of negotiations.
>
> (EPG Report, 1986: 119)

The important question, however, is how do we determine the success or failure of the EPG mission considering the overall negotiated transition in South Africa? What was its most important significance and contribution? I argue that determining the success of the EPG mediation effort must depend on the examination of the time horizon of the South African conflict and on the contribution that mediation played in improving the relationship between the parties, or in some way defining the process of negotiation. Putting it in a more pointed way, what role did the EPG mission play in getting each party to agree that they have a shared understanding of the conflict or problem, a shared understanding that a negotiated solution is possible, producing a commitment towards a negotiated solution, and overcoming preconditions as a barrier towards the opening of settlement negotiations? The Possible Negotiating Concept was prophetic – not only did it contain the basic points of the Groote Schuur Minute, i.e. the first meeting between the government and the ANC in 1990; it embodied the elements which formed the basis of the pre-negotiations in South Africa.

The ANC's search for dialogue

After the EPG mission, Tambo embarked on a diplomatic mission in the United Kingdom and Unites States to generate international support and consensus on preconditions for settlement negotiations. The target was Britain's ruling Conservative Party of Prime Minister Margaret Thatcher and their allies. On 24 June 1986, he addressed a large audience of businessmen at the Connaught Rooms in London. The participants included Lord Barber (fresh from the EPG mission); Sir Timothy Bevan, chairman of Barclays Bank; Sir Alistair Frame; Lord Greenhill of SG Warburg; Sir Martin Jacomb; Evelyn de Rothschild; George Soros; Sir James Spooner; and Michael Young from Consolidated Goldfields. The second state of emergency changed the businessmen's perspectives of South Africa; they were anxious and trying to rethink their policies towards South Africa. The chairmen of the two biggest banks in South Africa, Lord Barber of Standard and Sir Timothy Bevan of Barclays, were at odds with Margaret Thatcher over Britain's relationship with South Africa. They took turns talking privately with Tambo. Bevan was openly confronting the Botha government and refused to lend money to South Africa until apartheid "had been abolished." Lord Barber had also boldly stated that it was unreasonable to expect the ANC to renounce violence unconditionally (Sampson, 1987: 25).

Michael Young, the public affairs director at Consolidated Goldfields approached Tambo privately and asked him what Consolidated Goldfields, with its large interests in South Africa, could do to assist. According to Young's account of the conversation, Tambo asked if he could assist in creating a secret communication channel between the ANC and the government; specifically, Tambo requested building a bridge between the ANC and Afrikaners close to the government as a first step. Tambo told Young that no means of communication existed and, without this, the ANC's diplomacy towards a peaceful resolution of the conflict was impossible (Young, 1999). Mbeki requested that Young arrange a meeting between Tambo and Lynda Chalker, the foreign office minister in charge for Africa (Harvey, 2001: 23). Because of Young's proximity to the Conservative Party, Chalker agreed to meet Tambo in late June 1986. This meeting was the first official-level meeting between the ANC and a British cabinet minister. Chalker effectively placed the ANC-British government relationship "on an entirely different and more proactive footing" (Harvey, 2001: 24).

The Tambo-Chalker meeting had far-reaching implications for the ANC. A few days later the United States State Department publicly announced it was planning closer and official contacts with Tambo. In September 1986, Tambo met Sir Geoffrey Howe, the British foreign secretary, for a two-hour official-level discussion in his country house. Also, in September 1986, Tambo also held official discussions with Chester Crocker, Ronald Reagan's special envoy for Africa. According to Crocker, he met with Tambo to lay groundwork for an October 1986 official visit by George Schultz, the United States Secretary of State, to the ANC headquarters in Lusaka, and an official visit by Tambo to the United States State Department, on invitation by Schultz the following year. Schultz stressed the importance of a negotiated solution to the South African crisis, and "spoke of his firm plan to advance [a negotiated process] by meeting with the ANC leader in exile, Oliver Tambo" (Crocker, 1993: 324).

The Tambo-Schultz meeting was an important diplomatic breakthrough for the ANC. On 28 January 1987, Tambo led a delegation of four to Washington that included Mbeki, Makhathini, Barbara Masekele (the ANC's representative in the United States) and Neo Mnumzana, the ANC's chief representative to the United Nations. On the US side, Schultz was accompanied by a delegation of eight, which included Crocker; his deputy Chas Freeman, a representative of the National Security Council; the State Department spokesman, Charles Redman; and the US ambassador to Zambia, Paul Hare (US-ANC Meeting, 1987). Minutes of the meeting reveal elements of the Possible Negotiating Concept as the basic points of moving to negotiation. Schultz opened the meeting, referring to the ANC leader as "President" Tambo, and stated the position of the United States government towards South Africa:

> The Secretary of State said the U.S. Administration is against apartheid and that the sooner that system goes the better. However, they were against all violence from whichever side it came. They wished to see an open, democratic state with equal opportunities for all to participate in government and in the economy of the country. This should come through negotiations. While the U.S. Administration has its own ideas, it does not wish to prescribe solutions. This is a task for South Africans. To that end the Pretoria regime should release the political prisoners, unban political parties and involve everybody in negotiations. The U.S. Administration has been talking to South Africans as well as talking to the ANC to convey its views about the need for negotiations. It recognised the ANC as an important player in South Africa. He had read the ANC's January 8th statement with interest and noted what it said about a non-racial democracy.
>
> (US-ANC Meeting, 1987: 1)

Schultz outlined the US government's areas of concern:

> [Schultz] wanted to make it clear that the U.S. Administration was opposed to violence and viewed the "practice of necklacing" as horrible. He also wished to take up the issue of Soviet influence over the ANC rather than the question of communism.
>
> (US-ANC Meeting, 1987: 2)

Tambo stated that the US and the ANC agreed about the overall objective: "the goal of a united, democratic and non-racial South Africa" (Tambo, 1987: 1). Their major difference was on "what action to take to achieve this result." Tambo also presented other issues to Schultz:

> 6. We believe that the policy of constructive engagement has not succeeded to move Botha towards this goal. Instead, Pretoria read it as encouragement to dig in; 7. We are also aware that your stated policy is to bring about negotiations. Our view is that Botha is not ready because pressure is still insufficient; 8. Therefore we urge strict implementation of the present set of U.S. sanctions.
>
> (Tambo, 1987: 1)

Tambo described a possible scenario around the issue of the release of political prisoners: "To unblock the political process we urge the U.S. Administration to do everything possible to secure the unconditional release of all political prisoners. There is a way of handling Botha's expressed concerns" (Tambo, 1987: 1). Schultz stated that the US was in favour of the release of political prisoners, and this had been communicated to the South African government. He asked whether the ANC would be prepared to renounce violence if Botha were to agree to "serious negotiations." Tambo explained that the ANC "could not agree to a unilateral cessation of hostilities but that hostilities could end because of negotiations during which both sides could agree to end the use of force." Further, the ANC would "need strong signals, and not words, to convince [the ANC] that Pretoria was serious about negotiations" (US-ANC Meeting, 1987: 3). Tambo and Schultz appreciated they had met in an official capacity and stated that the meeting was the beginning of an official dialogue between the United Sates and the ANC. Originally scheduled for 30 minutes, Tambo and Schultz spoke for over an hour. The meeting signalled the official recognition of the ANC by the US government.

The meeting in the Connaught Rooms was crucial; Tambo requested international assistance for the negotiated ending of apartheid. Young came to his assistance in two ways. First, he offered to create a communication channel between the ANC and South African government. To this end, Young would facilitate building a bridge between ANC and Afrikaners close to the government as a first step. Second, Young facilitated the first official-level meeting between the ANC and a British cabinet minister. This was complimented by George Schultz's official visit to the ANC headquarters in Lusaka, and Tambo's official visit to the United States State Department. By 1987 a consensus on preconditions for negotiation, evolved out of the EPG's Negotiating Concept, had emerged and was supported by the United States: the unconditional release of political prisoners and unbanning of political parties.

Acting on Tambo's request, Young, with the assistance of his colleague, Fleur de Villiers, assembled a team of professors from Stellenbosch University who were known to have close contacts with senior members of the government: Willie Esterhuyse, Willie Breytenbach and Sampie Terreblanche. All three had gained some reputation as notable reformers with important links to the NP government. Soon, Neil Barnard, the director-general of the NIS, approached Esterhuyse and requested he report to him on the discussions with the ANC. Esterhuyse agreed provided he informed his ANC equivalent, which would turn out to be Mbeki. This informal dialogue thus became a shield for the secret channel between the government and the ANC.

Secret conversations

Six meetings took place in England between elite Afrikaner academics, led by Esterhuyse, and several ANC officials, led by Mbeki, between October 1987 and February 1990. The meetings were held on average every four months, and follow-up meetings continued after the beginning of official negotiations. Each of the meetings in England lasted three days, were typically over a weekend, with formal sessions on Saturday and Sunday extending to the mid-afternoon (Lieberfeld, 2005: 111).

The first meeting was held in Henley, England, between the 31st October and 1st November 1987. The conversation that followed revealed the divisions in Botha's government over negotiations. In the first session, Breytenbach opened the discussion and gave a background of the perceptions of the hard-liners in Botha's government. Breytenbach stated that the hard-liners believed the South African conflict and prevailing impasse "required a political solution." This was dependent on the support and "buy-in" of the black population:

> The approach of the "securocrats," other than the inner group of "controllers," is that political stability requires 20% coercion, 80% political solution. The political solution depends on the support of the mass of the blacks and in the short/middle term the question is whether this support can be won.
>
> (ANC, 2010: 638)

There were two important groups in the government, each with a different interpretation on how to reach such a political solution: one group, associated with the military intelligence believed that the black population should be co-opted within the existing framework of reform; and another, associated with the national intelligence, recognised the ANC and argued that the way out of the stalemate was to enter negotiations with them (ANC, 2010: 638). For the latter group, the possibility of negotiations with the ANC arose because the second state of emergency had effectively diminished two of the ANC's three options: mass mobilisation and the creation of alternative structures. Thus, while the ANC could continue to prosecute the armed struggle, it would be deploying its weakest arm against the government's strongest point – the military. The conclusion was that the ANC would inevitably run out of options, and would have to negotiate (ANC, 2010: 638).

Breytenbach stated that the hard-line security experts were more amenable to negotiation than the politicians as they did not possess the "ideological emotionalism" of politicians, i.e. they were more pragmatic. Their view of a political solution was premised on two main realisations: first, that the second state of emergency, and the accompanying political stability, had created conditions for the opening of serious negotiations; and second, that any future political system to replace apartheid would have to "provide for all [the races] at the highest level," i.e. at the level of the central state.

In the final session, Breytenbach and Esterhuyse were more precise about actual initiatives. First, the security experts viewed the release of political prisoners as crucial to a political solution and a priority matter. Second, for the security experts, it was not a condition of negotiation that the ANC relinquish violence. This however was an issue for the electorate, i.e. for politicians: "They are interested in results (i.e. a political solution) and they do not demand that the ANC abandon violence as a condition of negotiation." Esterhuyse qualified that "a response from the ANC which included something about the armed struggle would be necessary if the release [of political prisoners] was to be a step forward" to put the politicians at ease.

Third, the important sequential steps were to release Govan Mbeki followed by Mandela, and then the unbanning of the ANC. However, the security experts regarded the release of political prisoners and the ANC's unbanning as two separate issues. Their willingness to release Mbeki and Mandela was purely an issue of timing; before the state of emergency, this would not have been possible as it would have been interpreted as buckling under the pressure of the uprising, i.e. "it would have been interpreted as violence paying off." However, the second state of emergency and the restoration of stability had created more favourable conditions; they were now prepared to release Mbeki and then Mandela (ANC, 2010). The immediate goal of releasing political prisoners was to relieve international pressure to revive the economy. However, by responding positively to this, the ANC could seize the initiative and insert itself more constructively in an evolving political solution.

The central issue was for the government to release prisoners without losing face, i.e. "without stoking white fears about violence and without giving the [Conservative Party] the opportunity to make capital out of the release and what the response of the ANC will be." However, before the government embarked on the process, the security experts were concerned and wanted to know what the response of the ANC would be –

> if there is not some sort of positive response (in the sense of welcoming the release and treating it as a step towards negotiations) from the ANC, if the ANC downgrades the step and simply moves the goal posts, then there will be a blockage. Negotiations will lose, not the [government].
>
> (ANC, 2010: 638)

Aziz Pahad, a senior ANC representative in London, led the ANC response. The ANC, he stated, would welcome the release of some prisoners but preferred to deal with the issue on political terms; they would call for the release of all political prisoners. Breytenbach and Esterhuyse regarded this as a positive response. Pahad then pointed out that while the issue of political prisoner release had previously been handled by lawyers, it was now necessary to shift it to the political; the government had to communicate directly with the ANC on this issue (ANC, 2010).

The logic of the security experts, however, was clear; the government was aware that without the release of political prisoners, the stability created by the second state of emergency was unsustainable. By releasing political prisoners, space would open to make viable Botha's reformist political measures and, in that way, weaken the position of the ANC if it continued to stay outside the reformed structures (ANC, 2010). The strategy of negotiation, therefore, was a continuation of reform and not the consequence of its failure. More importantly, the military intelligence and national intelligence position was taken from a position of relative strength; they believed that the ANC had little room to manoeuvre and were thus engaged in a process of co-opting them. However, for reform to be viable, the government needed the ANC on board. This was a bilateral solution to their goal of reform.

The second meeting was held in Eastwell Manor Hotel in Kent between 21 and 24 February 1988. The ANC team was led by Thabo Mbeki. Esterhuyse was accompanied by Terreblanche and Marinus Wiechers. Three issues dominated the meeting. First was the renunciation of violence as a precondition for opening negotiations. While the government could not relax its requirement that the ANC declare a cessation of violence before settlement negotiations could begin, they realised that the ANC alone could not end the violence (Harvey, 2001: 133). Therefore, the government were prepared for a dialogue without a cessation of violence.

Second, Mbeki outlined the conditions for the beginning of settlement negotiations: the release of all political prisoners and the unbanning of all political organisations. Mbeki added that their newfound relations in the United States and United Kingdom had confirmed this: "All Western countries support us on this. There is an international consensus" (cited in Harvey, 2001: 133). For the ANC, this was non-negotiable. What was up for discussion, Mbeki continued, was the logistics of these conditions: "of course, the 'how' of the conditions has to be discussed. The ANC would like to talk about their implementation. But we seek in principle acceptance, even if it's not via a public announcement" (Harvey, 2001: 133).

Further meetings were held in August and December 1988. In the August meeting at Mells Park in Somerset, Mbeki stated that the ANC would be prepared to abandon violence if the "political struggle," i.e. negotiation, yielded results and proved effective in bringing about a non-racial constitutional order: "violence can be unnecessary" (Esterhuyse, 2012: 143). The meetings in April 1989, however, were crucial. The most important issue was the political context; Botha had suffered a stroke, and with F.W. de Klerk as National Party leader, Willem de Klerk (F.W. de Klerk's brother) took over the leadership from Esterhuyse. Willem de Klerk revealed that his brother had little patience with the security experts; he had a civilian inner circle with close ties to the Transvaal business community alienated by Botha. His rise was "viewed with suspicion by the military and security apparatus . . . which feared that a major purge could get under way should he become president" (Esterhuyse, 2012: 164).

According to Esterhuyse, the discussion that followed focused primarily "on the question as to when the time would be ripe for the two contending parties to start talking directly to each other." By April 1989, the conditions for settlement negotiations had been clearly defined:

> By [April 1989] the conditions set by both the ANC and the NP had been clearly defined for some time, with the release of Nelson Mandela one of the non-negotiable conditions on the part of the ANC. For Botha and his government, the insistence on a renouncement of violence by the ANC was of prime importance. Naturally, none of the participants at our meeting had the mandate or power to give any authoritative view in this regard. This was a matter the contending parties themselves had to discuss.
>
> (Esterhuyse, 2012: 192)

Botha's stroke was a turning point. Esterhuyse reported that Botha's stroke had impaired his judgement and temperament. His illness had stalled his communication with Barnard over the secret channel with the ANC. Mbeki responded by stating that it would therefore be better to delay the impending talks, Mandela's release and the unbanning of the ANC until after De Klerk was inaugurated as the president; this would give his Presidency enormous impetus, credibility and legitimacy, all of which were crucial for any settlement talks with the ANC (Esterhuyse, 2012: 167).

Barnard, however, did not hold the same view. He told Mbeki's biographer that he learned two things from Esterhuyse's reports: "Firstly, it was reassuring that there were South Africans on the other side who were interested in finding a solution, and secondly, reaffirmation that we should not find the solution outside the country. We had to bring them home" (cited in Gevisser, 2007: 545). Botha's stroke, however, had prevented him getting the necessary instruction. Barnard found other means to secure the necessary orders. On 16 August, the State Security Council, chaired for the first time by F.W. de Klerk, approved a resolution carefully drafted to provide authorisation of the first official meeting between the South African government and the ANC:

> It is necessary that more information should be obtained and processed concerning the ANC, and the aims, alliances and potential approachability of its different leaders and groupings. To enable this to be done, special additional direct action will be necessary particularly with the help of the National Intelligence Service functionaries.
>
> (cited in Saunders, 2006: 248)

First encounters: the South African government and the ANC

The first official, but secret meeting, between the government and the ANC was a top-secret intelligence operation called Project Flair. Project Flair was preceded by two important developments that set the ANC irreversibly onto the part of negotiations: the resolution of the Angolan civil war, and the drafting of the Harare Declaration.

In 1989, MK was plunged into an indefinite crisis effectively rendering the armed struggle obsolete. On 22 December 1988, two important agreements were signed in New York, bringing a temporary end to over 20 years of civil war in Angola and Namibia. The first agreement, signed by Angola, Cuba and South Africa, set 1 April 1989 for the beginning of the implementation of UN Security Council Resolution 435. The resolution contained a plan for

> achieving the independence of Namibia, under which a 7,500 strong UN military force . . . was to be inserted into Namibian territory to ensure suitable conditions for the holding of 'free and fair elections' for a constitution-making assembly in November 1989, seven months after the implementation of the resolution commenced. Formal independence would follow shortly afterwards.
>
> (Berridge, 1989: 463)

The second agreement provided for the "total withdrawal of Cuban troops from Angola, in stages, by July 1991, and was signed by Cuba and Angola" (Berridge, 1989: 463).

Implicit in both agreements was a non-aggression pact like the Nkomati Accord. Principle G of the New York Principles stated that the signatories should "not allow their territory to be used for acts of war aggression, or violence against other states" (Crocker, 1993: 500). Consequently, in return for South Africa's dropping UNITA, the Angolan government would cease offering military facilities to the ANC. In early January 1989, Oliver Tambo announced the decision to abide by the New York Accords and closed all MK military bases in Angola. According to the chief mediator in the Angolan conflict, Chester Crocker, the New York Accords were of historical significance for Southern Africa:

> The principles contained potent symbolism and it would set new standards of regional conduct. UNITA would lose its regional military ally at the same time the MPLA would lose the Cubans. The ANC would lose its last remaining sanctuary within reach of South Africa just when SWAPO [South West African People's Organisation] would become free to return home and seek power through elections. South African would put Namibia on the path to independence and begin shedding their interventionist military role in neighbouring countries.
>
> (Crocker, 1993: 442)

The New York Principles would serve as a resolving formula for civil wars in Angola and Namibia, and consequently, begin the path to the negotiated end of apartheid. The New York Accords had a profound impact on MK. A large exodus of MK fighters moved across the Angolan border into Zambia "where the ANC did not have permanent military camps, but rather an agreement with the

Zambian government that it could use 'transit' residences for its military personnel headed towards South Africa" (Simpson, 2009b: 508). Morale was at its lowest. Bill Anderson, a senior ANC intelligence officer in Zambia, stated that after the New York Accords MK was "in a state of absolute chaos with [MK fighters deployed] without briefings, without proper preparations of documents, without proper clothing" (Anderson, 1991: 5). Keith Mokoape, a senior MK intelligence officer, told Anderson that

> because the number of MK operations was perceived to be declining, "there was one objective and one alone" for the intelligence department in helping to plan operations: this was "to make the graph of actions go up, irrespective of what actions were undertaken, irrespective of basing cadres, and so on."
> (Anderson, 1991: 5)

Chris Hani, the MK Chief of Staff, stated that "of about 240 MK cadres deployed from Zambia in 1989, a third had defected, a third were captured or killed, while a third were somehow in place, whether active or drifting" (Anderson, 1991: 5).

The resulting uncertainty led to increasing levels of frustration and ill-discipline in MK, with serious diplomatic implications for the ANC's relationship with the Zambian government. As a result, the ANC's Security Department (Mbokodo) and Zambia's intelligence service carried out regular raids to disarm MK fighters (Simpson, 2009b: 509). The violence within MK continued; "on 30 July [1989] an explosive device detonated at a house belonging to the ANC in Kamanga township in Lusaka" (Simpson, 2009b: 509). Mbokodo became more ruthless in its policing, and a vicious cycle ensued. Things came to a head in August 1989 when Mbokodo agents arrested and detained four MK fighters who had applied for refugee status with the United Nations High Commission for Refugees (UNHCR) and awaiting resettlement. The Zambian government, furious with this heavy-handed response, demanded their release (Simpson, 2009b: 510).

When allegations of torture and abuse in Mbokodo custody surfaced, the Zambian government had enough; on 16 August, Alfred Nzo announced that over 5,000 MK fighters in Zambia would be relocated to Tanzania and Uganda. A second exodus of MK took place within just a month, this time from Zambia, the ANC's most loyal ally in the region (Simpson, 2009b: 510). This was of extreme significance for the ANC's external mission and the armed struggle; the infiltration of MK into South Africa was no longer an option. In the aftermath of the Nkomati and New York Accords, MK's military camps in Tanzania and Uganda faced an enormous strip of territory preventing any significant deployment of MK fighters into South Africa. It became impossible for the ANC to pursue the armed struggle in any meaningful way; armed struggle had reached its endgame, and MK was checkmated in August 1989.

As the Angolan and Namibian political settlements came to an end, Oliver Tambo realised that the ANC was losing control of events. If the ANC wanted to control the unfolding process, it would have to embrace the principles of negotiations as a first preference. Simon Makana, now the ANC's chief representative in the Soviet Union, stated that political events in Southern Africa isolated the ANC; the Front-Line States were tired of decades of war in Southern Africa and by 1989, were actively pushing the ANC toward a negotiated settlement with the NP government (Gevisser, 2007: 545).

In the immediate aftermath of the New York Accords, Tambo instructed Mbeki to organise an internal committee to draft an ANC bottom line for settlement negotiations. Tambo's strategy was to draft a document to be endorsed by the Front-Line States, the Organisation of African Unity (OAU) and the United Nations (UN) as a basis for the ANC's negotiation with the government (Gevisser, 2007: 549). The document, known as the Harare Declaration, was drafted by Tambo and Mbeki, and accepted by the OAU on 21 August 1989 (less than week after MK's relocation to East Africa) and by the UN on 14 December 1989.

The preamble declared apartheid "an obstacle to peace and an affront to justice and human dignity, and must be abandoned" (Harare Declaration, 1989). The declaration encouraged the negotiated end to the apartheid system and the creation of a non-racial democracy and constitutional order, with "universally recognised human rights, freedoms and civil liberties, under an entrenched Bill of Rights." It stated that it was essential for a necessary climate of negotiations to be created before any negotiations can take place and placed the responsibility on the South African government to create this climate. Accordingly, the government, at the very least, was called to:

> release all political prisoners and detainees unconditionally and refrain from imposing restrictions on them; lift bans and restrictions on all proscribed and restricted organisations and persons; remove all troops from the townships; end the state of emergency and repeal all legislation . . . designed to circumscribe political activity; and cease all political trials and political executions.

These measures were essential and necessary to produce conditions in which "free political discussion can take place."

The declaration defined how the process of negotiation should unfold:

> Discussions should take place between the liberation movement and the South African regime to achieve the suspension of hostilities on both sides by agreeing to a mutually binding ceasefire; negotiations should then proceed to establish the basis for adoption of a new Constitution by agreeing on, among others, the Principles enunciated above; having agreed on these principles, the parties should then negotiate the necessary mechanism for drawing up the new Constitution; the parties shall define and agree on the role to be played by the international community in ensuring a successful transition to a democratic order; the parties shall agree on the formation of an interim government to supervise the process of the drawing up and adoption of a new constitution . . . ; after the adoption of the new Constitution, all armed hostilities will be deemed to have formally terminated.
>
> (Harare Declaration, 1989)

Following Barnard's instruction, Esterhuyse informed Mbeki that the NIS was ready to meet and to begin to negotiate preconditions for settlement negotiations. Project Flair was carried out by Louw and Spaarwater on the government side. On the ANC side was Mbeki and Jacob Zuma, the deputy director of the ANC's Security Department.

The first meeting took place on 12 September 1989, at the Palace Hotel in Lucerne, Switzerland. The meeting lasted seven hours. The agenda covered substantive issues: the necessity of a negotiated settlement; the release of Mandela; the state of emergency; the ANC's relationship with the SACP; and the armed struggle. The government was seeking assurance that the ANC was ready to talk and negotiate. Louw and Spaarwater were given this assurance. The second item discussed was the role of would-be facilitators and mediators. Both sides agreed that only direct dialogue between the ANC and the government would lead to progress. Esterhuyse writes that what was primarily intended as a clarification of positions became also an unofficial declaration of intent: "we have to make peace with one another and among ourselves" (Esterhuyse, 2012: 224).

The second meeting took place on 6 February 1990, in Lausanne, Switzerland. The ANC delegation comprised Mbeki and Pahad, and for the NIS, Louw and Spaarwater. According to Pahad, concrete details were discussed about

> the release of Mandela, structures to be established to manage the return of the exiled ANC leadership, and preparations for the first [public] meeting between the ANC and the government in South Africa, the issue of indemnity, the definition of a political prisoner and the cessation of violence.
>
> (Pahad, 2010: 23)

Issues pertaining to removing obstacles for settlement negotiations had to be dealt with, indemnity had to be arranged, and the question of who a political prisoner was had to be resolved. There was agreement that the negotiation process would need to have an initial phase of talks about talks, i.e. of deciding who would represent whom, and on the form the process would take (Sparks, 1994: 116). Louw cautioned that De Klerk was about to take enormous political risk, and the ANC would need to respond positively to keep the momentum. Specifically, Louw wanted "a positive response from the ANC's executive committee, 'greater discipline' in controlling the protest campaign inside South Africa, and an agreed formula for ending guerrilla struggle" (cited in Sparks, 1994: 116).

Mandela and De Klerk met on the morning of 13 December in Tuynhuys. In attendance were Barnard, Louw, Willemse and Coetsee. Mandela raised the issue of "group rights," which was contained in the National Party's recently introduced five-year plan, arguing that "it was not in his interest to retain this concept, for it gave the impression that he wanted to modernise apartheid without abandoning it." Mandela said the concept must be "entirely cast aside" as "the ANC had not struggled against apartheid for seventy-five years only to yield to a disguised form of it" (Mandela, 1994: 664). De Klerk stated that the National Party's support for group rights was a mechanism to provide "structural guarantees that majority rule would not mean the domination of the white minority by blacks" (De Klerk, 1998: 158).

Both Mandela and De Klerk have pleasant recollections of the meeting. Mandela's impression of De Klerk was a reasonable leader who was a very good listener (Mandela, 1994: 663–665). De Klerk's impression was that Mandela conveyed "dignity, courtesy and self-confidence [and] had the ability to radiate unusual warmth and charm – when he so chose." De Klerk saw him as "every inch of a Thembu patriarch [who] bore the mantle of authority with the ease of those who are not troubled by self-doubt" (De Klerk, 1998: 157). They both reached the same conclusions: that it would be possible to do business together.

Success or failure?

As discussed previously, the meaning of success is disputed among scholars of international mediation, and indicators vary. As discussed, Frei (1976: 69) explains mediation success "as a situation in which both parties accept a mediator and mediation attempt within five days after the first attempt." Other scholars move from this position and equate mediation success with effectiveness in taking the mediator's objectives as a starting point (Touval and Zartman, 1985). While other scholars measure successful mediation as producing an agreement, i.e. "by successful outcomes we mean producing a ceasefire, a partial settlement or a full settlement" (Bercovitch et al., 1991: 8) or "when it leads to the termination of hostilities and the advent of democratic governance" (Nathan, 1999: 3).

What is clear from the discussion is that neither the government nor the ANC accepted the Negotiating Concept in early 1986, especially in the way it was packaged. While both parties accepted the mediation attempt, they were not ready for mediation in early 1986. In less than a few months, this changed considerably. In June 1986, less than a month after the EPG departure, Tambo accepted Young's request and defined the type of mediated assistance required, i.e. assistance in creating a secret communication channel between the government and the ANC, using intermediaries as a first step. This would be a communication-facilitation mediation role. The government used Esterhuyse as their intermediary. As Young's secret facilitative meetings progressed, so the profile of government intermediaries and ANC representatives was raised, leading to the first direct meeting between the government and the ANC. Therefore, while the government and the ANC were not ready to accept the EPG mission in early 1986, they did ultimately accept mediation to begin the process of dialogue, on their own terms.

The interrelated issues here are with regards to the attributes of the mediator, and timing. Regarding the former, there was simply insufficient trust between the government and the EPG as a product of the Commonwealth. Given the history of the South African question inside the Commonwealth, it would have taken close to a miracle for the government to accept the Commonwealth as a trusted mediator; it took Thatcher's intervention for the government to even agree to listen to what the EPG had to say. The ANC, as discussed, were equally suspicious. Furthermore, the EPG's formulation strategy, involving a redefinition of the issues, and then in turn putting them to the parties, was a miscalculation; the ANC and the government had already begun exploring negotiation possibilities. The EPG, however, could not know this. By the time the parties opted for mediation, it was for the communication-facilitation type, i.e. a more passive role of mediation, largely keeping channels of information open and passing along information to each other, on their own terms.

Regarding the matter of timing, neither the ANC nor the government were amenable to accepting any third party at the beginning of 1986. In the search for negotiation possibilities, the focus on both sides was inner-directed, i.e. both the government and the ANC were internally considering alternative negotiating scenarios, reflecting varying degrees of scope for the potential negotiation, and successive steps towards increasing communication towards a solution. Passive facilitative mediation through Young was important in assisting this process. The Negotiation Concept came too soon for the parties, and the attributes of the mediator were unattractive. This however does not mean that the parties were not willing to accept mediation; it was the type of mediation and its appropriateness for the stage of the conflict in the search for negotiated solutions.

If, however we examine the time horizon of the conflict and examine success or failure within that context, we would have to ask what contribution the mediation effort played in terms of getting the parties to the table. In this light, the negotiating concept was significant; while the ANC and the government did not accept the negotiating concept in 1986, the document embodied all the elements which formed the basis of negotiations between the government and the ANC. These were the basic points in the pre-negotiation phase, i.e. the release of political prisoners and unbanning of the ANC and other banned political organisations (for the ANC), and the renunciation or suspension of violence (for the government). The fundamental issue was about synchronisation, i.e. reaching prior agreement between both to act simultaneously in fulfilling their respective commitments as the basis for starting dialogue. How to achieve this was what pre-negotiation was about. George Schultz, the US Secretary of State, offered a solution: the renunciation of violence if Botha were to agree to serious negotiations. Tambo however explained that hostilities could end because of negotiations. By 1987, the US government supported the ANC's eventual precondition for negotiations: the unconditional release of political prisoners and unbanning of prohibited political parties. The renunciation of violence would be a consequence of this.

At the secret meeting in Henley-on-Thames in England, the government, through intermediaries, was precise on its formula to the ANC; the security experts in the government viewed the release of political prisoners as crucial to a political solution and a priority matter. Further, it was not a condition of negotiation that the ANC relinquish violence. Esterhuyse qualified that a response from the ANC which included something about the armed struggle would be necessary if the release of political prisoners was to be a step forward to put the politicians at ease (ANC, 2010: 638). For the government, the release of political prisoners and the ANC's unbanning were two separate issues. The willingness to release Mandela was purely an issue of timing; before the state of emergency, this would not have been possible as it would have been interpreted as buckling under the pressure of the uprising. The second state of emergency and the restoration of stability had created more favourable conditions; they were now prepared to release Mandela. The immediate goal of releasing political prisoners was to relieve international pressure to revive the economy.

Therefore, for the government this was not interpreted as buckling under pressure but as a strategic matter: their logic was that without the release of political prisoners, the stability created by the second state of emergency was unsustainable. By releasing political prisoners, space would open to make viable Botha's reformist political measures and, in that way, weaken the position of the ANC if it continued to stay outside the reformed structures. The strategy of negotiation, therefore, was a continuation of reform and not the consequence of its failure, i.e. for reform to be viable, the government needed the ANC on board. This was a bilateral solution to their goal of reform.

At the secret meeting in Eastwell Manor in Kent (February 1988), the government realised that the ANC alone could not end the violence. As a result, they were prepared for a dialogue without a cessation of violence. Mbeki also outlined the conditions for the beginning of settlement negotiations: the release of all political prisoners and the unbanning of all political organisations. What was up for discussion was the logistics of these conditions. Mbeki proposed a controlled introduction of freed political prisoners into the community. Further, released political prisoners, who enjoyed significant status in most communities, could play a constructive role in reducing levels of violence, thus transforming them into part of the evolving political solution. At the meeting held in Mells Park (August 1988), Mbeki stated that the ANC would be prepared to abandon violence if negotiations yielded results and proved effective in bringing about a non-racial constitutional order. If this were the case violence would be unnecessary (Esterhuyse, 2012: 143). For this to happen, there had to be a strong commitment to a meaningful process that would lead to a non-racial democratic settlement.

After Botha had his stroke, the ANC and the government reached a turning point of seriousness, i.e. the perception by each side that the other is serious about finding a negotiated solution – that the other is willing to lose a little to win a little rather than lose all or win all. At this point Mbeki suggested that they delay the impending talks, Mandela's release and the unbanning of the ANC until after De Klerk was inaugurated as the president; this would give his Presidency enormous impetus, credibility and legitimacy, all of which were crucial for any settlement talks with the ANC (Esterhuyse, 2012: 167). Barnard was equally ready to talk. He told Mbeki's biographer that he learned two things from Esterhuyse's reports: "Firstly, it was reassuring that there were South Africans on the other side who were interested in finding a solution, and secondly, reaffirmation that we should not find the solution outside the country. We had to bring them home" (cited in Gevisser, 2007: 545).

The Negotiating Concept was therefore the living document of the pre-negotiation phase; not only did it contain the basic point of negotiation during this period, but it also mirrored the basic points of the Harare Declaration, and De Klerk's major announcements at the opening of parliament in February 1990.

Bibliography

African National Congress. 1987. "Report on a meeting held in Henley-on-Thames, England, with three Stellenbosch Academics, October 31–November 1, 1987" (abridged). Document 146 in Gail Gerhart and Clive Glaser, *From Protest to Challenge: A Documentary History of African Politics in South Africa, 1882–1990, Volume 6: Challenge and Victory 1980–1990*. Bloomington: Indiana University Press, 2010.

Bercovitch, J., T. Anagnoson and D. Wille. 1991. "Some Conceptual Issues and Empirical Trends in the Study of Successful Mediation in International Relations," *Journal of Peace Research* 28(1): 7–17.

Berridge, G. 1981. *Economic Power in Anglo-South African Diplomacy: Simonstown, Sharpeville and After*. Basingstoke: Palgrave Macmillan.

Berridge, G. 1989. "Diplomacy and the Angola/Namibia Accords," *International Affairs* 65(3): 478–500.

Carter, G. 1956. "The Expanding Commonwealth," *Foreign Affairs*, October.

The Commonwealth Accord on Southern Africa, 20 October 1985, Lyford Cay, Nassau, Bahamas.

The Commonwealth Report. 1986. *Mission to South Africa*. London: Penguin Books.

Crocker, C. 1993. *High Noon in Southern Africa: Making Peace in a Rough Neighbourhood*. Johannesburg: Jonathan Ball.

"Declaration of the Organisation of African Unity Ad Hoc Committee on Southern Africa on the Question of South Africa" (Harare Declaration), August 21, 1989. Document 174, in Gail Gerhart and Clive Glaser. 1989. *From Protest to Challenge: A Documentary History of African Politics in South Africa, 1882–1990, Volume 6: Challenge and Victory 1980–1990*. Bloomington: Indiana University Press, 2010.

De Klerk, F.W. 1998. *The Last Trek – A New Beginning: The Autobiography*. London: Macmillan.

Dubow, S. 2017. "The Commonwealth and South Africa: From Smuts to Mandela," *Journal of Imperial and Commonwealth History* 45(2): 284–314.

Esterhuyse, W. 2012. *Endgame: Secret Talks and the End of Apartheid*. Cape Town: Tafelberg.

Frei, D. 1976. "Conditions Affecting the Effectiveness of International Mediation," *Peace Science Society (International) Papers* 26(1): 67–84.

Harvey, R. 2001. *The Fall of Apartheid: The Inside Story From Smuts to Mbeki*. Hampshire: Palgrave.

Gerhart, G. and C. Glaser. 2010. *From Protest to Challenge: A Documentary History of African Politics in South Africa, 1882–1990, Volume 6: Challenge and Victory 1980–1990*. Bloomington: Indiana University Press.

Gevisser, M. 2007. *Thabo Mbeki: The Dream Deferred*. Johannesburg: Jonathan Ball.

Hyam, R. and P. Henshaw. 2003. *The Lion and the Springbok*. Cambridge: Cambridge University Press.

Iliffe, J. 2011. *Obasanjo, Nigeria and the World*. Woodbridge: James Currey.

Ingram, D. 2008. "Thatcher and Ramphal: A Long and Turbulent Relationship," *Round Table* 97(398): 781–790.

Lee, K. 2000. *From Third World to First: The Singapore Story 1965–2000*. New York: Harper Collins.

Lieberfeld, D. 2005. "Contributions of a Semi-Official Prenegotiation Initiative in South Africa: Afrikaner-ANC Meetings in England, 1987–1990," in R. Fisher, ed. *Paving the*

Way: Contributions of Interactive Conflict Resolution in Peacemaking. Lanham: Lexington Books.
Mandela, N. 1994. *Long Walk to Freedom*. Edinburgh: Little, Brown and Company.
Mayall, J. 2010. *The Contemporary Commonwealth: An Assessment 1965–2009*. London: Routledge.
McIntyre, W. 1991. *The Significance of the Commonwealth, 1965–1990*. Basingstoke: MacMillan.
Melunsky, J. 2002. The Rejection of Silence and Desolation: Explaining Political Transition in South Africa. Doctoral Dissertation. London: School of Oriental and African Studies.
Miller, J. 1961. "South Africa's Departure," *Journal of Commonwealth Political Studies* 1(1): 56–74.
Mole, S. 2012. "Negotiating With Apartheid: The Mission of the Commonwealth Eminent Persons Group 1986," *Round Table* 101(3): 253–260.
Murphy, P. 2011. "Britain and the Commonwealth: Confronting the Past – Imagining the Future," *Round Table* 100(414): 267–283.
Nathan, L. 1999. "When Push Comes to Shove: The Failure of International Mediation in African Civil Wars," *Track Two* 8(2): 1–23.
Nyerere, J. 1971. *South Africa and the Commonwealth*. Dar es Salaam: Government Printer.
Onslow, S. 2015. "The Commonwealth and the Cold War, Neutralism, and Non-Alignment," *International History Review* 37(5): 1059–1082.
Pahad, A. 2010. "Nine Days that Shook the World," *The Thinker: For Thought Leaders* 13.
Pottinger, B. 1988. *The Imperial Presidency: PW Botha the First 10 Years*. Johannesburg: Southern Book Publishers.
Ramphal, S. 2014. *Glimpses of a Global Life*. Toronto: Dundurn.
Report of Meeting Between President of the ANC Oliver Tambo and the U.S. Secretary of State, George Schultz: State Department: 28 January 1987. BC 1081 (P14.1) Manuscripts and Archives Department, University of Cape Town [US-ANC Meeting].
Robertson, P. 2008. "Ramphal and Southern Africa," in R. Bourne, ed. *Shridath Ramphal: The Commonwealth and the World*. Hertford: Hansib Publications.
Sampson, A. 1987. *Black and Gold: Tycoons, Revolutionaries and Apartheid*. London: Hodder and Stoughton.
Saunders, J. 2006. *Apartheid's Friends: The Rise and Fall of South Africa's Secret Service*. London: John Murray.
Schrire, R. 1991. *Adapt or Die: The End of White Politics in South Africa*. London: Hurst and Co.
Simpson, T. 2009b. "Toyi-Toying to Freedom: The Endgame in the ANC's Armed Struggle, 1989–1990," *Journal of Southern African Studies* 35(2): 508–520.
Singapore Communiqué of 1971, at: http://thecommonwealth.org/history-of-the-commonwealth/commonwealth-heads-government-meeting-singapore-singapore-14-%E2%80%93-22
Singapore Declaration of 1971, at: http://thecommonwealth.org/history-of-the-commonwealth/commonwealth-heads-government-meeting-singapore-singapore-14-%E2%80%93-22
South African Institute of International Affairs (SAIIA). 1985. *The Commonwealth at Nassau: Initiating Intervention in South Africa*. Johannesburg: SAIIA.
Sparks, A. 1994. *Tomorrow Is Another Country: The Inside Story of South Africa's Negotiated Revolution*. Sandton: Struik Book Distributors.

Srinivason, K. 1998. "What Are Commonwealth Values? Traditional Ones: Against Aggression and Authoritarianism," *International Journal* 53(4): 624–627.

Tambo, O. 1987. Notes for Meeting with Secretary of State, Mr George Schultz. BC 1081 (P14.1) Manuscripts and Archives Department, University of Cape Town.

Taylor, I. 2000. "Legitimisation and De-legitimisation Within a Multilateral Organisation: South Africa and the Commonwealth," *Politikon* 27(1): 51–72.

Thatcher, M. 1993. *The Downing Street Years*. New York: Harper Collins.

Touval, S. and I.W. Zartman. 1985. "Introduction: Mediation in Theory," in S. Touval and I.W. Zartman, eds. *International Mediation in Theory and Practice*. London: Westview Press.

Transcript of Bill Anderson interview by Howard Barrell, 8 April 1991, Folder 1 Part 1, Karis-Gerhart Collection, Historical Papers, University of the Witwatersrand.

Transcript of Kobie Coetsee interview with Padraig O'Malley, 6 November 1999.

Transcript of Michael Young interview by John Carlin, 25 May 1999.

Transcript of Niel Barnard interview with Padraig O'Malley, 17 September 1998.

Transcript of Pik Botha interview by Sue Onslow, 13 December 2012, Institute of Commonwealth Studies, University of London.

Vale, P. and D. Black. 1994. *The Prodigal Returns: The Commonwealth and South Africa, Past and Future*. Belville: Centre for African Studies.

Ziegler, P. 2010. *Edward Heath: The Authorised Biography*. London: Harper Collins.

5 Getting to agreement

The United Nations Observer Mission to South Africa

Between 15 and 16 May 1992, the second plenary of the Convention for a Democratic South Africa (CODESA 2) reached a crisis; the impasse was in regards to a critical point of disagreement arising out of Working Group 2 – the number of votes in a constituent assembly required to take decisions on issues affecting regions. While a high-level De Klerk-Mandela meeting momentarily rescued talks, it failed to resolve the disagreement; the suspicion, mistrust and tension between the ANC and government negotiators was simply too high. CODESA 2 failed to reach a political settlement. As the deadlock sunk in, frustration within the ANC alliance over the negotiations reached an apex. Hard-line ANC power-brokers, exasperated with the government, shifted the fight from the negotiating table back to the streets. The plan was a four-phase rolling mass action plan: "first, local and regional strikes; second, a phase of industry-specific strikes; third, a four- to five-day general strike on 3 August; and finally, a phase purportedly culminating in the resignation of the De Klerk government" (Sisk, 1995: 212). Anxiety was heightened when the Goldstone Commission, formed to investigate political violence, issued an interim report that confirmed the long-held suspicion that Inkatha and the government were a contributing factor to political violence, and that the major cause was the ANC-Inkatha rivalry.

The explosion happened on the evening of 17 June 1992; over 200 Inkatha members, in a murderous campaign, rampaged through the ANC stronghold of Boipatong. In a gruesome attack, over 49 were killed with spears, knives and machetes. A usually calm Mandela could not hide his anger:

> I can no longer explain to our people why we continue to talk to a government which is killing our people. We are now convinced that his [De Klerk's] method of bringing about a solution to this country is war. We will respond to that. One thing is clear: we are back in the Sharpeville days.
>
> (cited in Sisk, 1995: 213)

As storm clouds gathered over South African skies, the international community intervened; the UN secretary-general sent a special envoy to South Africa, former US Secretary of State, Cyrus Vance. The outcome of Vance's mission created the necessary climate that ushered in the formal end of apartheid.

To understand the success of this mission, and its contribution in getting parties to the table, it is important to trace the negotiation process in South Africa after Mandela was released and parties committed to negotiations and to discussing the fundamental issues of contention. Vance's mediation and formula came at a specific point in this process. At the heart of the matter was the issue of political violence and its relationship to the negotiation process.

Preliminary talks: negotiating preconditions, 1990

The transition from secret and informal to open and formal negotiations was signalled by the parties' going public with their intent to replace violence with talking. This was an important turning point; it shows that political leaders were willing to accept the inevitable risks and costs of negotiations. This public acknowledgement radically changed the dynamics of the conflict: "it unleashes a new, uncertain interregnum" (Sisk, 2009: 66). De Klerk's seminal address to the Tricameral Parliament in February 1990 was broad in scope. De Klerk responded positively to several demands made in the Harare Declaration, signalling a commitment to negotiate. De Klerk announced a series of immediate, short and longer-term initiatives that profoundly changed the course of pre-negotiation.

In the immediate measures, the prohibitions placed on the resistance organisations, i.e. the ANC, PAC, SACP and several subsidiary organisations, were rescinded. Political activists who were serving prison sentences for membership in the above resistance organisations, or who had committed offences because a ban on these organisations was in place, would be identified and released. The short-term measures included the unconditional release of Nelson Mandela. Mandela, De Klerk stated, could make a constructive contribution to a peaceful political process in South Africa. Long-term measures included a request to the South African Law Commission to examine suitable constitutional models for a new South Africa that could safeguard the government's mix of individual and minority rights.

Mandela was released on 11 February 1990 after 27 years in prison. His release was accompanied by a wave of township demonstrations reflecting both the excitement at political liberalisation and the impatience for an end to the hardships of life under apartheid (Jeffery, 2009: 236). Protests were held on the Reef in Thokoza (80,000 residents), Daveyton (60,000), Alexandra (50,000) and Tembisa (20,000) (Jeffery, 2009: 237). These demonstrations highlighted local grievances and targeted the discredited system of black local authority. Mandela's release was also accompanied by a wave of unrest in the homelands. It was in the KwaZulu homeland and Natal where political violence intensified, transforming the conflict in that region effectively into a low-intensity civil war. In the weekend of Mandela's release, more than 50 people were killed as armed gangs rampaged through urban townships, fighting, looting and burning homes (Jeffery, 2009: 240). The violence was particularly intense in the Edendale Valley outside Pietermaritzburg, with the body count reaching 700 by the beginning of March 1990.

Despite the mounting violence, the government and the ANC began to assemble their negotiating teams and positions. The government negotiating team was essentially the cabinet. The Department of Constitutional Development was transformed into a structure that would initiate, direct and support the government negotiations' team and strategy (De Klerk, 1998: 176). De Klerk appointed Gerrit Viljoen as its minister and Roelf Meyer as his deputy. Barnard was removed from the NIS and appointed the director-general of constitutional development. Viljoen, Meyer and Barnard's task was to "develop the government's negotiation's policy into more detailed concepts" to "put well-considered proposals and fall-back positions on the table when the real negotiations began" (De Klerk, 1998: 176).

The government's negotiating strategy rested on five assumptions:

> the NP could stay united and hold off the far right during the process; Western countries would accept some notion of group rights and lift sanctions; sufficient numbers of conservative black leaders would rally to an anti-ANC alliance to destroy the ANC claim to majority representation; state power could be used to sap the demands of the ANC negotiators, forcing them into compromise; and the ANC was controlled by strong leaders who could command compliance from their radical constituents.

The foundation of their constitutional strategy was based on the 1989 Broederbond guidelines: "[each] 'component unit' of the population would control its 'own affairs,' with 'general affairs' decided by consensus between the majority of each such unit in the national legislature" (O'Meara, 1996: 404–405).

Four principles that formed the basis of an envisioned constitutional dispensation emerged from this internal NP debate. First, the group rather than the individual would provide the basis for political representation and would be the primary repository of constitutional rights and protections (Price, 1991: 142). Second, South Africa was understood to be a country of minority groups with no majority. Third, a system of minority protection was fundamental. And fourth, all racial groups should be allocated separate legislative institutions to decide their "own" affairs. In short, the basic notion was that the South African population

> would be statutorily differentiated into a variety of groups (white, "coloured," Indian, urban black, ethnic homeland, national state). The groups would participate in central government through representation in an executive institution, within which the principle of "co-determination" (or mutual veto) would govern decision-making.
>
> (Price, 1991: 143)

The ANC's constitutional policy can be traced back to the principles laid out in the Freedom Charter. Albert Luthuli writes that the Freedom Charter was not only a product of its time but also the most agreed-upon articulation of an alternative South Africa (Luthuli, 1962: 157). It presented an unambiguous non-racial alternative to Verwoerdian apartheid (Corder and Davis, 1989: 635). The ANC's constitutional proposals for going into a formal negotiation process were contained in a document called the "Constitutional Guidelines for a Democratic South Africa" that was published by the organisation's Constitutional Committee chaired by Zola Skweyiya.

The guidelines guaranteed freedom of association, expression, thought, worship and the press. These freedoms were subject to the qualification that the "advocacy or practice of racism, fascism, Nazism or the incitement of ethnic or regional exclusiveness or hatred shall be outlawed" (Constitutional Guidelines, 1988: 131). They guaranteed social and economic rights – "the state would be obliged to protect the right to work, to guarantee education and social security, and to take active steps to eradicate, speedily, the economic and social inequalities produced by racial discrimination" (Dugard, 1990: 451). The guidelines also made the case for a Workers' Charter, protecting the right to strike and collective bargaining, to be incorporated into the constitution, and provided for affirmative action to redress past inequalities (Constitutional Guidelines, 1988: 132). The NP's proposals on the constitutional protection of group rights were denounced with the argument that such protection would simply perpetuate apartheid (Dugard, 1990: 451). Simultaneously, the guidelines did declare that "the state shall recognise the linguistic and cultural diversity of the people and provide facilities for free linguistic and cultural development" (Constitutional Guidelines, 1989: 131).

While the guidelines reflected the ANC's first order preferences, the Harare Declaration outlined the preconditions to official negotiations and contained a brief section describing the ANC's view of a future state. The Declaration called for negotiation but with conditions; the bottom line would be the creation of a non-racial majoritarian democracy. Mandela however was flexible; the importance of addressing white fears, an outcome of secret talks with Barnard's team, poured cold water over the Declaration's bottom line. After Mandela was released, he began to emphasise addressing minority concerns in the constitution, to the consternation of many in the ANC (cited in Sisk, 1995: 152).

The preconditions for negotiations

Three main issues shaped the process leading to the first official meeting between the South African government and the ANC: the issue of indemnity (the release of political prisoners and return of exiles), the political violence in Natal and the escalation of violence beyond Natal's borders.

The release of political prisoners and return of exiles

The ANC had made it clear that it was only prepared to enter negotiations after preconditions set out in the Harare Declaration had been met, the most important being the unconditional release of all political prisoners. By contrast the government team wanted to ensure that the ANC renounce violence in exchange of lifting the state of emergency. In response to the ANC's demands, the government conceded that it was willing to release select political prisoners as a gesture and those serving sentences merely because they were members of a banned organisation or because they committed an offence because a prohibition on the respective organisation was in force. While the government's intention was to break a logjam, it created another impasse; the government position, articulated in the 2 February announcement, fell short of the Harare Declaration. This is because political prisoners who committed offences in the category affected by De Klerk's announcements essentially committed "pure" or "absolute" political offences. These are offences that do not involve the commission of common law crimes. Essentially, they are aimed directly at the government, do not involve injury to private individuals and property, and include treason, sedition and espionage (McDougall and Soberbergh, 1990: 5).

The problem was that given the nature of the South African conflict, most political prisoners were convicted of common offences such as murder, assault, robbery, public violence, malicious damage to property, etc. (Keightley, 1993: 336). What complicated matters was the nature of these offences given the South African conflict; they frequently involved elements of extreme violence against private individuals (Keightley, 1993: 337). To avoid the impasse standing in the way of the first bilateral, ANC and government officials came to a compromise; the category of political prisoner release would be negotiated, defined and placed on the agenda of the first formal bilateral. This was acceptable to both parties.

The causes of political violence

Preparations for the first ANC-Government bilateral also provided a glimpse of trends to follow. The first trend was that it became clear that the ANC and government were not the only role-players in the unfolding political process; the sustainability of the process would also depend on the alliances and relationships that these two players were able to develop. The most important role-player in this regard was Inkatha, and its leader Chief Mangosuthu Buthelezi.

Inkatha had an awkward relationship with the ANC. On the one hand, Inkatha had fought running battles with the UDF in Natal in the 1980s, effectively transforming Natal's Midlands region into killing fields. At the same time, Inkatha had refused to negotiate with the South African government until the ANC was legalised and all political prisoners released. To compound matters, Inkatha was also essentially a regional political organisation, trapped in ethnic mobilisation, and formed to preserve Zulu cultural traditions (Maré, 1991). While this "ethnonationalist" character fitted very well with its relationship with the government, it did not sit well with the ANC and UDF, especially their Natal Midlands leadership.

The second trend was that political violence regularly interrupted the political process, but at the same time drew the parties closer together in their commitment to negotiation. There were two sources of this violence. The first is rooted in the relationship between the UDF and Inkatha. The political direction of Inkatha in the 1980s, particularly its consolidation as a Zulu ethnic movement entrenched as a regional (Bantustan) and local government, set it on a path that led to regionalism, federalism and increasingly to militant Zulu ethnic mobilisation (Maré, 1991: 195). This set it apart from the UDF, which was riding on a wave of popular revolt, directed at the very regional, local government and the ethnic divisions of apartheid in which Inkatha became entrenched and sought to defend. The 1980s uprising intensified the tension between the UDF and Inkatha, and transformed them into enemies; when it appeared that the state would lose all control over the structures it had created among African people, when township councils came under massive political and physically violent attack, when revolt spread to the Bantustans, Inkatha defended those structures, attempted the incorporation of even more people under its jurisdiction and extended it repressive apparatus through the formation of the notorious Zulu Police.

The second source of violence is rooted in the networks of the government's security services, notably the South African Police and to a lesser extent the SADF. These networks became known as the Third Force. While the idea of the Third Force can be located in the 1960s counterinsurgency strategies of the South African security forces, its 1990s manifestation can be traced to senior security service official discussions in the 1980s. Between 1985 and 1986, the State Security Council (SSC) discussed the establishment of a Third Force as a parallel structure to the SADF and SAP on a number of occasions (Saunders, 2006: 256). The most important was a document circulated by the Secretariat of the SSC on 9 May 1986 entitled "Creation of a Special Counter-Revolutionary Capacity (Including a Third Force)." The document "defined 'special capacity' as 'specifically organised, equipped and trained to plan, co-ordinate and set up counter-revolutionary actions to fight internal unrest and terrorism'" (Saunders, 2006: 257). Inkatha became central to this project and a close relationship between Inkatha and the Third Force soon developed.

The third trend was that the government wanted to ensure that it had allies in the negotiation process. To this end, government strategists began to apply to South Africa the techniques drawn from the decolonisation process in Namibia where SWAPO's electoral power had been considerably reduced (Ellis, 1998: 283). Government strategists calculated that they could form a right-of-centre alliance with conservative homelands leaders which could defeat the ANC at the polls. Viljoen was identified as a key architect and leading advocate of this strategy (Giliomee and Schlemmer, 1989: 200). Viljoen argued that this would be achieved "by negotiating full citizenship rights for all in a constitution with strong guarantees for minority rights and a powerful second chamber" (Giliomee and Schlemmer, 1989: 284). The strategy depended crucially on Inkatha, as this was the only organisation outside of the ANC alliance with which the NP government could reasonably hope to build an alliance. Not only did Inkatha have a substantial power base in Natal, but it had a long historical presence and pedigree in that region.

The escalation of violence

By early March, the Steering Committee had set aside 11 April as the date for the first bilateral between the ANC and the government. However, political violence after Mandela's release escalated in scope and intensity, putting enormous pressure on these preparations. Two incidents are significant, both occurring towards the end of March. The first happened in the Edendale Valley in the Pietermaritzburg area and was the worst violence at the time in the conflict between the UDF and Inkatha (Jeffery, 1997: 218–219). This fresh outbreak of violence signalled a new phase of major, calculated escalation of fighting. The violence began on 25 March 1990 after an Inkatha political rally in Durban addressed by Buthelezi. Inkatha warlords organised and mobilised an army of 12,000 militants from the outlying Inkatha-controlled areas and divided into separate battalions armed with shotgun rifles and spears. These legions, numbering several thousand a piece, "mounted a full-scale assault from the KwaZulu territory on ANC [residential] strongholds in the embattled Edendale complex" (Murray, 1994: 99). In what was to become known as the "Seven Days War" (25–31 March 1990), "Inkatha battalions, ferried by bus from place to place by the KwaZulu Police [KZP], fought pitched battles with UDF/ANC supporters." By the time the fighting subsided, "whole communities lay in ruins, dozens of houses had been set ablaze, hundreds killed or seriously injured, and thousands of people had fled for their lives." In terms of the body count and levels of destruction, Inkatha scored an impressive victory; "over 200 people were killed and 20,000 were made refugees, almost all of them UDF supporters or people not prepared to show allegiance to Inkatha" (Murray, 1994: 99).

In response, Mandela and Buthelezi scheduled a joint peace rally on 2 April at Taylor's Halt, an Inkatha stronghold, where both leaders were meant to share a platform. However, hard-liners in the UDF/ANC's Natal leadership rejected Mandela's peace gesture to Buthelezi and summarily cancelled Mandela's participation. In a public show of defiance, Harry Gwala led a 70-strong delegation from the Edendale "Valley of Death" to lobby against the meeting arguing that "the intensity of the war [with Inkatha] is such that an ANC-Inkatha rally could reduce Taylor's Halt to a battleground." The prevailing atmosphere, Gwala continued, was not ideal for a joint peace rally in Natal (Jeffery, 1997: 219). Gwala had the support of influential power-brokers in the ANC's Natal leadership such as Archie Gumede (the national UDF co-president) and Diliza Mji, the ANC's Natal secretary. The issue created major divisions in the ANC about how to manage and resolve the Inkatha matter; with Mandela arguing for a rapprochement with Inkatha, while Gwala insisted that this was counterproductive when it was ANC members filling the mortuaries. In the face of the peace rally cancellation, Mandela addressed an audience of 2,500 in Edendale and stated that Inkatha was not the enemy, and that Inkatha had to know that the ANC wanted to make peace (Jeffery, 1997: 219).

The second incident occurred in Sebokeng, in the Vaal Triangle. On 26 March, police opened fire on an unarmed crowd of 50,000 people; an incident that became known as a second Sharpeville. The UDF had called a march to protest the chronic housing shortage, unaccountable councils, rentals and a persistent education crisis. Sixty rounds of buckshot ammunition, one of the most lethal, were fired in two seconds, five people were killed, and 161 injured, and all were shot from behind. Despite these incidents, the first round of talks would go ahead on 2 May.

The Groote Schuur Minute

The first formal bilateral between the ANC and the NP government began on 2 May 1990 at Groote Schuur. The meeting lasted three days. There were 11 delegations on each side. The first day of the bilateral was exploratory and was spent getting acquainted. Journalists who observed the mood on the first day of the first encounter wrote about the cordiality of the talks, as participants mingled freely and socialised openly (Mkhondo, 1993: 40–41). On the second day, the parties discussed a range of issues to define mutual differences, lay the foundations for compromise solutions and thus clear the obstacles to negotiations. The groundwork for these matters was laid by the Steering Committee, and included the release of political prisoners, the safe return of exiles, the lifting of the state of emergency, the suspension of political trials, withdrawal of troops from the townships and the steps to be taken to curb political unrest in the townships.

The most urgent matter for the ANC was the release of all political prisoners, and the safe return of all exiles. The ANC also demanded the immediate release of all detainees who had not been charged or convicted of any offence, and the repealing of apartheid security legislation in terms of which the detainees were held in prison (Savage, 2000: 2). However, given that no register of political prisoners existed, reaching agreement as to who constituted a political prisoner was a crucial precursor to any further negotiations. Consequently, the primary issue discussed was the definition of political prisoners.

The government, consistent with the February 2 announcement, argued for a narrow definition of political prisoners, essentially defined as those who had committed "pure" or "absolute" political offences. By contrast, the ANC, in demanding the release of all political prisoners, argued for a broad definition, defined as those who had also committed "related" political offences. The parties' positions on the issue were strategic; the government wanted to restrict the number of people who would qualify for an indemnity, and negotiate the release of the remainder, thus using the political prisoner release issue as leverage, which would enable them to gain a strategic advantage. The ANC wanted "any person who was convicted for an offence that was politically motivated [to] qualify for an indemnity" (Mandela, 1994: 570). Essentially, they wanted all their supporters out of prison. The parties agreed on the general question of whether political prisoners should be released. However, they deadlocked; they could not agree on a mutually satisfactory definition of "politically motivated" crimes, which would primarily affect the identification, number and timescales of political prisoner releases. To manage the deadlock, the ANC and the government established a "Working Group" with a mandate to develop a definition of political offence and a plan for indemnity for political prisoners and exiles.

The meeting produced a working agreement known as the Groote Schuur Minute, which committed both parties towards the resolution of the existing climate of violence and intimidation, to political stability and to a peaceful process of negotiations. Flowing from this commitment, the parties agreed to five points. First, following the disagreement and deadlock on the definition of political prisoners and exiles, the parties agreed to establish a "Working Group on Political Offenses" to make recommendations on a definition of political offences, to discuss timescales, and to advise on norms and mechanisms for dealing with the release of political prisoners and the granting of immunity in respect of political offences (Groote Schuur Minute, 1990: paragraph 1). Second, temporary immunity from prosecution for political offences committed by ANC national executive members, and selected exiles, would be considered on an urgent basis to enable them "to return and help with the establishment and management of political activities, to assist in bringing violence to an end and to take part in peaceful political negotiations." Third, the government undertook to review the existing security legislation to bring it into line with the unfolding liberalisation process. Fourth, the government committed to work towards the lifting of the state of emergency. In this context, the ANC would work towards the resolution of political violence and commit to political stability to assist the government in this regard. Fifth, channels of communication between the parties were established to curb violence and intimidation (Groote Schuur Minute, 1990: paragraph 1).

Important features of this agreement stand out. First, the Groote Schuur Minute committed the parties to working towards a common definition of political crimes (Mallinder, 2009: 16). While it did not provide much description on the form this would take, it awarded the government considerable discretion in considering other "political parties and movements and other relative bodies" (Groote Schuur Minute, 1990: paragraph 1). Second, the reference to Namibia's experience pointed the Working Group to consider the Norgaard Principles, which used the approach of extradition law to define political crimes (McCarthy, 1997). Within these principles, it was unclear "whether serious human rights violations would be treated as political due to their gravity and the proportionality test" (Mallinder, 2009: 17). Third, paragraph 1 stipulated that individuals who left the country illegally and joined the prohibited organisations would immediately receive attention for these offences, "which were deemed to be purely political" (Mallinder, 2009: 17). This corresponded to De Klerk's February 2 announcement and was heavily biased in favour of the older generation, and a select group, of ANC leaders. Fourth, the Groote Schuur Minute granted immunity from prosecution of political offences committed before 4 May, to enable the ANC leadership to return to South Africa and participate in the negotiations (Groote Schuur Minute, 1990: paragraph 2). ANC members who continued their involvement in activities "related" to the armed struggle would be acting in violation of the agreement and would thus not be entitled to protection under its terms (Simpson, 2009: 516).

Following the Groote Schuur Minute, the NP government successfully passed the Indemnity Bill through parliament on 7 May, and the Indemnity Act was signed by De Klerk on 15 May. This new piece of legislation was needed to permit the return of ANC exiles that had yet to be charged as per the 2 February announcement and Groote Schuur Minute (Parker, 1996: 4). The act gave the president enormous discretion in granting immunity "either conditionally or on conditions he may deem fit." The effect of the indemnity was that no civil or criminal proceedings would be instituted against any person granted the indemnity

> during the period stipulated in such notice in respect of him, in respect of anything done or omitted by him any date prior to the announcement of that period, and such person shall not be detained during such periods of immunity.
> (Mallinder, 2009: 18)

This provision implemented paragraph 2 of the Groote Schuur Minute by "permitting ANC operatives to return to South Africa to participate in the negotiations without facing legal sanctions."

Following the Minute, the Working Group on Political Offences began functioning with members drawn from both the government and the ANC. The Working Group submitted its report on 21 May as per the Groote Schuur Minute. The Working Group followed the Norgaard Principles in approaching the contentious issue of political crimes recommending that they "form the basis of guidelines to meet the South African situation" (Pedain, 2004: 785). The report also acknowledged that "related" political offences may be regarded as political (Working Group Report, 1990). The Working Group further stated that indemnity would be assessed and implemented individually. Significantly, neither the Indemnity Act nor the mechanism established following the Working Group's report required individuals to renounce violence to gain indemnity (Mallinder, 2009: 21).

The escalation of violence

Despite the timeous tabling of the Working Group report, and the resultant raised expectations of a breakthrough toward settlement negotiations, political violence increased, politics became increasingly uncertain, and mutual suspicion and mistrust remained. The main culprit was the escalation, and spill-over, of Natal's violence into the Reef. The "Seven Days War" had a significant impact on the country's political landscape. It created important differences within the ANC on how to manage the Inkatha question. Two groups emerged. One group, sympathetic to Mandela, wanted immediate peace talks with Inkatha. The second group was sympathetic to Natal Midlands leader Harry Gwala. According to Gwala, the non-violence Mandela and his team of negotiators preached was misguided. Gwala saw no merit in sending an olive branch to Inkatha. The war with Inkatha, as Gwala saw it, was not between the ANC and Inkatha, nor was it between the government and the ANC, but rather between those who wanted to preserve apartheid (which included Inkatha) and those who wanted a democracy. The immediate strategy against Inkatha, Gwala therefore added, was not to talk peace but to fight back.

As the violence spiralled out of control, with Gwala creating a vast network of highly armed and trained self-defence units in Natal's townships, ANC regional leaders descended into the Natal Midlands to learn how Gwala and his units repelled Inkatha attacks. De Klerk's introduction of the South African Special

Forces, and counterinsurgency units, into the Natal Midlands escalated the conflict. As the body count mounted, with academics, churchmen and lawyers becoming the targets of Inkatha assassination squads, the ANC began to take a harder position towards Inkatha, weakening Mandela's group (Mkhondo, 1993: 135).

With no end to the violence in sight, hard-liners in the ANC alliance decided to raise the temperature. On 25 June, COSATU mounted a successful nationwide work-stoppage in order to draw attention to the violence in Natal and isolate Inkatha. The demands included an end to the state of emergency in Natal, the disbanding of the KwaZulu Bantustan, the withdrawal of 32 Buffalo Battalion from the townships and the arrest of Inkatha warlords. Over three million workers stayed at home, and tens of thousands of people marched through South Africa's cities and towns in support of COSATU's demands.

The strategy backfired horribly. COSATU's call for a national stayaway had coincided with an Inkatha political strategy of realignment; in a calculated manoeuvre designed to adapt to the changing circumstances of 1990, Buthelezi sought to remould Inkatha from an ethnic-based regional movement into a national political party, the Inkatha Freedom Party (IFP). In particular, the idea was to extend Inkatha's constituency into the greater Johannesburg region. The first step towards this end was a massive recruitment drive targeting the 56 single-sex hostels in the region, housing Inkatha's natural social and political base – over 175,000 Zulu-speaking migrant men who had come to Johannesburg from Natal in search of work (Murray, 1994: 101). The new IFP's intention was clear: "to reclaim its self-professed mandate to speak on behalf of Zulu-speakers, despite the diaspora that left them stranded on the fringes of the Rand townships" (Murray, 1994: 101). ANC supporters resented this attempt by the IFP to establish a permanent base in traditional, and predominantly, ANC strongholds. It was a matter of time before Natal's conflict was "transported like an airborne virus to South Africa's industrial heartland as the power struggle between the [ANC and Inkatha] assumed a wider, national political significance" (Murray, 1994: 101).

The violence exploded on 22 July, after an IFP rally in Sebokeng. Armed IFP militants went on a rampage in a residential area killing over 30 people in a very gruesome attack (Mandela, 1994: 579). The violence spread like wildfire and very quickly developed a logic and momentum of its own (Taylor, 1991: 8). The fighting primarily involved Zulu-speaking migrants in hostels and residents of squatter camps in the established townships; both were desperately seeking permanent and stable working and living space in the cities (Murray, 1994: 103). Murray writes that labour-market segmentation created deep divisions between professionals and skilled workers with a modest stake in the system and unskilled workers and the unemployed who competed for temporary and casual work. The resulting competition for scarce resources "led to social tensions" that "coalesced around 'tribal' identities, political affiliations, and geographical affinities" (Murray, 1994: 103). The dynamic of the ensuing conflict followed a very clear logic:

> As the battle lines were hastily drawn, Inkatha loyalists in the squalid hostels forcibly evicted non-Zulu speakers and those who refused to swear allegiance

> to the IFP. The hostels became paramilitary staging areas from which vigilantes planned and executed their forays into the townships. When young comrades mounted counter-attacks, the hostels became fortresses in which to retreat.
>
> (Murray, 1994: 104)

In the midst of the escalation of violence, and spill-over of Natal's killing fields into South Africa's industrial heartland, debate arose on three questions: whether an interim government was necessary to oversee an election before drafting a new constitution; whether the new constitution should be drafted by a constituent assembly, in particular whether it should happen before or after an election; and whether the notion of group rights had a place in a new constitution. There were two competing scenarios.

The perspective of the NP government was that "the present government would remain intact while a Great Indaba [i.e. a conference] representing different parties would negotiate a new constitution" (Ebrahim, 1998: 50). The Tricameral Parliament would then pass this constitution. On constitutional issues, the government argued forcibly on the issue of the protection of minority rights; Viljoen stated this "could be used as a temporary nation-building measure rather than being permanently enshrined in the constitution" and their argument "was an assurance for minority groups that they will have a particular say in the new constitutional system, by way of representation and decision-making, in spite of the fact that they are not part of the majority" (SAIRR, 1990: 734). Viljoen further added that the NP government would go to formal roundtable negotiations to negotiate the protection of minority rights, and that this was a significant departure from the original group rights preference.

The ANC's perspective was premised on the Harare Declaration. Thabo Mbeki explained that the Groote Schuur Minute set into motion a process of removing obstacles to negotiations. The next step was to determine the participants at the negotiating table. The ANC wanted an elected constituent assembly, which would decide who should sit together to draw up a new constitution. Mbeki added that "before a new constitution is adopted, and before political structures change on the basis of it, there would need to be an interim government which [enjoyed] the confidence of all political groups" (SAIRR, 1990: 680).

The question of the suspension of the armed struggle, a key government demand, remained very tricky for the ANC; despite the closure of MK's Angola camps, and resultant endgame for the military wing, MK remained a symbolic hope for the ANC. Yet MK's circumstances revealed the hard truth that political power would not come from the "barrel of a gun." Sticking to this trump card invited more problems after the Groote Schuur Minute; the government inevitably became more hesitant in allowing exiles to return and in releasing political prisoners while the ANC maintained its policy of armed struggle. The ANC soon began to recognise that it was not possible for the government to address all obstacles identified in the Harare Declaration, and that it needed to be flexible in its demands.

The Pretoria Minute: suspending the armed struggle

In August 1990, the ANC announced the unilateral suspension of the armed struggle. This was a major breakthrough for the political process as it dealt with the government's core demand. This was also a strategic move by the ANC on two counts. First, while the Working Group on Political Offences had produced a final report on 21 May, concerns over its content had delayed an ANC-government meeting scheduled to consider the report. By August, "there had been little or no progress towards resolving the form and timescale for meeting these commitments." As a result, those affected political prisoners and exiles began to pressure the ANC negotiators to deliver results (Haysom, 1992: 29). Second, in order to resolve the issue with a favourable concession from the government, the ANC needed to meet a core government demand. But this had to appear not at government insistence in order to save face. The suspension of the armed struggle was thus made unilaterally before the scheduled meeting and was intended to give the ANC the moral high ground in the process, thus setting a positive tone to the meeting.

The ANC and government met at the Presidency in Pretoria on 6 August. The meeting lasted 13 hours and gave birth to the Pretoria Minute. In the meeting, the Groote Schuur Minute and the Working Group report were accepted by both parties. The Working Group report had made provisions for the formulation of guidelines to be applied in dealing with members of all organisations who committed political offences (Working Group Report, 1990). However, the Working Group report was subsequently amended; the previous acknowledgement that murder could be a political crime was left out, an omission that caused significant problems later (Keightley, 1993: 338).

The Pretoria Minute generated a joint Working Group on indemnity, and this new group was instructed to draw up a plan "for the release of ANC-related prisoners and the granting of indemnity to people in a phased manner and to report before the end of August" (Pretoria Minute, 1990: paragraph 2). The minute also agreed on specific target dates. The mechanism to implement the indemnity process, recommended by the report of the Working Group on Political Offences, would be created by 31 August 1990. The release of political prisoners was scheduled to start on 1 September 1990, and for the granting of indemnities as from 1 October 1990. Indemnity for categories of persons was to be completed by the end of 1990, and on an individual basis by April 1991 (Pretoria Minute, 1990: paragraph 2).

The ANC suspended the armed struggle, with the Minute stating that "no further armed actions and related activities by the ANC and its military wing Umkhonto we Sizwe will take place" (Pretoria Minute, 1990: paragraph 3). The minute established another Working Group, the Armed Action Working Group, to resolve all outstanding questions arising out of this decision to report by 1 September 1990. The government undertook to lift the state of emergency in Natal and to review the Internal Security Act. Both parties also committed themselves to steps and measures aimed at "normalising and stabilising the situation in line with the spirit of mutual trust obtaining among the leaders involved" (Pretoria Minute, 1990: paragraph 4). Paragraph 8 of the Pretoria Minute reasserted a strong commitment by the parties to the goal of negotiated change. Finally, in order to facilitate movement on substantive issues, paragraph 9, the concluding section of the agreement, stated, "Against this background, the way is now open to proceed towards negotiations on a new constitution. Exploratory talks in this regard will be held before the next meeting which will be held soon" (Pretoria Minute, 1990: paragraph 9). To give expression to this clause, another joint Working Group, the Paragraph Nine Working Committee, was established to discuss procedural and agenda items for an as-yet-defined constitutional conference (Sisk, 1995: 95).

The Pretoria Minute was the beginning of the most complex phase in the pre-negotiations. Three issues deserve attention: the political fall-out emanating from the ANC's suspension of the armed struggle; continued dispute and uncertainty around the indemnity process; and the escalation of violence. After the unilateral suspension of the armed struggle, Joe Slovo told Patti Waldmeir that 98 percent of ANC supporters, both in and outside the NEC, "thought the decision was a sell-out." Mandela was convinced that "time was not on our side that the longer the process stretched out the more time would be given to those who would like to sabotage the process" (Waldmeir, 1997: 166). The ANC's anxiety found its way into the Armed Action Working Group; the group could not arrive at a definition of "armed action." The ANC contended that the "training and recruitment of soldiers were not armed activities, and that the cessation of armed activities did not bind the organisation to reveal arms caches inside the country or hand those over to the authorities" (Haysom, 1992: 29). According to Ivan Pillay, a senior ANC intelligence officer, his reading of the Pretoria Minute was that "it doesn't say we will stop shipping weapons, it says we will stop, we won't carry out armed action" (Pillay, 2002). Pillay admitted that he and his commanders continued to ship arms into South Africa, and train and arm the ANC's self-defence units (Pillay, 2002).

By contrast, government security officials within the committee continued to pressure the ANC to reveal armed caches, "arguing that the release of trained MK personnel could not take place as long as their arms were still readily available to them." In this way, the government "sought to use the frustration of political prisoners awaiting release as a pressure on the ANC to extend its definition of armed actions to incorporate the delivery and surrender of arms to the authorities" (Haysom, 1992: 29). The ANC countered and insisted that the government first disband covert security force units if it was to reveal arms caches and stop recruiting and training soldiers. The ANC also objected to the government linking the release of political prisoners and indemnity of exiles to the suspension of the armed struggle in order to force further concessions from the ANC (Ebrahim, 1998: 66).

The Groote Schuur Minute, the Pretoria Minute and the indemnity process that flowed through them contained one political problem: whether indemnity would be applied to all political prisoners or just high-profile political prisoners needed for pre-negotiations. While the ANC simply wanted all their people out of prison and back into the country, the government only wanted to release select high-profile and senior ANC leaders needed to legitimise their strategy of pre-negotiation (Mallinder, 2009: 13).

The escalation of violence

Political violence flared immediately after the signing of the Pretoria Minute. It began in the Vaal Triangle and further attacks brought the death toll in the East Rand to 140 within a few days, with more than 300 injured. In the coming weeks, political violence grew in intensity and brutality. Twenty-four ANC supporters died in the Crossroads shack settlement (Jeffery, 2009: 257). By late August, security forces were brought in to stem the slaughter. Designating 27 townships "unrest areas," and providing the police with extensive powers of search and arrest without a warrant, "a police dragnet of the hostels and [informal settlements] produced an awesome armoury of deadly weapons ranging from primitive spears and axes to limpet mines, machine guns and hand grenades" (Murray, 1994: 105).

To end the violence in Natal and related killings in the Transvaal, the ANC compiled a list of six demands. First, the KwaZulu police had to be disbanded and cease to exist. Central government should be responsible for security in Natal. Second, security forces should be impartial. Third, a liaison and monitoring machinery between the ANC and the government should be established to monitor the outbreak of violence. Fourth, individuals who are alleged responsible for earlier incidents of violence should be prosecuted. Fifth, the state of emergency should be lifted. And finally, a high-level joint Working Group of representatives of the government and ANC "should be established to oversee the implementation [of] such agreements" (ANC, 1990: 1). The primary responsibility, Mandela concluded, rested with the South African government.

On 15 September, De Klerk ordered a massive security crackdown. Code-named Operation Iron Fist, the crackdown involved "the large-scale deployment of SADF and police riot units to the war-torn townships, the cordoning off migrant workers' hostels with razor wire, and the imposition of night-time curfews" (Murray, 1994: 105). These measures bore strong resemblance to the states of emergency and drew the ire of ANC activists (Garson, 1990: 47). Township residents accused the police of favouring Inkatha, "providing them with armed escorts," and allowing them to brandish what were euphemistically termed "traditional weapons," such as spears, axes, pangas and clubs known as knobkerries, while tear-gassing and disarming their opponents (Murray, 1994: 105).

The intervention of the security forces failed to explain why the violence spread so quickly, why it affected specific townships, and why the political violence was essentially between the most impoverished township communities, particularly those in informal settlements and hostel dwellers. As ANC intelligence officers uncovered more security force complicity in the violence, ANC supporters began to cast serious doubt on the negotiating team's ability to move the government on the ANC's core demands, in particular the issues of political prisoners, political exiles and violence. The perception grew that "the aged Mandela was getting the run-around from a younger, wily, and politically deft de Klerk" (Sisk, 1995: 96). By the end of the year, and after heated public exchanges, the relationship between Mandela and De Klerk deteriorated. In the face of mounting pressure from hard-liners in the ANC, a disillusioned Mandela took the gloves off; he told an ANC rally in Johannesburg that the ANC would suspend its participation in the Working Group on Political Offences and set unilateral deadlines for the implementation of the agreement on exiles and political prisoners (Sisk, 1995: 97).

Tactical changes: moving towards multi-party negotiations

On the back of a consultative conference that had imposed new and tight deadlines for the ANC's negotiating team, Mandela and his negotiators had to move quickly in order to neutralise the militant threat. To this end, the NEC had to take the initiative in the pre-negotiations and alter their tactics. First, Mandela used the occasion of the ANC's annual January 8 Statement to propose a political solution; he called for the convening of an All-Party Congress on constitutional negotiations. The proposed All-Party Congress "would constitute the first step in the process leading to the adoption of [a] new constitution" (ANC, 1991: 1). The All-Party Congress would only be convened after all obstacles to negotiations had been removed and would have three tasks:

> To set out the broad principles within which the detailed constitutional work would be carried out; to determine the make-up of the body, such as an elected Constituent Assembly, that would draw up the constitution; [and] to establish an interim government to oversee the process of transition until a new parliament was elected, and a democratic government formed on the basis [of a new] constitution.
>
> (ANC, 1991: 1)

Since the All-Party Congress would not be established by a general election based on a universal franchise, it could not have the power to draw up a new constitution. According to the ANC, only an elected sovereign Constituent Assembly comprising of elected members of the assembly could have such powers. Therefore, having performed the three identified tasks, "the All-Party Congress would then dissolve, unless . . . it obtained a specific popular mandate to continue as a constitution-making body, an interim government or both." The installation of an interim government was critical for the ANC (ANC, 1991: 1).

Second, in seeking ways to arrest the escalating violence, the negotiating team decided to reach out to the IFP and arranged a meeting with Buthelezi. This acknowledgement of a role for Buthelezi in the unfolding political process was a political triumph for the IFP; the political standing Inkatha was unable to achieve through diplomacy, "it was able to acquire through an orchestrated campaign of social violence" and in the process "ensured itself a place in negotiating stability in the townships" (Murray, 1994: 107). After behind the scenes preparations, both leaders and their delegations met for an all-day session at the Royal Hotel in

Durban on 29 January. At the end of 13 hours of talks, a peace accord, the Royal Hotel Minute, was concluded. Both parties called for an end to violence, made a commitment to political tolerance and freedom of activity, and promised to take steps to peacefully reintegrate divided communities. The parties resolved to create a high-level joint committee to facilitate local level peace initiatives and act as a crisis contact point.

De Klerk welcomed the idea of a multi-party conference. However, their interpretation on its role was that the conference "would work out 'common ground' and 'basic principles' before deciding the composition of the 'more formal body' to draw up the new constitution" (O'Meara, 1996: 408). This position offered the prospect of a semantic compromise on the ANC's preference for a Constituent Assembly; "[p]arties to the conference would be offered a limited decision-making role in a form of a 'council of state' during the transition process" (O'Meara, 1996: 408).

Breakdown: the Mandela ultimatum

An agreement was brokered on the meaning of the "suspension of armed action and related activities." The agreement, the DF Malan Accord, was confirmed at DF Malan Airport in Cape Town on 12 February 1991. In terms of the agreement, the ANC undertook not to carry out armed attacks or infiltrate men or weapons inside South Africa (Ebrahim, 1998: 71). The creation of underground structures and training of fighters inside South Africa would cease. Further, statements inciting violence and threatening armed action would cease (DF Malan Accord, 1991: 493). However, there was no agreement on the surrender of ANC weapons, the identification of arms caches, the demobilisation of MK or the disestablishment of self-defence units. Membership of MK would continue to be lawful and individual weapons would be licensed (Ebrahim, 1998: 71).

De Klerk felt that the terms of the DF Malan Accord could be a major contribution to the restoration of peace and stability (De Klerk, 1998: 205). For the ANC, their assumption in the aftermath of the DF Malan Accord was that their concessions would pave the way for their core demands to be met as per the Harare Declaration, i.e. loosen the logjam on the release of political prisoners and the return of exiles, in effect setting the stage for the meeting of the 30 April deadline set at the ANC consultative conference (Collinge, 1992: 11).

But this was not to be. The major culprit was the implementation of the indemnity process. Under Government Notice 3013 of 18 December 1990, there was a requirement that to obtain indemnity, individuals had to complete application forms. While applications by persons who had committed "non-violent" crimes went relatively quickly, "cases involving more serious acts required greater individual consideration" (Mallinder, 2009: 27). The cumbersome procedure of application and review led to persistent delays and resultant tensions. A period of bitter accusations and counter-accusations ensued in which "the government blamed the ANC for failing to meet its commitments to provide lists of prisoners and exiles, and the ANC accused the government of delaying the process to pressure the ANC into further concessions on the armed struggle" (Mallinder, 2009: 27).

As the 30 April deadline drew nearer, only 900 prisoners had been released and 364 had been refused release because of the seriousness of their offences. The slow pace of the political prisoner release process finally took its toll; "ANC political prisoners went on a hunger strike, raising the tension between the government and the ANC, and between the ANC leadership and the political prisoners" (Collinge, 1992: 11). The ANC's negotiating strategy was bearing no fruit; the organisation had essentially interpreted its commitments regarding the fate of MK as dependent on sufficient progress in removing obstacles towards constitutional negotiations and they were nowhere near the removal of such obstacles. For his part, De Klerk failed to empathise with a moderate ANC coalition, under pressure from militants, who were willing and anxious to begin official negotiations. According to an observer of the times, De Klerk was pursuing "a myopic strategy of going for maximum short-term gains at ANC expense, seemingly oblivious to the eroding effect this tactic was having in prospects for obtaining a larger settlement" (Ottaway, 1993: 113).

The balance of power in the ANC began to shift in favour of hard-liners. At the end of a top-level ANC meeting, in which Mandela had apologised for misleading the organisation for calling De Klerk "a man of integrity," the ANC issued an ultimatum in the form of an open letter. The ultimatum listed seven demands: the immediate dismissal of defence minister Magnus Malan and law and order minister Adriaan Vlok; legislative action to outlaw the carrying of cultural weapons (spears, shields, knives, etc.) used in township violence; the visible, public dismantling and disarming of certain units in the SADF; the immediate suspension of all police who were involved in the Sebokeng shootings; assurances that the SADF would use restraint in crowd control; the phasing of single-sex worker hostels and their transformation into family housing; [and] the establishment of an independent commission to hear complaints about security-related issues (cited in Sisk, 1995: 104).

If these demands were not met by 9 May, the ANC would suspend all talks with the government. The ANC now realised that negotiations could no longer be driven by an apparent "chemistry" between Mandela and De Klerk or abstract talks about a future democratic country, while low-intensity civil war waged in the townships. Whereas months earlier Mandela had depicted De Klerk as a man dedicated to a new South Africa, "now he was being depicted . . . as a crafty and ruthless rival, prepared to give free rein to elements within the state security apparatus which sought to destabilise government opponents" (Mkhondo, 1993: 100).

De Klerk was not able to meet the demands set out by the ANC. The ANC announced that they were pulling out of constitutional talks with the government; they called for mass protests, a consumer boycott and a two-day general strike. This was the climate in which the ANC held a leadership conference in July 1991. While Mandela remained at the helm of the party, the conference witnessed the ascension of an important group of Young Turks, led by Cyril Ramaphosa, who became the new brains trust of the negotiations. Ramaphosa assembled a far more formidable negotiating team that was less compromising and drove a hard bargain. The conference reaffirmed the importance of the following steps: the convening of the All-Party Congress; the installation of an Interim Government; the election of a democratic Constituent Assembly; and the adoption of a democratic constitution and the election of a parliament representative of all the people of South Africa.

Changing power-balance: Inkathagate and the moment of convergence

The balance of power between the ANC and the government was to shift fundamentally. Barely two weeks after the conference, the *Weekly Mail* published an explosive series of articles revealing the existence of a secret state project for funding the IFP. The articles revealed that, with the knowledge of senior cabinet ministers, the security police in Natal had provided R250,000 to the IFP to help it organise and finance mass rallies. The smoking gun of police collusion with Inkatha had been discovered and details spread through the domestic and international press with lightning speed (Sisk, 1995: 111).

The leaked documents decisively altered the balance of power perception in favour of the ANC in the final stages of pre-negotiation. It presented the NP government with a legitimacy crisis with perceptions that they were not honest negotiators. Inkathagate had important consequences. First, Inkathagate was the beginning of the parting of ways between the government and IFP. In the process, the government "lost its only possible black partner with significant support and thereby its chances of building a substantive conservative alliance," an important strategic goal (Van der Westhuizen, 2007: 191). Second, for the ANC, the revelations were proof why an interim multi-party government should preside over the constitutional negotiation process and not the NP government; as Ramaphosa pointed out, it "confirmed the ANC's suspicion that the [government] was prone to abusing state resources to bolster its position [for the roundtable talks]." Consequently, ANC pressure for an interim government grew immensely (Van der Westhuizen, 2007: 191). Third, Inkathagate undercut the government's ability to control the pre-negotiation process; it could no longer claim that it could negotiate a transition away from apartheid while "keeping its hands firmly on the tiller of the ship of state." While it had to a large extent driven the pre-negotiation process since 2 February 1990, its strategy was now fully exposed; "it could not be a player in the process and a legitimate referee too. An interim government framework, which the ANC had been demanding, became an imperative" (Sisk, 1995: 112). For his party, De Klerk supported the ANC's position on a speedy path towards a multi-party congress.

Negotiations towards an interim government thus became crucial. This mean resuming talks with the government. Some, but not all, of the ANC's demands were met, but it nevertheless returned to pre-negotiations. The ANC's core power-brokers, Mandela and Ramaphosa, implied that returning to pre-negotiation towards an All-Party Congress was necessary because violence and mayhem would persist for as long as the NP government remained in power. Therefore, "only an interim government, in which the ruling [NP] would be forced to share power, could address the problem, and only negotiation could achieve that"

(Friedman, 1993: 16). For its part, the government conceded that such transitional arrangements would have to result from negotiations (De Klerk, 1998). The government and the ANC had reached a point of convergence. This is the point when the ANC and the government commit to begin settlement negotiation. The All-Party Congress could not wait for the removal of other obstacles to negotiations. The two processes could proceed at the same time.

With preconditions no longer seen as an obstacle for the commencement of an All-Party Congress, the debate shifted to what type of congress, i.e. what would it do? Despite divergent views on the type and nature of the institutions to debate, draft and implement a new constitution, the government and the ANC agreed in principle to an exploratory All-Party Congress to pave the way to official negotiation. Their agendas for this body, however, differed. For the ANC, the task of the All-Party Congress was to draw up the broad principles of a constitutional framework, to determine the make-up of a constituent assembly and to establish in interim government. The ANC's core preference was for the election of a constituent assembly on a proportional representation list basis in a single national constituency. This constituent assembly would negotiate and draft a new constitution (Sisk, 1995: 170). Their primary interest was to "prevent minority powers from producing deadlock in the constituent assembly." As the constituent assembly would provide legitimacy to the new constitution, the assembly would be transformed into a new legislature (Sisk, 1995: 170). According to the ANC, the All-Party Congress went beyond the agenda items. They saw it as a process that would "seek the broadest possible consensus within society around the transitional process [i.e. the constituent assembly] and the broad outcome of negotiations [i.e. a new constitution]." The All-Party Congress had to therefore be as inclusive as possible (ANC, 1991: 6).

The government envisaged a more open-ended process where De Klerk would issue initial invitations, and thereafter the All-Party Congress would be "free to elect its own chairman and determine its own agenda and working procedures" (Welsh, 1991: 743–744). They anticipated that the Congress would deliberate on two critical issues: "the composition, functioning and decision-making process of the actual constitutional negotiation conference, and the broad principles to be contained in a new constitution" (Welsh, 1991: 744). The government's core preference was that the All-Party Congress be transformed into a forum for the negotiation of a new constitution. These negotiations would include leaders of all other political parties. The new constitution would then be placed "before the electorate with full enfranchisement in a yes-or-no referendum." If approved, the constitution "would be enacted by the Tricameral Parliament in order to give it legal force" (Sisk, 1995: 168). Only after this process could a founding election take place. The primary interests for the government were that the transitional process had to operate within the prevailing constitutional framework.

There were thus some important points of general agreement. Both sides were ready and willing to formally negotiate in an All-Party Congress. It was agreed that an interim authority had to be in place while the constitution was negotiated. There was also tacit agreement that the government "could not be both referee and player at the same time" (Ebrahim, 1998: 88). The differences, however, were more substantial. Three questions had to be addressed:

> the constitutional framework within which the interim authority would operate; whether it was necessary for such an interim authority to be elected at all; and what authority such an interim authority would have – whether it should act as a government with effective authority, or only have limited responsibility.
>
> (Ebrahim, 1998: 89)

These issues were to dominate the agenda of the first phase of official negotiation.

Mutual security agreement: the National Peace Accord

With pre-negotiation gathering apace, the focus shifted to the Preparatory Committee of the National Peace Initiative. As discussed, De Klerk had convened a two-day conference on 24–25 May on violence. The conference, however, was not a success; the ANC, COSATU, the PAC, AZAPO, the SACC and other civil society organisations refused to attend. They viewed De Klerk as partisan on the issue of violence, regarded his conference as inappropriate as a result, and would have preferred the conference be convened by an independent mediator. Given the centrality of the ANC in the politics of violence, their non-attendance hampered the conference's ability to constructively deal with the issue of violence. This was a major impediment; the conference's decisions could not be binding on those not attending.

During discussions on the first day of the peace conference, Professor Johan Heys, a former moderator of the Dutch Reformed Church, proposed that Dr Louw Alberts, a prominent scientist and former chairman of the Atomic Energy Board, and Reverend Frank Chikane, the general secretary of the SACC, act as facilitators for an all-party peace conference to follow the peace summit. The conference agreed to appoint Alberts as a "one-man facilitation committee" for a second peace conference with the power to include other members (Gastrow, 1995: 25). The ANC welcomed the appointment of Alberts.

Alberts set about establishing the facilitation committee the very next day. He recruited Chikane to assist him in identifying individuals in whom the relevant participants in a peace conference would have confidence. Chikane, who had access to influential power-brokers in the resistance organisations, "undertook to find names that would be acceptable to the ANC, the PAC, COSATU, AZAPO, the [SACP], and other like-minded civil society organisations while Alberts sought representatives who would garner the trust of the government and the IFP" (Gastrow, 1995: 25). Alberts was particularly interested in involving the church and business leaders "because they interacted with a large proportion of the population" (SAIRR, 1992: 69–70). A facilitation committee of 13 individuals from church and business was constituted, and decided to work under a rotating chairperson.

A turning point happened when the facilitation committee successfully convened a meeting on 22 June at the Barlow Rand headquarters in Johannesburg. The meeting included the ANC, AZAPO, the NP government, the IFP, the SACP, COSATU, the IFP affiliated United Workers Union of South Africa, representatives of parliamentary parties, and various church and business organisations. The meeting decided that Roelf Meyer, Thabo Mbeki and Frank Mdlalose (representatives of the NP government, the ANC and the IFP respectively), together with representatives of the facilitation committee, "would form a 'preparatory committee' which in turn would form Working Groups to draft proposals on issues identified as necessary to end the violence" (SAIRR, 1992: 70). Under the chairmanship of John Hall, the preparatory committee met two days later on 24 June, and formed five Working Groups to look at the following identified issues: Working Group 1 would look at codes of conduct for political parties; Working Group 2 would look at codes of conduct for security forces; Working Group 3 at socioeconomic development; Working Group 4 at implementation and monitoring; and Working Group 5 at the peace process, the establishment of a secretariat and the media (Gastrow, 1995: 32).

Each Working Group consisted of three members from the NP government, three from the IFP, three from the ANC, one religious leader and one business representative from the preparatory committee. Each Working Group subsequently met on numerous occasions in order to produce a draft consensus document on the issue assigned. These draft documents were then "referred to the various principals for approval before being referred back to the negotiators to seek fresh consensus for a next draft" (Gastrow, 1995: 32).

In the changed political environment after Inkathagate, the work of the preparatory committee gathered pace. In August 1991, the Working Groups all presented their reports to a meeting of the preparatory committee. The meeting reached consensus on a draft peace accord arising from these reports (SAIRR, 1992: 70). The preparatory committee decided to fix 14 September 1991 as the target date by which the five Working Group reports had to be completed. On that day, a national peace conference would be convened to ratify and sign the combined Working Group reports, and these would form the basis of a peace agreement (Gastrow, 1995: 32).

The reports from the Working Groups were agreed to only a few hours before the national peace conference was to commence. The reports were collated to form a draft text of a peace agreement.

The peace conference was held at the Carlton Hotel in Johannesburg on 14 September 1991. The outcome was the signing of the first ever multi-party agreement in South Africa, the National Peace Accord, which was formally adopted on 16 September at an occasion attended by all the major players and political organisations, parliamentary and extra-parliamentary, church and business groupings, and trade unions. As the first ever multi-party agreement, it laid the foundation for the All-Party Congress. This was most evident in its preamble and chapter one, which related the accord to the process of democratisation: "The establishment of a multi-party democracy in South Africa is our common goal. Democracy is impossible in a climate of violence, intimidation and fear" (Sisk, 1995: 114).

The accord was built around "legally enforceable codes of conduct" for political organisations and security forces. These legally enforceable codes of conduct were located within a hierarchical set of committees from national to regional to local. A national peace committee assisted by a national peace secretariat stood at the apex of a pyramid based on local dispute resolution committees (Haysom, 1992: 34) The peace accord thus attempted "to make the obligations under the accord enforceable either in terms of legally enforceable obligations or in terms of the political process that violation of the accord would occasion" (Haysom, 1992: 34). The strategy was based on the belief that a multilateral accord would be more effective than previous bilateral agreements between the ANC and Inkatha. A multilateral accord would bind all political players in South Africa into a common agreement, thus increasing the political costs for parties who wished to move in and out of the accord as and when it suited them.

The important impact of the National Peace Accord was that it allowed violence to be managed. While this management was not perfect, it created conditions for non-violent peaceful protest to continue but not to escalate or otherwise threaten negotiations. This illustrates that pre-negotiation cannot develop into settlement negotiations if violence is simultaneously escalating or becoming widespread. The management of violence is therefore a crucial issue. This responsibility cannot be left to the main actors; each will have too many incentives to use violence to advance their interests. The signing of the National Peace Accord was a turning point; it signalled the establishment of a detailed set of multi-party transitional arrangements. Most importantly, it signalled the end of the phase of negotiation over preconditions, which had dominated stages three and four. This phase had been drawn out considerably, exposed important weaknesses in the ANC's negotiation strategy and had confirmed the pre-eminence of the ANC and the NP government as the principal players in the negotiation process (Haysom, 1992: 34). The negotiation process would now primarily be a multi-party process, with the ANC and NP government serving as important anchors of the process.

Following the signing of the National Peace Accord, a steering committee chaired by Chief Justice Michael Corbett was established, through which details of the All-Party Congress would be negotiated. The committee agreed that the NP government, the ANC and the IFP convene a preparatory meeting of all parties to discuss the All-Party Congress. Set for 29 and 30 November, some 20 political parties, including homeland government representatives, attended. The parties and organisations included the PAC, the government and the NP (as separate delegations; the former as non-voting), ANC, IFP, Labour Party, Inyadza National Movement (KaNgwane), Transvaal and Natal Indian Congresses (joint delegation), Venda government, Bophuthatswana government, United People's Front (Lebowa), Solidarity, DP, Transkei government, National People's Party (opposition party in the Indian House of Delegates), Ciskei government, Kikwankwetla Party (QwaQwa), Itando Yesizwe Party (KwaNdebele), Ximoko Progressive Party (Gazankulu) and the SACP (Sisk, 1995: 203). In prior NP-ANC bilateral talks, agreement was reached on the decision-making rules for the All-Party Congress:

the principle of "sufficient consensus." This meant that if the NP government and ANC reached agreement, sufficient consensus existed (Friedman, 1993: 25).

The preparatory meeting agreed that the All-Party Congress would be called the "Convention for a Democratic South Africa" (CODESA). The meeting also agreed upon CODESA's nine-point agenda:

> the creation of a climate for free political participation; definition of general constitutional principles; agreement on a 'constitution-making body/process'; creation of 'transitional arrangements'; decision about the future of 'independent' (TBVC) homelands; agreement on the role of the international community in negotiation; selection of a time frame; creation of mechanisms for implementation; and discussion of other issues.
>
> (Sisk, 1995: 203)

The first plenary session of CODESA took place on 20 and 21 December 1991 and was chaired by Justices Ismail Mohamed and Piet Schabort. There were three important outcomes to this first historic formal roundtable. The first was the Declaration of Intent. The Declaration established a set of principles and purposes to guide CODESA, and all signatories declared and committed themselves to be bound by the agreements of CODESA. The parties and organisations declared their "solemn commitment" to "bring about an undivided South Africa with one nation sharing a common citizenship," to establish "a free and open society based on democratic values," to ensure "equal opportunities and social justice for all," to "create a climate conducive to peaceful constitutional change," and to "set in motion the process of drawing up and establishing a constitution" (cited in Ebrahim, 1998: 529).

The second important outcome was the creation of five Working Groups to negotiate broad sets of issues:

> the principles and structures of a new constitution; the creation of a climate conducive to peaceful political participation; the form of transitional or interim government and the future path of the transition; the constitutional future of the four homelands that had accepted nominal independence; and the implementation of agreements.
>
> (Sisk, 1995: 205)

The Working Groups served as the engines of the substantive and formal negotiation process. Working Group 1 considered the creation of a climate for free political participation and the role of the international community in the transition process. Working Group 2 was mandated to explore constitutional principles and the constitution-making body. Working Group 3 dealt with an interim government. Working Group 4 was tasked to debate the future of the homelands. And Working Group 5 dealt with timeframes.

The third important outcome, as mentioned, was a major concession by the NP government. In what was described as a "breath-taking policy switch," De Klerk proposed that the government

> would be prepared to consider a compromise to bridge the fundamental differences between the ANC's position that the new constitution should be drawn up by an elected constitutional assembly, and [the NP government] that it should be written by a multiparty constitutional convention.
>
> (De Klerk, 1998: 222)

De Klerk proposed "two-phased process of constitutional writing: a new interim constitution would be drafted by the CODESA process, in terms of which the first fully representative Parliament would be elected, which would in turn draft and adopt the final constitution" (De Klerk, 1998: 222). De Klerk's acceptance of an elected constituent assembly drafting the final constitution amounted to the NP government effectively ceding its power to exercise control over the final negotiations as the ruling party. This was the political solution, the resolving formula, that ushered in formal around-the-table negotiations.

Breakdown: CODESA 2, the white referendum and the escalation of violence

Serious discussions regarding international intervention in the unfolding political process emerged early in 1992. The issue was political violence; despite the implementation of the National Peace Accord, the body count mounted. Church leaders were the first to lobby the government. Archbishop Desmond Tutu led a delegation to De Klerk where he urged the government to recognise "the value of an international monitoring mechanism in coping with the violence" (Anglin, 1995: 522). De Klerk dismissed them with irritation. However, three months later, the government agreed and accepted international mediation. Two developments had occurred. First, the CODESA process collapsed and mistrust and suspicion reached an all-time high. Second, a horrific massacre happened in the ANC stronghold of Boipatong that exposed the inability of South Africa's major political actors to stem the tide of violence on their own. International mediation became necessary to save the political process.

Deadlock at CODESA 2

CODESA's Working Groups met for the first time on 20 January 1992. They were required to report back when the second plenary of CODESA was expected to convene in March or April 1992. There was a positive mood at the beginning of 1992. In their New Year's messages, both Mandela and De Klerk made clear that CODESA would quickly yield breakthrough. The ANC even called for an interim government by mid-year, calling 1992 "the year for democratic elections for a constituent assembly" (Sisk, 1995: 206). For their part, the government supported the agreement at CODESA 1 but with a qualification; any changes would require approval through a referendum with white votes counted separately. If approved by the electorate at large "and a majority of whites," elections to a transitional parliament would be held to draft the terms of a new constitution (Sisk, 1995: 206).

De Klerk was under a very different kind of pressure. While Mandela spent the most part of his time reigning in hard-liners in the ANC, De Klerk was put under constant pressure by the white right wing (supported by the CP), who felt that De Klerk had thrown them under a bus. The white backlash came to a head at a by-election in the rural and conservative town of Potchefstroom, in what was a major showdown between the NP and CP. When the right-wing candidate won by more than 2,000 votes, De Klerk announced that a white referendum would be held in March to test white attitudes on the transition. De Klerk's expectations were met; 68 percent voted in favour of the transition, leaving the right wing defeated by a landslide. While observers at the time lauded the victory, expecting a deal on an interim government by late April, this later turned out to be the seeds of disaster.

Victory made the government overconfident with disastrous consequences. Before the referendum, there was widespread agreement on basic principles for the interim government. After the referendum, the government submitted new proposals that envisaged a longer transition, preserving constitutional continuity, and countless opportunities for white vetoes on a regional and political party basis (Sisk, 1995: 209). An angry ANC rejected this and countered. Critical differences facing CODESA 2 surfaced; they centred on "the powers of an interim executive, the influence of minorities in the constitution-making body, and the length of time such a body would sit (the government favoured several years; the ANC four months)" (Sisk, 1995: 209).

After two days of intense talks, CODESA 2 reached an impasse. The government was buoyed by its performance in the referendum. The ANC and its allies were frustrated by the government's negotiating style and position after the referendum. Neither would budge, and the talks deadlocked. A high-level Mandela-De Klerk meeting could not resolve the impasse. ANC hard-liners pounced; they saw this as an attempt by the NP to prolong the transition as long as possible, and their proposals as gimmicks designed to preserve white minority privilege indefinitely. COSATU led the charge, and took the fight from the negotiating table back to the streets. The aim of the rolling mass action was clear: the public show of power, similar to the government's demonstration of strength in the referendum. Abandoning the negotiation table, ANC hard-liners proposed a four-phase coordinated mass action campaign: local and regional strikes, a phase of industry-specific strikes, a four- to five-day general strike and a general protest phase culminating in the resignation of the De Klerk government (Sisk, 1995: 212).

An enormous cloud of uncertainty and anxiety hung over South Africa as the negotiations hung in the balance. A series of violent incidences followed the breakdown of CODESA 2 and created the most serious crisis of the transition. On 16 June, Johannesburg was a ghost city; commuter trains ran almost empty, taxi ranks in the surrounding townships were desolate, while bus companies halted their services to townships. According to the Johannesburg Chamber of Commerce and Industries, "more than 89 percent of city employees stayed away from work" (Banda, 1992). Similar occurrences prevailed throughout the country.

The explosion came on 17 June 1992. On the night of 17 June, a group of 300 men from Kwa Madala Hostel, in nearby Sebokeng Township, attacked residents in the Joe Slovo informal settlement in Boipatong outside Vereeniging. In an orgy of slaughter, they hacked, stabbed and shot 38 people to death in their homes. Among the dead were a nine-month-old baby and a child of four (Sparks, 1994). The incident was political violence; Boipatong was predominantly ANC-aligned, its attackers came from Kwa Madala Hostel, a Vaal stronghold of the IFP. Further, evidence of prior IFP-state collusion in political violence in the Vaal, and in massacres elsewhere, as well as police complicity in the Boipatong massacre led to local and national and international outrage. Mandela expressed his anger:

> I am convinced we are no longer dealing with human beings but animals. . . . We will not forget what Mr de Klerk, the National Party and the Inkatha Freedom Party have done to our people. I have never seen such cruelty.
>
> (SA History, 1992)

He blamed De Klerk personally:

> I can no longer explain to our people why we continue to talk to a government which is killing our people. . . . We are now convinced that his [De Klerk's] method of bringing about a solution to this country is war. We will respond to that. One thing is clear: We are back in the Sharpeville days.
>
> (cited in Sisk, 1995: 213)

Mandela finally bowed to the hard-liners. He announced that a bilateral meeting between the ANC and the NP on 23 June would be cancelled; in its place the ANC's national executive would hold an emergency meeting: "The voice of our people is coming out strong and clear. Their demand is: no more contact with the regime" (cited in Simpson, 2011: 38). In line with Mandela's assurances, the ANC decided to break off both CODESA and bilateral talks with government. The ANC stated that "the deadlock could be ascribed to the NP's dogged refusal to prioritise democratic change over white minority veto powers" (ANC, 1992). The ANC then listed a broad range of demands that the state would need to work towards if negotiations were to reconvene. The ANC demanded that government "agree to the creation of a democratically-elected and sovereign Constituent Assembly to draft and adopt a new constitution, as well as the establishment of an Interim Government of National Unity"; that the state end "its campaign of terror against the people"; that the carrying of all dangerous weapons in public, including so-called cultural weapons, be banned; and urged the international community to place renewed pressure on the De Klerk regime to bring violence to an end and to commit itself to solutions based on internationally accepted democratic principles (ANC, 1992). Most importantly, it appealed to the United Nations Security Council (UNSC) "to convene as a matter of urgency to undertake measures which will help stop the violence and reinforce our efforts aimed at bringing about a democratic order" (ANC, 1992).

International intervention: United Nations mediation

Throughout June, South Africa was plunged into a deep crisis. The negotiation process was reduced to bitter and abusive exchanges between the government and the ANC, "replete with mutual recriminations and thinly veiled personal insults" (Sisk, 1995: 214). The international community stepped in. In a meeting with the Spanish prime minister, Felipe Gonzalez, Spanish official sources reported that De Klerk was willing to accept international mediation as long as there was no interference with South Africa's internal affairs (Simpson, 2011: 42). Chief Emeka Anyaoku, secretary-general of the Commonwealth, and the European Community (EC), were also considering sending observers to the country.

On 1 July, the British government stepped in. The British foreign Office invited UN Secretary-General Boutros Boutros-Ghali to London to discuss the South African crisis with John Major's government (Simpson, 2011). Boutros-Ghali accepted a government invitation to visit South Africa on a fact-finding mission. Late in June, Mandela had attended a meeting of the Council of Ministers of the OAU in Dakar, Senegal. There, he appealed once again for international intervention. The OAU mandated a ministerial delegation to take the South African case to New York, and agreed to call for the "urgent convening" of the UN Security Council "to examine the issue of violence in South Africa and to take all appropriate action to put an end to it" (Anglin, 1995: 522). While Boutros-Ghali was rumoured to have been averse to a Security Council meeting addressing the Boipatong issue and the breakdown of negotiations, "he now accepted the need for Security Council debate and expressed himself in favour of UN intervention" (Simpson, 2011: 43).

The focus of the crisis shifted to the United Nations headquarters in New York. On 15 July, the Security Council held a two-day debate on South Africa. More than 50 speakers from South Africa and other state representatives addressed this meeting. From South Africa, delegates included Mandela, Buthelezi, Pik Botha, Clarence Makwetu of the PAC, and leaders of Transkei, Bophuthatswana and Ciskei. Mandela told the audience that "an extremely critical situation has arisen" and that South Africa was trapped in "an escalating cycle of violence." He warned the delegates that the South African government was untrustworthy as it represented "a system of white minority rule to which the United Nations is opposed." Later at a press conference, he stated that the ANC "would like sanctions to be re-imposed" and chided US President George Bush for lifting them prematurely (Simpson, 2011: 43–44). Mandela requested the speedy appointment of a Special Representative to recommend action to help end the violence. In response, Pik Botha reiterated that only South Africans could resolve South African conflicts, including the political violence. He proposed "a meeting of De Klerk, Mandela and Buthelezi to consider the availability of a joint monitoring body of the three parties to defuse and solve problems that could give rise to violence" (Anglin, 1995: 523).

The mandate: Resolution 765 (1992)

After listening to a comprehensive list of allegations of state complicity in violence, and counter-accusations, the Security Council voted unanimously for UNSC Resolution 765 (1992) of 16 July 1992. The resolution condemned the escalation of political violence and urged the South African government to "take immediate measures to bring an effective end to the ongoing violence and bring those responsible to justice." It also called upon all parties to work together in combating violence and to ensure the implementation of the National Peace Accord. The Security Council authorised the secretary-general to appoint

> a Special Representative for South Africa in order to recommend [after discussions with the parties] measures which would assist in bringing an effective end to the violence and in creating conditions for negotiations leading towards a peaceful transition to a democratic, non-racial and united South Africa, and to submit a report to the Security Council as early as possible.

All parties were urged to cooperate with the Special Representative "in carrying out his mandate, and to remove the obstacles to the resumption of negotiations" (UN Resolution 765, 1992: 1).

Boutros-Ghali appointed Cyrus Vance, former US Secretary of State, as the Special Representative. He also requested Virendra Dayal, the former cabinet chief, to accompany Vance on the mission. Concerned that the ANC's planned mass action might result in an explosion before Vance could report back, Boutros-Ghali sent a provisional team from the secretariat to observe developments.

Vance's mission

Given the complexity of South Africa after the breakdown of CODESA 2, Vance sought to hold discussions with the widest range of parties in the country. The programme began with meetings with De Klerk and members of his cabinet (22 July), and these would be followed by a further round of talks between Vance and De Klerk on 30 July (UNSC Report, 1992: 3). Separate meetings were also held with Pik Botha (26 July) and Kobie Coetsee (31 July). Vance also held meetings with delegations of political parties on 23 July. These included the IFP (Buthelezi), PAC (Makwetu), ANC (Sisulu, Ramaphosa and Mbeki) and AZAPO (Phandelani Nefolovhdodwe). Meetings were also held with the Democratic Party (Zach de Beer and Colin Eglin) and the SACP (Slovo). Vance also received delegations from leaders of the homelands, other political parties involved in the negotiations and members of civil society organisations. Annex 2 outlines the programme of the mission.

Discussions between Vance and the government concerned the subject of violence and the CODESA process. The government emphasised that De Klerk had taken many initiatives to de-escalate and combat violence. These initiatives, the government argued, resulted in the National Peace Accord and the Goldstone

Commission. The government further stated that De Klerk had repeatedly invited Mandela and Buthelezi to a joint meeting in order to demonstrate that the principle actors could work together to end violence (UNSC Report, 1992: 5). The government stated that they had responded to the recommendations of the Goldstone Commission by drafting regulations to "prohibit the carrying of dangerous weapons in public spaces within 'unrest areas,' and that urgent attention was being given to the carrying of traditional weapons and to single migrant workers' hostels" (UNSC Report, 1992: 5). Referring to the ANC's mass action campaign, the government's view was that "it would provoke violence, delay the search for democratic solutions and disrupt the economy and social services" (UNSC Report, 1992: 5).

On the matter of negotiations, the government stated that there was substantial agreement with the ANC at the second plenary of CODESA. Differences were with regard to regions' devolution "with the government strongly supporting a regional government system where powers, functions, and boundaries would be agreed to prior to the adoption of the transitional constitution" (UNSC Report, 1992: 6). The government also denied that their proposals implied a veto power for white South Africans.

The ANC, on the other hand, emphasised the need for the speedy implementation of the Goldstone Commission, especially with regard to "the fencing of hostels, the disarming of their residents and the prevention of weapons leaving or entering those premises." The ANC further called for the disarming and confining to the barracks all SADF special force counterinsurgency units who bore enormous responsibility for the violence. The ANC specifically demanded a role for the United Nations in furthering the political process. They envisaged UN monitors in three critical areas:

> military (to monitor the disbanding and confinement to barracks of special force counterinsurgency units); security (to monitor the South African police); civilian (to monitor the implementation of the National Peace Accord, including the code of conduct for political parties and organisations).
>
> (UNSC Report, 1992: 7)

This role for the United Nations would be one where the organisation would maintain early warning offices that would "receive information from the public relating to possible or impending violence." In a working paper subsequently handed over to Vance's mission, the ANC further stated that UN monitors should not merely be symbolic; they need to have "freedom of movement and the independent resources needed to act as 'the eyes' of the international community" (UNSC Report, 1992: 8). Vance held a meeting privately with Mandela. Mandela wanted to return to negotiations but had specific concerns. These included the need to release all political prisoners, the problems encountered on constitutional matters and the current state of negotiations with respect to the creation and powers of a senate. On all other matters concerning violence, Mandela reiterated the position of the ANC.

In the meeting with the IFP, Buthelezi considered the structures of CODESA as weak as it lacked a dispute resolution mechanism at the level of head of the party. The IFP reiterated its position that only a federal constitutional model "could reconcile the disparate sectors of South African society and that the powers should be devolved from regional governments to the central government." Buthelezi slammed the ANC for violating the code of conduct for political parties as laid out in the Peace Accord, and while condemning the Boipatong massacre, the "IFP also deplored the comparative indifference of the international community to the slaying of its supporters at Crossroads" (UNSC Report, 1992: 6).

All the delegations Vance held discussions with, across the spectrum of South African politics, demanded a strong United Nations presence in the country to assist the political process. There was no disagreement amongst all parties on this point. The positive influence of Vance's team on the ANC's mass action demonstrators even reduced the South African government's paranoia regarding the UN's intentions (Anglin, 1995: 523–524).

Recommendations: Resolution 772 (1992) and international observer missions

In his report on Vance's mission to the Security Council, Boutros-Ghali recommended a strengthening of the National Peace Accord. The National Peace Committee and the National Peace Secretariat "needed to be more consistently and substantially supported from the highest political levels, as do the 11 regional dispute resolution committees covering all parts of the country" (UNSC Report, 1992: 17). Such action, Boutros-Ghali stated, would contribute to enhancing the capacity of indigenous structures in building peace. To this end, he recommended that the UN make available "30 observers to serve South Africa, in close association with the National Peace Secretariat, in order to further the purposes of this Accord" (UNSC Report, 1992: 17). The observers would be supplemented by observers from the Commonwealth, European Community and the OAU.

After considering the secretary-general's report, the Security Council adopted Resolution 772 of 12 August 1992. This resolution authorised the secretary-general to deploy United Nations observers in South Africa "in such a manner and in such numbers as he determines necessary to address effectively the areas of concern noted in his report, in coordination with the structures set up under the National Peace Accord." The resolution further invited the OAU, Commonwealth and the European Community to consider deploying their own observers in South Africa in coordination with the United Nations and the structures set up under the National Peace Accord (UN Resolution 772, 1992: 2). Accordingly, the Security Council sanctioned the establishment of the United Nations Observer Mission to South Africa (UNOMSA). An advance party of 13 arrived within a month (Anglin, 1995: 524). This was followed by observer missions from the Commonwealth (COMSA), the OAU and the European Community (ECOMSA).

While the four intergovernmental observer groups operated under UNSC Resolution 772, each maintained a separate identity, derived their authority from their own institutional structures and reported to those structures rather than to the UN (Anglin, 1995: 524). Although the immediate preoccupation of the four observer groups was the monitoring of violence, this role was preliminary to the ultimate purposes of promoting conditions conducive for a successful negotiation process, and conducive to free and fair elections. Angela King, a senior official of the UN from Jamaica, was appointed by Boutros-Ghali to head UNOMSA on 23 September. By the end of October 1992, 50 UNOMSA observers were deployed in all 11 regions of South Africa designated in the National Peace Accord.

Bisho massacre and the Record of Understanding

Despite the positive response from the international community, the ANC continued its programme of mass action as planned. ANC hard-liners, including former MK intelligence chief Ronnie Kasrils, felt compelled to demonstrate the ANC's popular support and reassert its militancy. On the heels of a successful general strike, ANC hard-liners took aim at what they thought would be an easy but symbolic target; protest action whose sole aim was the overthrow of the Ciskei homeland government. ANC tacticians had a provocative plan:

> while the bulk of the protesters marched into a soccer stadium on the edge of the town in accordance with the agreed plan, Ronnie Kasrils, would flank the Ciskei military and lead a breakaway group into the heart of Bisho.

Kasrils's group would then occupy the city centre "and stay there until Gqozo [the Ciskei leader] was forced from power" (Sisk, 1995: 218). The plan backfired horribly; the Ciskei military opened fire with live automatic weapons, killing 28 and injuring over 200. Despite calls by ANC hard-liners, notably Chris Hani, to break off all communications with the government, the combination of the Boipatong and Bisho massacres, and the positive responses from the international community for assistance, reinforced pressures to negotiate. Unlike the Boipatong massacre, the Bisho massacre did not scuttle talks; it pushed the parties back to the negotiating table.

Mandela and De Klerk and their delegations met on 26 September. After marathon eight-hour meeting, the parties reached a crucial agreement, the Record of Understanding, that brought the parties back to the negotiation table, and the set the country on the course to a democracy. The meeting was the culmination of a series of secret meetings held between Roelf Meyer and Cyril Ramaphosa. These meetings "entailed discussions with a view to remove obstacles towards the resumption of negotiations and focused on the identification of steps to be taken viewpoints on the relevant issues and obstacles" (Record of Understanding, 1992: 1). The crucial points of the Record of Understanding read as follows:

> b) The Government and the ANC agreed that during the interim/transitional period there shall be constitutional continuity and no constitutional hiatus. In consideration of this principle, it was further agreed that:

- the constitution-making body/constituent assembly shall also act as the interim/transitional Parliament;
- there shall be an interim/transitional government of national unity;
- the constitution-making body/constituent assembly cum interim/transitional Parliament and the interim/transitional government of national unity shall function within a constitutional framework/transitional constitution which shall provide for national and regional government during the period of transition and shall incorporated guaranteed justiciable fundamental right and freedoms. The interim/transitional Parliament may function as a one or two-chambered body.

c) The two parties are agreed that all prisoners whose imprisonment is related to political conflict of the past and whose release can make a contribution to reconciliation should be released. The government and the ANC agreed that the release of prisoners, namely, those who according to the ANC fall within the guidelines defining political offences, but according to the government do not, and who have committed offences with a political motive on or before 8 October 1990 shall be carried out in stages (as reflected in a separate document; Implementation Programme: Release of Prisoners) and be completed before 15 November 1992. To this end the parties have commenced a process of identification.

(Record of Understanding, 1992: 1–2)

The ANC and the government also agreed on a deadlock-resolving mechanism as recommended in the secretary-general's report to the UN Security Council, the principle of sufficient consensus: "through continuing negotiations, agreement would first be reached between the ANC and the government on a bilateral basis, then taken to other parties for multilateral negotiation." This was justified both on the grounds of efficacy and because of "the parties' converging interests in a successful outcome to the negotiation process they created" (Sisk, 1995: 220).

The road to the negotiated settlement

The Record of Understanding set the country back on the path of multi-party negotiations, the multi-party negotiating process in 1993. During the period of multi-party negotiations, UNOMSA observed demonstrations, marches and other forms of mass action; noted the conduct of all parties; and obtained information indicating the degree to which the parties' actions were consistent with the principles of the National Peace Accord and the Goldstone Commission guidelines (UN, 1994). Observers supplemented their field observations by establishing and maintaining informal contacts at all levels with existing government structures, political parties and organisations, as well as with civic associations (UN, 1994).

By late December, there were 17 observers from the COMSA, 14 from the European Community and 11 from the OAU. UNOMSA's observers was were mostly deployed to the Vaal and Natal, regions which had the highest occurrence of political violence (Reddy, 2015: 135). According to King:

> The aim (of UNOMSA) is to help open channels of communication between communities, reduce political intolerance and create a spirit of reconciliation among South Africans of all races and ethnic backgrounds. Observers from 36 different countries participate in demonstrations, marches, rallies and other forms of mass action and, over the last year, have covered more than 8 500 events and meetings throughout the country. They also maintain informal contacts at all levels with established governmental structures, political leaders and parties, as well as civic organisations and other groups.
>
> (King, 1993: 1)

In time, the deployment patterns of the four intergovernmental observer groups were broadly similar. All concentrated their energies and resources on Natal and the Vaal. Over the months, the role and functions of international observers in South Africa evolved considerably. Initially, the focus was on bringing an end to political violence and intimidation as a prerequisite for progress towards free and fair elections (Anglin, 1995). Specifically, this involved observing demonstrations, marches and other forms of mass action; noting the conduct of all parties; and obtaining information indicating the degree to which the parties' actions were consistent with the principles of the National Peace Accord and the Goldstone Commission guidelines. Observers would then supplement their field observations by establishing and maintaining informal contacts at all levels with existing government structures, political parties and organisations, as well as with civic associations.

The UN also stepped up efforts to resume talks after the Record of Understanding. Two special envoys of the secretary-general visited South Africa after the Vance mission: Virendra Dayal from 16 to 27 September 1992, and Tom Vraalsen, assistant secretary-general of the Ministry of Foreign Affairs of Norway and former representative of Norway to the UN, from 22 November to 9 December 1992 (Reddy, 2015: 135). A delegation of the Special Committee, led by its chairman, Ibrahim Gambari (Nigeria), also "visited South Africa for ten days in March 1993." These diplomatic interventions helped facilitate the resumption of negotiations (Reddy, 2015: 135). As diplomatic efforts from the United Nations increased, so the number of observers was also increased in 1993 to 60 in February and 100 in September. The number of local peace committees served by UNOMSA had risen from 23 to 120 in less than a year. By the end of 1993, UNOMSA observers had attended more than 9,000 meetings and events (Reddy, 2015).

In March 1993, representatives from 26 political parties and organisations held a multi-party planning conference at Kempton Park and agreed to resume constitutional negotiations as a Multi-Party Negotiating Council, i.e. the Multi-Party Negotiating Process. Beginning on 1 April, the essential task was to broaden acceptance and define details of the agreements reached in the Record of Understanding. The central decision-making structure of the 26-party parliamentary-style assembly was the ten-person negotiating council, "an effective decision-making body even though it still operated under the 'sufficient consensus' rule that governed CODESA" (Sisk, 1995: 226). Despite rising levels of political violence, the Negotiating Council adopted by consensus 27 constitutional principles which, along with a bill of rights, would be included in a new constitution (Reddy, 2015: 135). It was also decided that elections would be held on 27 April 1994. Furthermore, the South African parliament passed a bill on 23 September providing for the creation of a Transitional Executive Council (TEC) to oversee government operations and facilitate the transition to a democratic system of government by holding free and fair elections (Reddy, 2015: 235). The passing of the TEC legislation allowed Mandela to address the Special Committee on Apartheid at the United Nations and call for the end of sanctions against South Africa. In passing Resolution 48/1, the general assembly decided that

> all provisions adopted by the General Assembly relating to prohibitions or restrictions on economic relations with South Africa and its nationals . . . shall cease to have effect as of the date of the adoption of the present resolution, and requests all States to take appropriate measures within their jurisdiction to lift the restrictions and prohibitions they had imposed to implement the previous resolutions and decisions of the General Assembly.

It further decided that

> all provisions adopted by the General Assembly relating to the imposition of an embargo on the supply of petroleum and petroleum products to South Africa, and on investment in the petroleum industry there, shall cease to have effect as of the date that the Transitional Executive Council becomes operational, and requests all States to take appropriate measures within their jurisdiction to lift any restrictions or prohibitions they had imposed to implement previous resolutions and decisions of the General Assembly in this respect.
>
> (UNGA Resolution 48/1, 1993: 1)

In November 1993, the Multi-Party Negotiating Council approved the interim constitution and several constitutional principles and institutions were adopted by South Africa's Multi-Party Negotiating Council, which would guide South Africa during its transition. They included the Transitional Executive Council (TEC), the Interim Constitution, the Independent Electoral Commission (IEC), the Independent Media Commission (IMC) and the Independent Broadcasting Authority (IBA). The Interim Constitution stipulated that the future South Africa would be divided into nine provinces, each having a provincial legislature, government and executive council. The plenary session of the multi-party negotiating process also approved the involvement of the international community in the preparation and conduct of the elections and directed its Negotiating Council to work out the details (Anglin, 1995: 525–526). In a resolution ratified by the TEC on 9 December 1993 the four international organisations already present as well as individual foreign governments were asked "to provide a sufficient number of international observers to oversee the electoral process" (Anglin, 1995: 527).

This request was accepted by Security Council Resolution 894 (1994) as documented in the "Report of the Secretary-General on the question of South Africa" from 10 January 1994. In December 1993, the Security Council approved the UN Secretary-General's appointment of Lakhdar Brahimi as his Special Representative for South Africa. Angela King was appointed as the Deputy Special Representative of the Secretary-General for South Africa (UN, 1994). Security Council Resolution 894 expanded the mandate and size of UNOMSA; it created the Peace Promotion Division (PPD) and the Electoral Division. UNOMSA's mandate was subsequently expanded to include electoral observation and increased the number of observers, including additional international observers of the COMSA, the OAU and the European Union Election Unit in South Africa (EUNELSA). By April 1994, there were 3,000 observers stationed throughout South Africa (UN, 1994). Upon the election of Nelson Mandela and the establishment of a democratic South Africa, UNOMSA was terminated on 27 June 1994, through Security Council Resolution 930 (1994).

Bibliography

African National Congress, "Constitutional Guidelines for a Democratic South Africa." ANC policy paper, Lusaka, August 1988. Document 153 in Gail Gerhart and Clive Glaser, *From Protest to Challenge: A Documentary History of African Politics in South Africa, 1882–1990, Volume 6: Challenge and Victory 1980–1990*. Bloomington: Indiana University Press, 2010.

African National Congress. 1991. Statement of the National Executive Committee on the Occasion of the 79th Anniversary of the ANC, 8 January 1991.

African National Congress. 1992. Statement of the Emergency Meeting of the National Executive Committee, 23 June 1992.

Anglin, D. 1995. "International Monitoring of the Transition to Democracy in South Africa, 1992–1994," *African Affairs* 94(377): 519–543.

Banda, R. 1992. "First Day Largely Successful as Most Blacks Observe Stayaway Call," *South African Press Association*, 16 June 1992.

Collinge, J. 1992. "Launched on a Bloody Tide: Negotiating the New South Africa," in G. Moss and I. Obery, eds. *South African Review 6: From Red Friday to CODESA*. Braamfontein: Ravan Press.

Corder, H. and D. Davis. 1989. "The Constitutional Guidelines of the African National Congress: A Preliminary Assessment," *South African Law Journal* 106: 633–647.

De Klerk, F.W. 1998. *The Last Trek, A New Beginning: The Autobiography*. London: Macmillan.

DF Malan Accord. 1991. "Document 19 in Hassen Ebrahim," in *The Soul of a Nation: Constitution-Making in South Africa*. Cape Town: Oxford University Press.

Dugard, J. 1990. "A Bill of Rights for South Africa?" *Cornell International Law Journal* 23: 441–466.

Ebrahim, H. 1998. *The Soul of a Nation: Constitution-Making in South Africa*. Cape Town: Oxford University Press.

Ellis, S. 1998. "The Historical Significance of South Africa's Third Force," *Journal of Southern African Studies* 24(2): 261–299.

Friedman, S. 1993. *The Long Journey: South Africa's Quest for a Negotiated Settlement*. Johannesburg: Ravan Press.

Garson, P. 1990. "South Africa: The Killing Fields," *Africa Report* 35(5): 47–50.

Gastrow, P. 1995. *Bargaining for Peace: South Africa and the National Peace Accord*. Washington, DC: United States Institute for Peace.

Giliomee, H. and L. Schlemmer. 1989. *From Apartheid to Nation-Building: Contemporary South African Debates*. Cape Town: Oxford University Press.

The Groote Schuur Minute, 1990. reprinted in *South African Journal on Human Rights* 6.

Haysom, N. 1992. "Negotiating a Political Settlement in South Africa," in G. Moss and I. Obery, eds. *South African Review 6: From Red Friday to CODESA*. Braamfontein: Ravan Press.

Jeffery, A. 1997. *The Natal Story: Sixteen Years of Conflict*. Johannesburg: South African Institute of Race Relations.

Jeffery, A. 2009. *People's War: A New Light on the Struggle for South Africa*. Johannesburg: Jonathan Ball Publishers.

Keightley, R. 1993. "Political Offences and Indemnity in South Africa," *South African Journal on Human Rights* 9: 334–357.

King, A. 1993. "Violence: The Biggest Obstacle," *UN Chronicle*. New York, September 1993.

Luthuli, A. 1962. *Let My People Go: An Autobiography*. London: Fontana Books.

Mallinder, L. 2009. "Indemnity, Amnesty, Pardon and Prosecution Guidelines in South Africa," Working Paper No. 2 From *Beyond Legalism: Amnesties, Transition and Conflict Transformation*. Belfast: Queen's University

Mandela, N. 1994. *Long Walk to Freedom*. Edinburgh: Little, Brown and Company.

Maré, G. 1991. "History and Dimension of Violence in Natal: Inkatha's Role in Negotiating Political Peace," *Social Justice* 18.

McCarthy, E.1997. "South Africa's Amnesty Process: A Viable Route Toward Truth and Reconciliation?" *Michigan Journal of Race and Law* 3: 214–238.

McDougall, G. and C. Soberbergh. 1990. "The Release of South Africa's Political Prisoners: Definitions and Expectations," *Temple International and Comparative Law Journal* 4: 5–20.

Mkhondo, R. 1993. *Reporting South Africa*. London: James Currey.

Murray, M. 1994. *The Revolution Deferred: The Painful Birth of Post-Apartheid South Africa*. London: Verso.

O'Meara, D. 1996. *Forty Lost Years: The Apartheid State and the Politics of the National Party, 1948–1994*. Randburg: Ravan Press.

Ottaway, D. 1993. *Chained Together: Mandela, De Klerk, and the Struggle to Remake South Africa*. Toronto: Random House.

Parker, P. 1996. "The Politics of Indemnities, Truth Telling and Reconciliation in South Africa: Ending Apartheid Without Forgetting," *Human Rights Law Journal* 17: 1–12.

Pedain, A. 2004. "Was Amnesty a Lottery? An Empirical Study of the Decisions of the Truth and Reconciliation Commission's Committee on Amnesty," *South African Law Journal* 121: 785–808.

The Pretoria Minute, 1990. reprinted in *South African Journal on Human Rights* 6.

Price, R. 1991. *The Apartheid State in Crisis: Political Transformation in South Africa 1975–1990*. New York: Oxford University Press.

Record of Understanding, 26 September 1992, at: https://omalley.nelsonmandela.org/omalley/index.php/site/q/03lv02039/04lv02046/05lv02092/06lv02096.htm

Reddy, E. 2015. "The United Nations and the Struggle for Liberation in South Africa," in G. Houston, ed. *The Road to Democracy in South Africa, Volume 3, International Solidarity*. Pretoria: UNISA Press.

Report of the Secretary-General to the Security Council in pursuance of Security Council Resolution 765 (1992), S/24389, 7 August 1992.

Report of the Working Group Established under Paragraph 1 of the Groote Schuur Minute, 1990. reprinted in *South African Journal on Human Rights* 6.

Saunders, J. 2006. *Apartheid's Friends: The Rise and Fall of South Africa's Secret Service*. London: John Murray.

Savage, K. 2000. "Negotiating the Release of Political Prisoners in South Africa," Research Report written for the Northern Ireland Programme at the Kennedy School of Government at Harvard.

Simpson, T. 2009. "Toyi-Toying to Freedom: The Endgame in the ANC's Armed Struggle, 1989–1990," *Journal of Southern African Studies* 35(2): 508–520.

Simpson, J. 2011. "The Boipatong Massacre and South Africa's Democratic Transition," *African Studies Centre African Studies Collection* 35.

Sisk, T. 1995. *Democratization in South Africa: The Elusive Social Contract*. Princeton: Princeton University Press.

Sisk, T. 2009. *International Mediation in Civil Wars: Bargaining With Bullets*. London: Routledge.

South African History Online. 2012. "Boipatong Massacre – 17 June 1992," at: www.sahistory.org.za/topic/boipatong-massacre-17-june-1992

South African Institute of Race Relations. 1990. *Race Relations Survey, 1989/1990*. Johannesburg: Institute of Race Relations

South African Institute of Race Relations. 1992. *Race Relations Survey, 1991/1992*. Johannesburg: Institute of Race Relations

Sparks, A. 1994. *Tomorrow Is Another Country: The Inside Story of South Africa's Negotiated Revolution*. Sandton: Struik Book Distributors.

Taylor, R. 1991. "The Myth of Ethnic Division: Township Conflict on the Reef," *Race and Class* 33(2): 1–14.

Transcript of Ivan Pillay interview with Padraig O'Malley, 11 December 2002.

United Nations. 1994. "United Nations Observer Mission in South Africa (UNOMSA)," United Nations Archives, at: https://search.archives.un.org/united-nations-observer-mission-in-south-africa-unomsa

United Nations General Assembly Resolution 48/1, 48 U.N. GAOR Supp. (No. 49) at 12, U.N. Doc. A/48/49 (1993).

United Nations Security Council Resolution, S/RES/765, 16 July 1992.

United Nations Security Council Resolution, S/RES/772, 7 August 1992.

Van der Westhuizen, C. 2007. *White Power and the Rise and Fall of the National Party*. Cape Town: Zebra Press.

Waldmeir, P. 1997. *Anatomy of a Miracle: The End of Apartheid*. New York: Norton.

Welsh, D. 1991. "The Outlook for a Democratic South Africa," *International Affairs* 67(4).

6 Contrasting roles in international mediation

Lessons from South Africa

The mediation efforts by the EPG and Vance offer some strong similarities. Both were envoys mandated by international organisations. Both consulted as widely as possible all sectors of the South African society. Both viewed the process of fact-finding as an essential task in developing a resolving formula. And both developed a resolving formula, as the essential ingredient in mediation, and in response to the problems put before them. One could also conclude that their actions in the process of mediation, i.e. the process of fact-finding and the resolving formula, ultimately made contributions to the process of conflict resolution in South Africa.

A close examination, however, reveals two very different missions, facing very different challenges, using similar (but approached differently) strategies to help resolve the South African conflict. Essentially, both used formulation strategies, but their approach to this was shaped by the stages of the conflict-resolution process, and the parties' perception of them. For the EPG, the goal was to assist parties to get to the table, i.e. to get each party to agree that they had a shared understanding that a negotiated solution is possible, to produce a commitment to a negotiated solution and to overcome preconditions as a barrier to opening negotiations. It was to get parties to start talking. For Vance, the task was to assist in restoring communications between the parties and explore conditions each was imposing on the resumption of talks when negotiations reached a crisis and broke down. It was not to define issues for them but to assist them by providing supportive resources.

This chapter will contrast these approaches across several dimensions to develop a better understanding of the range of third-party actions that may be appropriate and effective in the different stages of the negotiation process. Moving from Curran et al.'s (2004) comparison of George Mitchell and Richard Holbrooke's mediation in Northern Ireland and Bosnia-Herzegovina respectively, the chapter will offer a set of categories into which the actions of the EPG and the United Nations can be characterised (Curran et al., 2004: 516). These categories are embedded in framework that analyses the basic choices for those involved in third-party roles. Third parties face three decisions (Curran et al., 2004: 516). First, they must "determine their basic objectives," e.g. to get parties to the table, to restore communication between parties once talks have broken, to foster an agreement, to delay the conflict, to model a more constructive process or to break a deadlock. A mediator's objective will be determined by the stage of the conflict-resolution process. Second, mediators must "choose their fundamental role," e.g. neutrality or bias. Mediators must decide how they want to alter the perception and behaviour of the belligerents. Some mediators don't simply listen and suggest; they steer the belligerents towards an agreement and some form of muscle might be necessary (but not always) in the context of an impasse. Third they must consider their "best means of influence on the situation," e.g. forceful, persuasive, facilitative, etc. With these choices, mediators must form a "winning coalition" (i.e. coalition strategy) which contains three overlapping strands: "an issues strategy, with respect to the substantive aspects of the agreements sought, a process strategy with respect to the choices of process for the mediation, and a timing strategy with respect to the timing of their efforts" (Curran et al., 2004: 516).

The fundamental choices

Basic objectives: the mandates

The EPG's basis objectives were in the Commonwealth Accord on Southern Africa. The mandate was to call on the South African government to initiate, in the context of the suspension of violence on all sides, "a process of dialogue with a view of establishing a non-racial representative government in South Africa" (EPG Report, 1986: 19). Getting parties to start talking was their goal. There were important limitations to these objectives. First, they had six months to do their work; after that period Commonwealth heads of government would have to consider additional measures if their progress was deemed insufficient. Second, their role was limited to simply "facilitating the process of dialogue for change" (EPG Report, 1986: 20). It was not in their mandate to determine the form of change or prescribe what form a political settlement might take.

Cyrus Vance's mandate was contained in UNSC Resolution 765. The objectives here were to recommend measures "which could assist in bringing an effective end to the violence and in creating conditions for negotiations." More specifically, the aim was to remove obstacles to resume negotiation (UNSC Resolution 765, 1992: 2). The goal was simple: provide assistance for the resumption of talks that had already made considerable progress, and identify areas to create a conducive environment for their sustainability. The mandates of both were therefore different and corresponded to different moments in the conflict-resolution process. The task of the EPG was to get parties to the negotiation table, i.e. to sound out parties and see if there might be any readiness to engage in talks, and what conditions might be imposed if the will exists on both sides. By contrast, Vance's task was to assist the parties to break the deadlock and resume talks to create conditions for the parties to reach agreement. The UN was responding to a breakdown in the negotiation process; their task was to restore communication between adversaries and explore conditions each was imposing on the resumption of talks. Most importantly, all parties requested this assistance and thus their basic objectives had a strong sense of legitimacy and corresponded to the needs of the parties. By contrast, the major parties in the South African conflict did not ask the Commonwealth for such assistance; their objectives were thus derived from their own interests and corresponded to the internal question of the organisation and how it understood and articulated the South African question. Therefore, even though the issues that they identified were the very obstacles being discussed between the parties, they did not carry the necessary legitimacy; there was the mistrust of the mediator.

Fundamental role

The roles of the EPG and Vance corresponded to their mandates. Both assumed the role of an advocate for the end of apartheid and creation of a democratic South Africa, with substantial clout from the Commonwealth and United Nations respectively. From this perspective they were not neutral, they did not simply listen and suggest; they steered discussion towards a resolving formula that had the goal of creating a united, non-racial and democratic South Africa. They were therefore active engineers in developing the resolving formula to meet the goals of their mandates. The EPG had the powers to punish; before the mission went underway, the Commonwealth had agreed on an arsenal of punitive action against South Africa: an arms embargo, discouraging sports contacts and various economic measures. If progress was not made within the six-months period, further economic measures would be considered including sanctions. This approach was problematic; the lack of neutrality in an environment where their assistance was not requested meant that in the end, the government would never have the political interest to accept their mediation. In the end, both the ANC and the government did accept a mediator, Michael Young, but it was on the terms that was acceptable to them, i.e. mediator as communicator using a secret channel, that corresponded to their political interests in that phase of the conflict. That they accepted working through Young (and in the process ironically with the elements of the negotiating concept) and not the EPG is crucial; it raises important questions about appropriateness of the mediation method and the attribute of the mediator, at specific moments of the conflict-resolution process.

By contrast, the UN was operating in a very different political environment. They did not need a carrot and stick approach; the major parties requested the mediator, were comfortable in working with the United Nations, and were committed to returning negotiations and reaching a settlement. Their United Nations role was to insert themselves in the unfolding political process to assist the parties in that endeavour. Once talks resumed, they needed to provide whatever resources requested that could sustain that climate. Thus, they were able to exercise some degree of neutrality as all major parties had agreed to move away from apartheid. Their role was derived from how they received their mandate; while the Commonwealth Accord should be viewed in the context of that organisation's consistent preoccupation with the South African question (a country that ironically ceased to be a member decades ago), and the consequent insertion into the South African political process, the United Nations was accepted by all parties into the political process and this considerably legitimised their role as a neutral and acceptable mediator, and legitimised their recommendations in the form of UNOMSA.

Means of influence: the mediator as formulator

Both the EPG and United Nations missions were examples of mediation as formulation. As discussed, in this method, redefining the issues in the conflict, and finding a formula for its resolution, is the key to its termination (Touval and Zartman, 1985: 12). Conflicting parties need assistance in finding a solution "hidden in the morass of bad relationships or in constructing a solution from the pieces of the conflict itself." The mediator as formulator, therefore, "helps the parties help themselves, by tactful, sympathetic, accurate, straightforward prodding suggestion" (Touval and Zartman, 1985: 12). How mediators approach formulation will thus depend on the stage of the conflict. In the process of getting to the table, the formulator will explore possibilities, determine readiness for negotiated solutions, encourage consensus on core issues and concessions and through this, develop a resolving formula to initiate or facilitate the process of talks. By contrast, in the process of reaching agreement, the formulator will facilitate, strengthen existing options and perspectives, provide new resources, provide insurance against the breakdown of talks and through this, accompany and assist the process towards the negotiated settlement.

For the EPG, the Negotiating Concept was the formula developed to initiate the process of dialogue. It linked the release of political prisoners and the moratorium on violence with the initiation of a political process. It embodied a package approach:

> its preamble constituted a firm statement of intent that apartheid would be ended; its operative paragraph set out measures that were needed to create a climate of confidence and enable all concerned to turn to the task of constructing a new South Africa; and the postscript embodied the statements made by the South African government [designed to] facilitate the negotiation process.
>
> (EPG Report, 1986: 103)

This formula became the basic point of pre-negotiation in South Africa. While the parties did not accept the terms of the EPG's mediation, they did accept the basic principles of their resolving formula, on their own terms. Therefore, it wasn't that they refused mediation; that they used Young to channel messages is testimony to their need for mediation. Mediation as formulation was just not appropriate for that moment in that phase of the conflict-resolution process.

In the UN case, the secretary-general's report on "The Question of South Africa," presented to the Security Council on 7 August 1992, was the formula developed to remove the obstacles to the resumption of talks, and create conditions for negotiations leading towards a peaceful transition to a democratic South

Africa. This involved the creation of a United Nations observer mission, which would work closely with the National Peace Secretariat. The intention was to strengthen and reinforce the National Peace Accord as an indigenous structure for it to play an important role in the building of peace. Resolution 772's significance went beyond that; it inserted the resources of the United Nations diplomatic system into the transition which enabled the negotiations to progress relatively quickly despite the persistence of political violence. The role of the UN, however, was still limited to formulation.

The fundamental choices of the EPG and Vance's mission, with reference to their objectives and roles, were therefore different; they corresponded to their mandates which spoke to issues specific to the phase of the conflict-resolution process. However, their method, i.e. their means of influence, was similar. This raises important questions about mediation as formulation and its appropriateness in the conflict-resolution process. Most importantly, it highlights the point about the fruitfulness of formulation as a mechanism in resolving a crisis in negotiations: the formulator helps the parties help themselves in the morass of bad relationships when talks breakdown. The formulator is more appropriate under these circumstances. By contrast, as Young's mediation efforts demonstrate, the communicator is more appropriate at initiating talks, i.e. to make the original and important contacts, and to serve as a telephone wire. Young played that role to perfection.

Political strategies: coalition, process and timing

Coalition strategy

The EPG and Vance's mission had similar political strategies. Both used fact-finding missions to get an accurate reading of the political climate. Consequently, both consulted as wide as possible all sectors of the society in the process of developing formulas. How they went about this differed.

Four items were at the heart of the EPG's operational principles. First, they chose to "work quietly and in non-public ways." Second, they chose to be non-confrontational; even when provoked they chose to maintain an atmosphere of cordiality and remain silent. Third, they chose to "vary their consultations and work in other ways than always as a full group." They subdivided, and this enabled them to make simultaneous visits. Fourth, to demonstrate their independence and gain access to as many people as possible, they travelled alone without any government security personnel, and were accompanied by the small secretariat. This allowed them to move extensively around the country, with freedom of access to all those they chose to meet, "contacting as wide a spectrum of opinion as possible and seeing as much in the townships and elsewhere" (EPG Report, 1986: 21–22). The list of consultations was impressive: "from the State President and senior Cabinet Ministers to displaced poverty-stricken refugees and squatters; from business magnates, prelates and members of the church and university dons, to industrial and agricultural workers; from political prisoners, exiles and prominent dissidents" (EPG Report, 1986: 101). The EPG's inclusive political strategy was shaped by the fact that they had inserted themselves into the political process in South Africa; neither side had requested mediation from the Commonwealth. Consequently, there was suspicion among most of the principle parties of the mission. By their own admission, inclusivity was in part a political strategy to resolve this dilemma: "To overcome perceptions and remove apprehensions about the work of the group, and to build confidence to a point from which meaningful discussions could begin, we agreed on a number of operational principles" (EPG Report, 1986: 20–21). There was no love lost between the government and the Commonwealth, while the ANC, despite close ties to Ramphal, perceived the mission as the product of the British government's wish to resist sanctions.

Vance by contrast was not a member of a group of eminent persons but was a Special Representative. His mission programme bears striking similarity with the EPG mission. The list and number of consultations was extensive given the limited amount of time Vance had in the country. Because of the limitations of Vance's mission, i.e. it was confined to assisting the parties in resuming talks, consultations would not be as in depth and extensive as the EPG (who also consulted presidents of neighbouring countries) and were confined to parties related to the mandate. Vance's mission, however, did not have the political problems of the EPG; all parties were willing to accept mediation and a United Nations observer group. The issue therefore was not about whether to intervene but how, i.e. logistics, timeframes, locations, etc.

Process strategy

Their process strategies however differed and corresponded to the political strategies and objectives. To operate in a hostile environment, the EPG mission was broken up into different parts. The first part was a preliminary visit to South Africa by Obasanjo and Fraser. They held conversations and meetings with leaders from across the political spectrum – cabinet ministers, prominent members of the internal anti-apartheid movement, churchmen and members of the political opposition inside parliament. Their key objective was to test the government's willingness to enter dialogue and open the way for negotiations with the ANC. Following this preliminary visit, five members of the group (Barber, Malecela, Scott, Barrow and Fraser) visited Botswana, Lesotho and Zimbabwe before proceeding to Zambia. In Zambia they met President Kaunda and Tambo. Here they were joined by Singh, Obasanjo and Ramphal. Before flying back to South Africa, they held talks with President Dos Santos of Angola. The important meeting was with the ANC in Lusaka.

At the beginning of March 1986, the EPG's four additional members joined the three on a full-scale visit to South Africa. They were struck by the desire of most South Africans for a non-violent negotiated settlement. After these consultations, the group was satisfied that sufficient ground existed based on which a negotiated solution could be attempted. On this basis, the EPG developed a "Possible Negotiating Concept." The concept was then put to all the parties as the basis of a second phase of consultations to initiate the process of dialogue. The air strikes by the South African Airforce in neighbouring countries, and resultant rejection by the government of the concept, put an end to this.

By contrast Vance's mission had a very focused and specific objective and thus occurred in just over a week. Resolution 765 was clear: the secretary-general had to submit a report to the Security Council as early as possible. Given the urgency of the situation, and the volatile political climate at the time, Vance's mission was impressive. Based on these consultations he reported back to Boutros-Ghali. The positive response from all parties is what made Resolution 772 possible. After Resolution 772, the United Nations infrastructure was brought to bear on the South African transition, i.e. the combination of diplomacy and observer missions. Thus, both the EPG and Vance used consensus strategies, consulting as widely as possible to develop a formula. The major difference is that there was hostility to the EPG in the final stages of their mission, a function of the mistrust of their intentions. This hindered their ability to insert themselves into the political process. The Negotiation Concept, however, did not die with the air strikes; it became the living document of the early pre-negotiation phase containing the basic point of negotiation during this period. Vance's mission did not have such problems; acceptance by all the major parties meant that consensus over which measures would serve as recommendations for resuming negotiations would not be a political struggle.

Timing strategy

The issue of timing is related to the moment that belligerents become amenable to accepting mediation to resolve the conflict. In the literature, this moment is defined as a ripe moment and was coined by Zartman (1989). Ripeness is a time-oriented view of conflict that posits the idea that at any moment policies are chosen among desirable goals based on comparative costs and benefits. Since these policies may be altered depending on the external context and interaction of parties, some moments are better than others for managing and resolving conflict. Zartman argued that mediation depends on the identification of a ripe moment. Metaphorically, the point when conflict is ripe for resolution is associated with two types of intensity called plateaus and precipice, which produce two types of pressure respectively called deadlocks and deadlines.

A plateau or a deadlock is a stalemate and begins when "one side is unable to achieve its aims, to resolve the problem, or to win the conflict by itself, and is completed when the other side arrives at a similar perception." A plateau must be perceived as a hurting stalemate, i.e. "a flat, unpleasant terrain stretching into the future, providing no later possibilities for decisive escalation of graceful escape" (Zartman, 1989: 263–268). Zartman views perceptions of an intolerable situation as important for conflict resolution. In this regard, the role of the mediator is essential: "the conciliator must persuade the parties that escalation to break out of deadlock is impossible. Indeed, the conciliator may even be required to make it impossible, if necessary" (Zartman, 1989: 268). The deadlock is not a temporary stalemate; "each party must recognise its opponent's strength and its own inability to overcome it." Each party's unilateral policy option must be a more expensive and less likely way of achieving a possible, acceptable outcome than the policy of negotiation. Mediation is critical to the stalemate: "for the conciliator this means emphasising the dangers of deadlock as each party comes to recognise the other's strength. . . . Successful conciliation produces a shift from a winning mentality to a conciliating mentality on the part of both sides" (Zartman, 1989: 263). This hurting stalemate is as much a matter of perception as of reality for the warring parties, and as much a subject of persuasion as of timing for the mediator.

A precipice and a deadline represent a catastrophe, i.e. a realisation by both sides that matters will get worse if they have not gotten better in ways that negotiation seeks to define. A catastrophe "threatens the mutual checks that parties impose on each other." The catastrophe can either be impending, narrowly encountered or just avoided. It may also have just occurred or one in which parties is sinking deeper into. The ripe moment frequently comes after a crisis has just occurred, with losses on both sides that has left a conflict unresolved (Zartman, 1989: 268–269). The second dimension of a ripe moment concerns policy tracks and alternatives. The task of the mediator is to deflect the parties from competing attempts to impose unilateral solutions and into a joint search for a bilateral solution. The proper moment for mediation occurs when the power relations in the parties' positions become symmetrical, i.e. "when the upper hand starts slipping and the underdog starts rising" (Zartman, 1989: 272).

Was the point of the Commonwealth Accord and the EPG mission a ripe moment? No; neither the government nor the ANC and its allied organisations were on a pain-producing path. Both parties did not perceive the conflict to be a hurting stalemate. While they were exploring negotiation possibilities, they were still seeking unilateral solutions. This does not mean they were not amenable to mediation however; Young provided a useful means of communication. The Negotiation Concept was significant in so far as it laid the basic points of discussion that defined the agenda during this process. The ripe moment in South Africa happened three years later with the signing of the New York Accords. The subsequent closure of MK camps in Angola, and relocation of MK into East Africa effectively rendered the armed struggle obsolete. The ANC would have to negotiate the end of apartheid. This happened while the government realised they need to negotiate with the ANC. South African government leaders, faced with a legitimacy crisis, and lack of black popular acceptance of constitutional reform measures, saw negotiations as a way out. Therefore, the period between December 1988 and August 1989 is when the South African conflict reached the point of seriousness where the NP government and ANC developed a shared understanding that negotiated solutions are possible. This is the perception by each side that the other is serious about finding a negotiated solution – that is, that the other is willing to lose a little to win a little rather than win or lose all in a non-negotiated approach. Mediation in the form of Michael Young's secret facilitation did assist the process in terms of defining the issues and maintaining a secret channel of communication. This however, came from a different source, had a different role, and a very different political strategy. From this perspective the EPG mission was three years too early, but it did make a significant contribution.

This has important implications for theories of mediation that assume a stalemate is a necessary condition for mediation. The EPG case, and Young's subsequent secret channel, assisted the parties in terms of developing a shared understanding of the problem (the negotiating concept), and a shared understanding about finding a negotiated solution (the secret communication channel). This highlights the significance of political leaders, who are party to the conflict, in initiating and driving the process of negotiation. The contribution of mediation is in regards to how they can assist the process.

Was the moment of Vance's mission a ripe moment? Yes; South Africa was plunged into a deep crisis after the Boipatong massacre. Communication between the parties effectively broke down; the negotiation process was reduced to bitter and abusive exchanges between the government and the ANC, "replete with mutual recriminations and thinly veiled personal insults" (Sisk, 1995: 214). The parties could not see a way out of the deadlock and approached the United Nation for assistance. Both parties ended up accepting mediation which came in the form of UNSC Resolution 765, and the accompanying observer missions.

Mediation and outcomes

As discussed, the perpetual question troubling mediation efforts and research concerns the criteria defining success. How do researchers find indicators that can assist in finding variables that can help describe the outcome? When is an attempt at mediation considered successful? Which strategies are more conducive for the successful outcome of a mediation process? Is it when a mediation attempt is accepted? Or when violent behaviour ends? Or is it when an agreement is produced? Distinguishing success from failure is further complicated when a mediation effort produces a ceasefire without achieving a lasting resolution of the conflict. Authors such as Beardsley (2008), Beardsley et al. (2006), Svensson (2009) and Gartner (2012) point to a more long-term perspective on mediation success that goes beyond the simple ending of violent behaviour. This, according to Wallensteen and Svensson (2014: 323), leads to the question of the occurrence of conflict; do mediated solutions lead to a lower chance that conflict and war will recur compared to alternative ends to conflict, such as victory or agreements reached directly between parties?

Given the discussion, for our purposes, we can evaluate the EPG and Vance's mediation in two ways: in terms of their basic objectives; and in terms of their value to the conflict-resolution process.

In terms of the EPG's stated objectives, the mission was a failure; it was not able to initiate a process of dialogue within the six-months period. But it is important to note that given the political circumstances, it could not do this. While both parties accepted the mediation attempt, they were not ready for mediation in early 1986. Coupled with the suspicions around the EPG, this was not going to work. In less than a few months, this changed considerably. In June 1986, less than a month after the EPG departure, Tambo accepted Young's request and defined the type of mediated assistance required, i.e. assistance in creating a secret communication channel between the government and the ANC, using intermediaries as a first step. This would be a communication-facilitation mediation role.

The interrelated issues here are with regards to the attributes of the mediator, and timing. Regarding the former, there was simply insufficient trust between the government and the EPG as a product of the Commonwealth. Furthermore, the EPG's formulation strategy, involving a redefinition of the issues, and then in turn putting them to the parties, was a miscalculation; the ANC and the government had already begun exploring such negotiation possibilities and did not need the EPG to do it for them. The EPG, however, could not know this. By the time the parties opted for mediation, it was for the communication-facilitation type, i.e. a more passive role of mediation, largely keeping channels of information open and passing along information to each other, on their own terms.

If, however we examine the time horizon of the conflict and examine success or failure within that context, we would have to ask what contribution the mediation effort played in terms of getting the parties to the table. In this light, the negotiating concept was significant; while the ANC and the government did not accept the negotiating concept in 1986, the document embodied all the elements which formed the basis of negotiations between the government and the ANC. These were the basic points in the pre-negotiation phase, i.e. the release of political prisoners and unbanning of the ANC and other banned political organisations (for the ANC), and the renunciation or suspension of violence (for the government). The fundamental issue was about synchronisation, i.e. reaching prior agreement between both to act simultaneously in fulfilling their respective commitments as the basis for starting dialogue. The secret channel created by Young resolved this. As for Vance's mission, it was a success and embodied all the elements of a successful mediation effort.

Lessons from South Africa

Mediators use their personal and structural resources to preserve the triangular relationship and move parties to agreement. The basic problem is identifying the optimal strategy to do this. As discussed in Chapter 2, the literature is in no agreement regarding the most effective strategy. Bercovitch et al. (1991) argue that directive strategies, i.e. forceful strategies, tend to be more successful even though facilitative approaches are more common (Curran and Sebenius, 2003: 3). Later, Bercovitch and Diehl (1997) concluded that fostering approaches, i.e. facilitative approaches, were more productive for intractable conflicts. Drawing on peace-making efforts in Africa, Nathan (1999) points to fostering rather than forceful strategies, arguing that the pressure that comes with power or pure mediation has greater potential to be counterproductive. By contrast, Sisk (2009) makes the case for powerful peace-making using incentives and sanctions to leverage parties to peace. In a similar vein Touval (1975: 68) argued that "the more powerful international actors are, the more effective they are as intermediaries." Gelpi

(1999) also concluded that great power mediation increases the chances for mediation success.

The South African case study has revealed that the methods of mediation should be determined by whether that method is appropriate for the certain phase of a conflict. Getting people to start talking requires a different strategy to packaging a formula for settlement. The forms of mediation are also determined by the type of conflict. The book is thus in agreement with Greig and Diehl (2012) who point out that conflict phases and resolution stages intersect and influence the process and strategies of mediation. Mediation is thus not unique to a certain phase of the conflict but occurs within many different contexts. We can therefore conclude the following lessons from the South African case:

1 Where the goal of mediation is to explore possibilities and determine readiness for negotiated solutions, to encourage consensus on core issues and concessions and to initiate the process of talks, the mediator as communicator is more appropriate.
2 Where the goal of mediation is to resolve an impasse, break a deadlock and get parties back to the table, the mediator as formulator is more appropriate; it is more appropriate in an environment where the breakdown in communication not only impedes but keeps the parties from conceiving a solution to meet the needs of both sides.

A related question regarding mediation strategies concerns the relationship between mediation strategies and outcomes, i.e. the criteria defining success. When is an attempt at mediation considered successful? Which strategies are more conducive for the successful outcome of a mediation process? Once again there is no consensus in the literature. Frei (1976: 69) explains success as "a situation in which both parties to the conflict formally or informally accept a mediator and a mediation attempt within five days of the first attempt." Bercovitch et al. (1991: 8) measure successful mediation as producing an agreement: "by successful outcomes we mean producing a ceasefire, a partial settlement or a full settlement." Nathan (1999: 3) goes further and defines success as "when it leads to the termination of hostilities and the advent of democratic governance." Other scholars have equated mediation success with effectiveness taking the mediator's objectives as a starting point (Touval and Zartman, 1985). Distinguishing success from failure is further complicated when a mediation effort produces a ceasefire without achieving a lasting resolution of the conflict. This book agrees with authors such as Beardsley (2008), Beardsley et al. (2006), Svensson (2009) and Gartner (2012) who point to a more long-term perspective on mediation success that goes beyond the simple ending of violence behaviour. This is what the South African case reveals. We can therefore conclude the third lesson from the South African case:

3 The failure or success of mediation depends on the examination of the time horizon of a conflict, and on the contribution the mediation effort plays in improving the relationship between the belligerents.

Therefore, the task of mediation is varied and is dependent on the phase of the conflict-resolution process. In the pre-negotiation phase, the goal of mediation is to explore possibilities and determine readiness for negotiated solutions, to encourage consensus on core issues and concessions, and to initiate the process of talks. During the negotiation process, the goal is to facilitate, provide new options and perspectives, provide new resources, provide insurance against the breakdown of talks and offer to guarantee durable solutions, and to legitimise the negotiated settlement. As for the South African case, while South Africa's players did initiate the negotiation process on their own and on their own terms, and in the process were able to resolve their conflict, international mediation did play an important role in crucial stages of the conflict-resolution process. While it did not come in the form of a Kofi Annan, Richard Holbrooke, George Mitchell or Jimmy Carter, its contribution was significant for the stages and phases of the political process it intervened in. Once we appreciate that international mediation can cover a wide range of third-party activities (from simply providing good offices for the parties to negotiate, to assisting them in formulating a resolving formula to their conflict), then we can begin to truly appreciate the complexity and enormous value external third parties play in resolving intractable conflicts.

Bibliography

Beardsley, K. 2008. "Agreement Without Peace? International Mediation and Time Inconsistency Problems," *American Journal of Political Science* 52(4): 723–740.

Beardsley, K., D. Quinn, B. Biswas and J. Wilkenfeld. 2006. "Mediation Style and Crisis Outcomes," *Journal of Conflict Resolution* 50(1): 58–86.

Bercovitch, J., T. Anagnoson and D. Wille. 1991. "Some Conceptual Issues and Empirical Trends in the Study of Successful Mediation in International Relations," *Journal of Peace Research* 28(1): 7–17.

Bercovitch, J. and P. Diehl. 1997. "Conflict Management of Enduring Rivalries: Frequency, Timing and Short-Term Impact of Mediation," *International Interactions* 22(4): 299–320.

The Commonwealth Report. 1986. *Mission to South Africa*. London: Penguin Books.

Curran, D. and J. Sebenius. 2003. "The Mediator as Coalition-Builder: George Mitchell in Northern Ireland," *International Negotiation* 8(1): 111–147.

Curran, D., J. Sebenius and M. Watkins. 2004. "Two Paths to Peace: Contrasting George Mitchell in Northern Ireland With Richard Holbrooke in Bosnia – Herzegovina," *Negotiation Journal* 20(4): 513–537.

Frei, D. 1976. "Conditions Affecting the Effectiveness of International Mediation," *Peace Science Society (International) Papers* 26(1): 67–84.

Gartner, S. 2012. "Civil War Peacemaking," in J. Hewitt, J. Wilkenfeld and T. Gurr, eds. *Peace and Conflict*. Boulder, CO: Paradigm.

Gelpi, C. 1999. "Alliances as Instruments of Intra-allied Control," in H. Haftendorn, R. Keohane and C. Wallander, eds. *Imperfect Unions: Security Institutions Over Time and Space*. Oxford: Oxford University Press.

Greig, J. and P. Diehl. 2012. *International Mediation*. Cambridge: Polity.

Nathan, L. 1999. "When Push Comes to Shove: The Failure of International Mediation in African Civil Wars," *Track Two* 8(2): 1–23.

Sisk, T. 1995. *Democratisation in South Africa: The Elusive Social Contract*. Princeton: Princeton University Press.

Sisk, T. 2009. *International Mediation in Civil Wars: Bargaining With Bullets*. London: Routledge.

Svensson, I. 2009. "Who Brings Which Peace? Biased Versus Neutral Mediation and Institutional Peace Arrangements in Civil Wars," *Journal of Conflict Resolution* 53(3): 446–469.

Touval, S. 1975. "Biased Intermediaries: Theoretical and Historical Considerations," *Jerusalem Journal of International Relations* 1(1): 51–69.

Touval, S. and I.W. Zartman. 1985. "Introduction: Mediation in Theory," in S. Touval and I.W. Zartman, eds. *International Mediation in Theory and Practice*. London: Westview Press.

United Nations Security Council Resolution, S/RES/765, 16 July 1992.

Wallensteen, P. and I. Svensson. 2014. "Talking Peace: International Mediation in Armed Conflicts," *Journal of Peace Research* 51(2): 315–327.

Zartman, I.W. 1989. *Ripe for Resolution: Conflict and Intervention in Africa*. New York: Oxford University Press.

Index